Writing a Convincing Business Plan

Fourth Edition

**Arthur R. DeThomas, Ph.D.,
Stephanie A. Derammelaere, M.B.A., and
Steven Fox, J.D., M.B.A.**

BARRON'S

All inquiries should be addressed to:
Barron's Educational Series, Inc.
250 Wireless Boulevard
Hauppauge, New York 11788
www.barronseduc.com

Library of Congress Catalog Card No.: 2014034543

ISBN: 978-1-4380-0480-8

Library of Congress Cataloging-in-Publication Data
DeThomas, Art.
   Writing a convincing business plan / Arthur DeThomas, Ph.D., Stephanie
Derammelaere, M.B.A., Stephen Fox, J.D., M.B.A., — Fourth edition.
      pages cm.
   Includes bibliographical references and index.
   ISBN 978-1-4380-0480-8 (alk. paper)
   1. Business planning.   2. Business writing.   I. Fox, Steven.   II. Derammelaere,
Stephanie A.   III. Title.

   HD30.28.D477   2015
   658.4'012—dc23   2014034543

PRINTED IN CHINA
9 8 7 6 5 4 3 2 1

Contents

Preface

During the many years we have worked with and studied small- and medium-sized businesses, we have found that the most nagging question for entrepreneurs is: What can be done to increase the chances of success for my new business or improve the performance of my existing business?

While the business environment continues to change, the answer to the question has not. What is this time-tested advice? It is simply to:

■ Carefully research the firm's existing or intended industry, market, and competition; identify the factors that do or will account for its success or its failure; and make an informed, educated estimate of the chances for success.

■ Develop a detailed plan for favorably influencing the factors that determine success; for operating the business; and for acquiring and managing the human, physical, and financial resources that are needed to operate it profitably.

In short, the entrepreneur needs to prepare a business plan, or, as it is occasionally referred to, a feasibility study. It is an important theme of this book and, hopefully, for the business plan that is prepared.

As important as the business plan is, the planning process and preparation needed prior to writing the formal plan is more vital. Gathering the information and data needed to prepare a complete business plan minimizes the possibility of failure and maximizes the likelihood of success. This is as true for an existing business as for a new venture. Preparing a business plan converts pipe dreams into realities by forcing the entrepreneur to:

■ Think carefully about each phase of the business, the details of its operation, and how the various details and parts must fit together to form a viable, ongoing business entity.

■ Gather the information needed to make an informed estimate of the firm's probability of success and the degree of risk to which it will be exposed.

■ Crystallize their thoughts and commit them to paper so they can be evaluated personally and by informed outsiders.

■ Examine the strengths and weaknesses of the firm relative to its industry, market, competition, and customers.

■ Evaluate the feasibility of the business concept and identify the specific factors that will determine the firm's success or failure.

■ Establish realistic, attainable goals that can serve as guidelines for making day-to-day operating decisions as well as standards for measuring the firm's progress.

■ Maintain an ongoing process of investigating, gathering and evaluating information, identifying needed resources, setting goals, and preparing a road map for achieving them.

These analyses are important to the effective operation of any business but are especially crucial to the entrepreneur seeking financing. The prevailing attitude among financiers is skepticism. Before the typical financier will consider making a loan to or investing in a business firm, the entrepreneur must demonstrate:

■ A clearly defined business concept.

■ A working knowledge of the major functions of the business: production, marketing, sales, finance, and human resource management.

■ A clear understanding of the industry, market, and competitive environment in which the venture operates or will operate, and a detailed plan for capturing the opportunities they present.

■ A true picture of the current financial position of the firm or new venture, its expected financial needs, and its financial projections.

■ Supporting documentation and convincing arguments for why and how the business will succeed.

A well-researched, carefully prepared business plan conveys this information and is unmistakable evidence of the entrepreneur's ability to plan his or her business operation. It is also the type of evidence for which the intended reader of the business plan will be carefully searching.

Business Plan Specifics

It is not uncommon for entrepreneurs to ask questions such as the following:

1. "Exactly what is a business plan?"
2. "Is a business plan hard to prepare, and can someone like me do it?"
3. "Exactly what is included in a business plan?"

The answers to these questions are straightforward.

(1) First, a business plan is exactly what its name implies. It is a blueprint, detailing what the business or business concept is, what is expected for the business, how management intends to get the firm to that point, and, of greatest importance, *the specific reasons why it is expected to succeed.* This last point is crucial whether the business plan is used to attract the interest of a prospective financier or is used internally as the master plan for operating the business.

To be effective, the business plan must detail what is possible for the business, how it will be done, and the reasons it will be successful.

(2) Preparing a business plan requires time and effort, but the task is certainly not beyond the reach of the typical entrepreneur. It involves performing the same activities that successful managers perform as a standard part of managing and operating a business.

(3) An effective business plan contains the same fundamental information needed to effectively manage an existing business or evaluate the merits of a new business. Included are specifics on the firm's product or service, its industry, the markets and customers it serves, how its product or service is marketed, how operations are conducted and what resources are required to do so, and financial goals and how they will be achieved. This is the same information that practicing managers use for planning, developing business strategies, and decision-making.

About This Book

Writing a Convincing Business Plan is a how-to book for practitioners. It is designed and written as a comprehensive tutorial for understanding how business planning is done, what information is needed to do it, where this information is found, and how it is organized and written. The book addresses the needs of both the new entrepreneur and the veteran manager faced with the prospect of preparing a complete business plan or any of its parts.

A number of attractive features combine to make *Writing a Convincing Business Plan* an easy-to-read authoritative guide to the how and why of business plan preparation. Included among these helpful features are:

▬ Real-world examples of prepared business plan components.

▬ Detailed illustrations of business plan tools and techniques.

▬ A comprehensive list of the major sources of industry, market, and competitive information as well as explanations of how they are used.

▬ Guideline questions for each business plan component that help identify the factors that should be gathered to prepare the business plan.

■ A glossary of definitions and explanations of key business terms and concepts.

The sequence in which chapters appear is neither the order in which business plan information is gathered nor the order in which a business plan is written. The rule of thumb for researching and writing a business plan is to begin with the critical components and end with the easier summary components. In general, this means starting with the industry and market analysis components and ending with the business plan summary. The chapter sequence of the book, however, reflects the order in which a complete business plan would typically be arranged for presentation to an outside reader. An excellent summary can be found at *www.sba.gov.*

> Arthur R. DeThomas
> Stephanie A. Derammelaere
> Steven Fox

SUPPORTING DOCUMENTS FOR THE PRESENTATION PACKAGE

Packaging the Business Plan

THE IMPORTANCE OF GOOD PACKAGING

Your business plan is your calling card and your best opportunity to introduce the business and yourself to others in the most favorable light. While a prospective financier or investor will ultimately make a decision based on the business merits of your plan, appearances are important. An attractively packaged business plan helps promote a favorable first impression. It sends an important message about the care and diligence used in preparing the plan and managing the business. On the other hand, a carelessly prepared or inadequate presentation package has the opposite effect.

After studying the material in this chapter, you will:
- Understand the importance of having an appealing presentation package.
- Know which supplements should be included with the presentation package.
- Know how to prepare the supplements to the business plan.

DEVELOPING THE PACKAGE

The way your completed business plan *looks* is almost as important as the information contained in the plan. When packaging your business plan, give primary consideration to your audience. Your goal is to present the material in the most reader-friendly manner. This means including a cover letter, a title page, and a table of contents. It means that the entire package should be assembled and enclosed in a folder or binder that makes it most accessible to the reader. Depending on the final size of your business plan, you may want to work with a commercial designer and printer to ensure the most professional appearance.

The Cover Letter

Your cover letter will introduce you, your referring source, if applicable, and your business plan to your intended audience. It should identify you, the reason the business plan is being presented, and the documents included in the presentation package. The cover letter should be brief, to the point, and written in clear, concise language. A busy financier or investor should not have to read several pages of text to determine the nature and purpose of the material. A sample cover letter appears on the following page as Figure 1-1. It should be noted that this document:

- Identifies the entrepreneur and the firm.
- Reminds the recipient of the initial contact.
- Is brief and to the point.
- Immediately identifies the nature and purpose of the presentation package.
- Identifies enclosures and their purpose.
- Conveys a positive but not presumptuous introductory message.

The Title Page

The title page should identify:

- The content of the package, which is normally the business plan.
- Your name, address, and telephone number.
- The name(s) and position(s), for example, president or chairman of the board, of the principal(s) in the business.
- The contact person in the firm, if different from the listed owner(s) above.
- The current date.

If the business plan contains confidential or sensitive information, such as the description of a new product or the explanation of a strategic advantage, a "confidentiality statement" should be included on the title page. One example of a confidentiality statement is shown on the sample title page of The Ideal Growth Company business plan (see Figure 1-2). An even better solution would be a nondisclosure agreement that creates contractual obligations between the parties to protect any proprietary information or trade secrets and what consequences will flow in the event of a breach. The entrepreneur should consult a lawyer if this is desired.

There is no one correct format for a title page. The rule of thumb is to arrange the information in an appealing yet conservative format. One such arrangement is illustrated on The Ideal Growth Company title page.

Table of Contents

The table of contents not only enhances the appearance of the plan but also eliminates the reader's need to search through the plan to find specific topics. The table of contents should be located immediately after the title page.

FIGURE 1-1 *Sample Cover Letter*

[*Date*]

Stacy King
Commercial Loan Officer
Royal State Bank
Lawrence, GA 30011

Dear Ms. King:

I appreciated the opportunity to meet with you on June 5, and am excited about moving forward with the development of my firm. The enclosed business plan will provide the background and data to support my request for a $100,000 loan. As outlined in my proposal, this $100,000 loan would be divided into a $30,000 line of credit which would be repaid in ten months and a $70,000 term loan which would be repayable in quarterly installments over a three-year period.

My management team and I are very confident in the future success of The Ideal Growth Company. The abbreviated business plan outlines anticipated market conditions and provides a sales forecast and an operating and financial plan—all covering a three-year period.

We are eager for your reply and look forward to a long and mutually successful relationship with your bank.

Sincerely,

Fran George, President
The Ideal Growth Company
500 Industrial Park Rd.
Unionville, GA 30012

Enclosures (2)

FIGURE 1-2 *Sample Title Page*

The Business Plan
of
The Ideal Growth Company
500 Industrial Park Rd.
Unionville, GA 30012
(492) 247-1000

Presented By:
Fran George, President
[*Date*]

The content of this report is confidential and is the sole property of The Ideal Growth Company. Its use is strictly limited
to those readers authorized by the Company. Any reproduction
or divulgence of the content of this report without the written
consent of the Company is prohibited.

There is no one correct format or style for a table of contents.
Your goal should be to present the information in an attractive, easy-
to-read format designed to assist the reader to most efficiently locate
information within your business plan.

TIPS FOR PACKAGING THE BUSINESS PLAN

▬ **Appearance is important.** Since the reader forms first impressions about you, your business habits, and your business or business
concept from the presentation package, it is important that the package have an attractive, professional appearance. The following minimum guidelines should be observed:

1. The package should be neatly prepared.
2. The content should be free of spelling and grammatical errors.

FIGURE 1-3 *Example Table of Contents*

3. The material should either be printed using a quality printer or photocopier or reproduced by a commercial printer.

At the same time, don't make your business plan unreasonably "glitzy." The impression you want to convey is of a responsible business person—not of someone who spends money unnecessarily and frivolously. You want the reader to recognize the merits of a sound business, not marvel at the use of graphic design elements.

■ **Write a good business plan.** While appearance is important, the content of the business plan is the critical component of the package. To stimulate interest, it must effectively address the reader's concerns. This means the business plan should be written as a good feasibility study. Each component of the plan should emphasize *what* is feasible, the reasons *why* the business or business concept is or will be successful, and *how* success will be achieved.

■ **Content will vary.** Although this book covers every aspect of a business plan, not every business plan will necessarily contain this amount of detail. The content of a particular business plan should be governed by its intended use and the targeted reader. For example, if the plan is intended only as a guide to internal management, its content would typically focus on a general plan of action and would not include a great deal of descriptive detail. What's more, such components as the cover letter, financing proposal, executive summary, and business description would not be included. On the other hand, if the plan were written for presentation to a venture capitalist, it would have to contain appropriate descriptive detail to be effective.

■ **Use business language.** The business plan and accompanying documents should be written in conservative business language. Business and financial terms should be used wherever possible, and superlatives or exaggerated claims should be avoided.

■ **Clearly identify supporting information.** The business plan's assumptions, forecasts, and projections *must* be clearly stated and supported with convincing rationale and creditable evidence. Doing so provides critical "why it will succeed" explanations. Also, make sure that your data and projections are in line with your marketing and operating strategies and vice versa. If your goals include a fifty percent increase in sales in the fourth quarter, for example, your spending on cost of goods, marketing, and production need to reflect that growth. Financiers, investors, and other experienced business-people are accustomed to dealing with facts and informed judgments, and to basing decisions on the merits of underlying assumptions, justifications, and supporting evidence. If this information is missing, the reader will regard the business plan as nothing more than wishful thinking.

▬ Highlight key numerical values. Discussions involving numerical values such as cost figures, sales quantities, and cash-flow projections can often be enhanced through the use of tables and graphs. These tools highlight key points that may be overlooked or unappreciated if confined to text material. There are software packages that will readily allow you to portray numerical information in a variety of graphic formats. While you should not be overly reliant on these graphic aids, it is important to consider the method of presentation that will be most easily understood and most quickly grasped by your audience.

▬ Know the reader. If the business plan is to attract and hold the reader's interest, it must be written with the reader's concerns in mind. To do so effectively, it is necessary to understand the reader's business and the nature of his or her potential involvement with the firm. Frame the information you present from the point of reference of the reader. For example, the emphasis in a business plan that is used to support a loan request from a commercial bank should be different from what is stressed in a venture-capital proposal. When written as part of a loan request, the business plan should highlight the firm's ability to generate the cash flow necessary to repay the loan and the availability of suitable collateral. In the case of a venture-capital proposal, emphasis should be on such considerations as the existence of a market opportunity that promises heavy sales volume and large profit potential and on a timetable for the liquidation of the venture capitalist's interest in the business.

▬ Get feedback on your plan. Make sure that your final plan has been thoroughly proofread and seek feedback on the plan's content from people whose opinions you value and trust. Talk to local lenders, potential customers, and industry experts, and be open to constructive input on ways you can improve the plan.

CHAPTER PERSPECTIVE

Since opinions are often formed on first impressions, it is important that the business plan be well prepared, attractively packaged, and targeted to the intended audience. Three important elements that add to the professional appearance of the presentation package are: the cover letter, title page, and table of contents. The business plan and supplements should be intelligently written using appropriate business language, neat and free from errors, and packaged conservatively and attractively. Then, get a second opinion of the plan from a professional you trust, and modify accordingly. The plan must be as clear and uncluttered as possible.

The Executive Summary

WHAT IS AN EXECUTIVE SUMMARY?

An executive summary is a thumbnail sketch of the business plan. The primary purpose of the executive summary is to present the information contained in the financing proposal and business plan in an abbreviated format. The summary should spark the reader's interest and encourage further examination of the complete plan. It should adequately cover the key points of the plan and be presented in a succinct and clear manner.

After studying the material in this chapter, you will:

- Understand the purpose of the executive summary.
- Know what information to include in the executive summary.
- Know when to include an executive summary.
- Understand the two formats used to prepare an executive summary.

INFORMATION NEEDED TO PREPARE THE EXECUTIVE SUMMARY

The executive summary is a synopsis of the key issues in the business plan that are of primary interest to the intended reader. Normally, these include a concise description of the following:

- The firm's basic business.
- How business is or will be conducted.
- The firm's success thus far, if applicable, or a forecast of intended quantifiable success.
- The intended market for the firm's products or services and the sales potential of this market.
- How and why the firm can penetrate this market.
- The competitive or marketing advantage the firm has over its competition.
- The resources and amount of financing needed to implement the business plan.

WHEN TO INCLUDE AN EXECUTIVE SUMMARY IN THE PACKAGE

An executive summary should be included in the presentation package when a complete or essentially complete business plan is presented to the intended reader. A busy venture capitalist would normally look to the summary and then the business description (discussed in Chapter 4) to decide whether the business concept has merit and whether it is consistent with his or her investment interests.

If only selected portions of the business plan will be presented to an outside reader, an executive summary would normally not be included. For example, if the entrepreneur is making a routine loan request from a banker familiar with the business, the presentation package might consist of only a cover letter, a detailed loan proposal, and updated information from the firm's internal marketing and financial plans. For situations such as this, there is no need to summarize an already limited package.

CHOOSING THE APPROPRIATE FORMAT

The summary should be written using either of two styles: topical or narrative.

The most straightforward and least difficult to prepare is the *topical format*. This format consists of the essential points or conclusions presented in the business plan. For example, the operating plan (see Chapter 8) describes how management intends to conduct business and the resources needed to do so. If the firm's operations are crucial to the success of the business, a synopsis should be included in the executive summary. It should address implied questions of *how* operations are conducted and *why* this method of operation contributes to the success of the firm. The contribution can result from factors such as greater cost efficiency, better technology, superior product quality, or a more attractive store location.

An alternative to the topical format is the *narrative format*. The narrative style, as illustrated in Figure 2-1 at the end of this chapter, uses descriptive prose to tell a story about the business or business concept. This approach is most effective when used to describe a start-up firm, a planned venture, or an existing business that has developed a unique competitive advantage such as revolutionary cost-saving technology or an exciting new product or service.

If done well, the narrative style conveys the entrepreneur's message more effectively and offers a better chance of stimulating the reader's interest than its topical counterpart. It allows the writer to get more in depth with the background of the business idea and illustrate the potential success of the venture. The key to success with the narrative style is to write provocative prose and yet avoid hyperbole or misrepresentation. As a general rule, it is easier to write an acceptable topical summary than a stimulating narrative summary. The topical summary simply condenses key points or conclusions contained in the business plan. A tantalizing narrative summary, however, requires creativity and a higher level of writing ability.

TIPS FOR PREPARING AN EXECUTIVE SUMMARY

■ **Write it last.** Whether the topical or narrative format is used, the summary should be prepared after the entire business plan has been written. You will find your task much simplified by following this tip and will ensure accurate and thorough coverage of the key points contained in the plan.

■ **Keep the main theme in mind.** It cannot be overemphasized that a professional reader of the business plan will be most concerned with *why* and *how* the business or business concept is expected to succeed, and *what* factors will account for this success. Since the summary is normally read first, a clear and convincing case for the *why* and *how* of success must be made here. However, also remember the purpose. A business plan written with the intention of receiving grant funding and one written to secure venture capital financing will have different executive summaries, highlighting those factors that pertain to each situation and that will most benefit achieving the overall purpose.

■ **More risk means more proof.** To a business or financial professional, a new business or an untried business concept represents more risk than an established firm or a proven method of doing business. Because of this, the intended reader will be skeptical about claims for success. Consequently, the summary written for a new business or an untried business concept must make a stronger case for commercial and economic success than one written for an existing business. The supporting documentation must be carefully detailed in the body of the business plan and more convincingly articulated in the summary.

■ **Avoid hype.** Although the executive summary must be convincing and use positive language, the temptation to make exaggerated claims or to misrepresent facts must be avoided. A sophisticated reader will immediately recognize hype for what it is and the business plan loses credibility along with the chance to stimulate the reader's interest.

■ **Length is important.** Regardless of the format used, the executive plan summary must clearly convey the entrepreneur's message but, at the same time, be brief and to the point. Although there is no hard-and-fast rule governing length, a summary is customarily no longer than two pages and may be as short as one page. The purpose of the executive summary is to provide a brief snapshot of the overall plan, enticing the reader to further delve into the plan.

■ **Know the target audience.** The executive summary should be written with the intended reader in mind. To be most successful at capturing the interest and, ultimately, the support of your audience, you should attempt to respond to the issues and questions that the reader may have. This requires a good understanding of the reader's frame of reference and business issues. For instance, when writing for a potential investor, knowing the degree of risk the investor is willing to assume can help you more effectively develop your proposal.

A SAMPLE EXECUTIVE SUMMARY

Figure 2-1, a sample executive summary for Industrial Metal Finishing, uses the narrative style to support the firm's objectives and the owner's plans for introducing a business concept that capitalizes on new technology. In writing the summary, Paul and George Freund are able to demonstrate *how* and *why* success for the new business concept can be expected. For example, it is made clear that:

■ This new application process offers customers high quality, durability, and endurance when compared to other market alternatives.

■ Expectations for future success are based on sound research and reasoning, including the success of the business during its first 19 months of operation and clearly identified market potential in specific industry segments.

■ The owners are openly enthusiastic and have made a sizable commitment of equity funds in support of the business.

CHAPTER PERSPECTIVE

It is common practice to summarize the key issues from the business plan in a separate document known as the executive summary. The summary is a convenience the intended reader expects to find in the presentation package. It can be written in either a topical or narrative style. Regardless of which format is chosen, it is important that the summary pique the reader's interest by clearly articulating why the plan is feasible and how it will lead to the success of the firm. Remember that the executive summary will be the first text your reader will see.

FIGURE 2-1 *Sample Executive Summary for Industrial Metal Finishing*

Industrial Metal Finishing (IMF) is a company that provides state-of-the-art finishing as an alternative to painting in industrial metal finishing applications. Superior durability, reduced costs, and environmental considerations have played a role in the movement of manufacturers throughout the world from liquid paint to industrial metal finishing.

IMF was established by Paul and George Freund in 2006 and has been in operation since that time. IMF began operations in a manufacturing facility where the Freunds currently lease 2,500 square feet of manufacturing space and a 250-square-foot office. The operation is staffed by the two owners, one full-time employee, and one part-time employee. The addition of four additional employees within the next year of operation, with growth to approximately 12 employees within the next three years, will be required to meet identified market demand and potential.

During the first 19 months of operation, IMF established an operation with more than 20 industrial customers within a 50-mile radius and from as far away as 600 miles. An initial market survey of manufacturers in a 100-mile radius has identified more than 350 potential customers for the metal finishing services.

Applications for the use of industrial metal finishing vary widely and include the appliance and automotive industries. Industrial metal finishing is also appropriate for applications such as architectural metal, industrial equipment, furniture, and sporting goods.

The mission of IMF during its first three years of operation will be to provide quality metal finishing services to a variety of clients. IMF's long-term goal will be to identify areas of opportunity in the industry that will allow us to begin the manufacturing of value-added businesses that utilize metal finishing in the process. In an effort to move us toward this goal, the Freunds have developed several consumer products that will be marketed by a recently formed sister corporation. Additionally, IMF has recently obtained a distributorship for metal finishing products. These products will be a good complement to IMF's existing services since the market is very similar.

FIGURE 2-1 *(continued)*

IMF's equipment currently includes high-pressure cleaning and phosphatizing equipment, a spray booth and sprayer, and an oven. The start-up cost for equipment, fixtures, materials, and working capital was approximately $50,000. To date, the business has been financed by the stockholders in the business and from operations. In anticipation of future demand for IMF's services, a detailed expansion plan has been drafted and price quotations have been obtained. The expanded plant would include an automated metal finishing line that would increase capacity approximately ten times over current levels.

With current equipment IMF's production capacity is at approximately $28,000 per month in sales. With the addition of a larger oven, four additional employees, and 1,200 square feet of manufacturing space, IMF projects increased revenue to approximately $60,000 per month.

As discussed in our Loan Proposal and Financial Plan, an estimated $300,000 of total financing is needed by buy the equipment, land, construct additional manufacturing space, hire staff, and maintain working capital. We propose that the required financing be in the form of debt capital. A suggested maturity and repayment schedule for the proposed debt financing are detailed in the Loan Proposal and Financial Plan.

The Financing Proposal

WHAT IS A FINANCING PROPOSAL?

A financing proposal is a supporting document for the business plan and an integral part of most presentation packages. As its name implies, the proposal is a formal request for financial backing and an effective summary of the key issues in the financial plan.

The financing proposal makes two important contributions toward an effective presentation package. First, if the business plan is prepared to support a financing request, the financier expects a financing proposal to be included in the presentation package. Failure to provide a busy financier with the summary information found in the financing proposal may be ample reason for an out-of-hand rejection of the business plan.

Second, a well-prepared financing proposal is unmistakable evidence of the entrepreneur's financial savvy and ability to do the type of investigation and planning that is characteristic of effective managers. This is often the inducement needed for the financier to read the complete business plan.

After studying the material in this chapter, you will:

- Understand the role of a financing proposal.
- Know what information is needed to prepare a financing proposal.
- Know the steps to preparing a financing proposal.

INFORMATION NEEDED TO PREPARE THE FINANCING PROPOSAL

Since the financing proposal is essentially a summary of the financial plan, the information needed to prepare it comes directly from that document and other business plan components. For example,

- An analysis of the financing required to support working-capital needs such as inventory or the purchase of fixed assets such as equipment or buildings should be contained in the financial plan.
- A description and justification of the land and buildings needed to support expansion plans should be contained in the operating plan.

■ An explanation of the amount of financing needed to implement management's promotion and advertising strategy should be contained in the marketing plan.

As illustrated in the sample loan proposal at the end of this chapter (see Figure 3-1), when the discussion involves points summarized from other areas of the business plan, it is a good idea to reference the pages on which the information appears. These citations will help the reader quickly locate desired background information.

WHEN TO INCLUDE THE FINANCING PROPOSAL WITH THE PACKAGE

As a general rule, a financing proposal should be included in the presentation package whenever the business plan has been prepared to support a financing request. In some cases, an expanded financing proposal *may* serve as a substitute for a complete financial plan. This is true when the necessary financial information can be included in the proposal without making it inordinately long or when a detailed financial plan is unnecessary. For example, when working-capital financing is sought from a banker familiar with the firm and its management, only the proposal, a cash-flow projection (cash budget), and the most recent set of financial statements are usually needed.

STEPS TO PREPARING THE FINANCING PROPOSAL

The key to preparing the financing proposal is to divide the task into a series of small, manageable steps. The seven steps discussed below offer a logical sequence for gathering information from the financial plan and preparing the proposal. However, because financing needs differ for different businesses, each step need not be included in every proposal. Some steps may be omitted because they are inappropriate, some may be combined for clarity or convenience, and some may have titles or headings different from what is suggested here.

1. **Identify the amount needed.** The exact dollar amount of the financing requested should be clearly indicated and, as discussed below, tied directly to the intended use(s) of the funds. Resist the temptation to state a broad dollar range rather than a specific amount. Expressing financial needs as a range implies a lack of careful investigation and planning.

2. **Explain how the financing will be used.** A prospective financier is as concerned about the intended use(s) of the financing as the amount requested (use of proceeds). For example, will the proceeds be used for start-up expenses or operating expenses. Before a financial commitment is made, the financier must be satisfied that

the funds will be used wisely and that the expected returns for both parties are consistent with the level of risk involved. These considerations should be explicitly addressed in the proposal.

For example, if financing is needed to support seasonal upswings in normal operations (working-capital needs), each component of working capital to be financed should be identified. Or, if financing is needed to purchase fixed (plant) assets, a detailed description of the asset(s) should be provided. In each case, it is important to explain *how* and *why* the planned uses for the funds will contribute to the success of the business.

3. **Specify the type of financing needed.** The proposal should indicate whether borrowed funds (debt) or owner's invested capital (equity) are needed. As explained in greater detail in Chapter 10, debt financing is money borrowed under a contractual agreement. This contract legally obligates the borrower for repayment of interest and principal and for compliance with all other provisions of the agreement. Failure to meet debt obligations constitutes a breach of contract; possible resulting litigation could mean bankruptcy for the firm. On the other hand, equity financing is the owner's own capital. Raising ownership funds avoids the burden of mandatory debt payments but forces the entrepreneur to relinquish some portion of his or her interest in the business.

4. **Specify the maturity of the financing needed.** Will short-term, intermediate-term, or long-term financing be needed? A prospective financier will be concerned that the intended uses of funds are properly matched with an appropriate maturity period for the financing. In general, short-term debt financing is used to meet temporary or seasonal working-capital needs. This financing should be repaid within the firm's normal working-capital cycle as inventory and customer accounts (accounts receivable) are converted to cash.

Intermediate-term financing typically takes the form of an installment loan with periodic payments that amortize interest and principal over a maturity of two to ten years. This financing is usually used to acquire assets with a life span that approximates the maturity of the loan. Fixed assets such as vehicles, machinery, or computer equipment are common purchases made with intermediate-term credit.

Long-term financing represents the more permanent component of the firm's financial structure. In general, financiers expect equity financing to be the largest percentage of these dollars. A solid equity base protects the financial commitment of creditors and increases the firm's likelihood of surviving a business downturn. Lenders often use the size and strength of the firm's equity base as an indicator of the maximum amount of debt financing the firm should carry. For example, a long-established rule of thumb among bankers is the 50%-50% financial structure where amount of debt financing used does not exceed 50% of the firm's total financing.

5. **Suggest a payment schedule.** The proposal should *suggest* a timetable of when and in what amounts the financier will be repaid. In this way, the entrepreneur sends a clear message that he or she understands the financier's major concerns. A financier wants assurances that the entrepreneur recognizes the importance of:

- The legal and/or moral repayment obligation associated with the financing received.
- Generating cash flows that will support operating plans and meet financial obligations.
- A repayment plan that is consistent with the needs of the financier and the cash-flow pattern of the firm.
- Sound financial management principles for the successful operation of the firm.

Unless the financing proposal and financial plan provide these assurances of repayment, financing will not be forthcoming.

If debt financing is sought, a *proposed* repayment schedule covering interest and principal should be offered. If equity financing is needed, a schedule of the amount and timing of expected cash flows, profits, and owner withdrawals (dividends if the firm is incorporated) should be provided.

In the case of venture-capital financing, the proposal should also identify dates or milestone events that indicate the firm's progress toward a specified liquidation date of the venture capitalist's interests in the business. The typical venture capitalist is not interested in owning or operating the business. Most venture capitalists are high-risk investors who provide financing by buying an ownership interest in the business. They expect to earn a return on their equity investment that adequately compensates for the degree of risk assumed, and to liquidate this investment at some definite date through a public offering of the firm's stock or a planned buy-out agreement.

6. **Identify available collateral.** If debt financing is sought, the proposal should contain a detailed description of the type and market value of assets that can be pledged as collateral, if required, to secure the loan. The existence of collateral reduces the risk of loss for the lender in the event the borrower is unable to make the required loan payments.

For an established, profitable firm with a proven credit record, the pledge of collateral may not be necessary for obtaining a loan. On the other hand, if the firm is new or has an unproven or questionable credit standing, pledging collateral may be the only way to obtain debt financing. This is true even when the loan is sound and the prospects for repayment are strong. The reverse, however, is not true. Since the return on a loan is limited to the interest received, a creditor must limit default-risk exposure. Rarely, if ever, will a creditor accept collateral as a substitute for poor repayment prospects. An old banking adage describes this situation: "Good collateral does not make a bad loan good."

7. **Indicate the owners' investment.** The financing proposal should also provide a detailed description of the amount invested by each existing owner and the percentage of total equity financing each investment represents. If the firm is incorporated, the proposal should indicate the number of shares of common stock held by each major stockholder and the percentage of the total number of shares outstanding that each holding represents.

TIPS FOR PREPARING THE FINANCING PROPOSAL

▬ **Write the proposal last.** Although the financing proposal should be located immediately after the executive summary in the presentation package, it should be one of the last components written. Since the information needed to write the proposal comes from the financial plan and other relevant business plan components these documents must be completed before an effective summary can be written. In addition, completing the financial plan prior to writing the proposal allows you to fully understand your firm's financial picture and identify how much outside funding will really be necessary.

▬ **Do not rewrite the financial plan.** While the financing proposal identifies the key elements of the financing request, it should be written as a supporting *summary* document. Avoid a lengthy rehash of the financial plan. Readers of the business plan will be able to reference the financial plan for more detailed information. Like the executive summary, the financing proposal should offer only a sound overview and motivate the financier to continue reviewing the plan and seriously consider the proposal. As a general rule, the proposal should not exceed two pages in length.

▬ **Appreciate the importance of this component.** Since financing is critical to the question of feasibility, the information provided in the proposal will be carefully evaluated by the prospective financier. It is important, therefore, that you address the implicit questions of *how* and *why* the financing will contribute to the success of the venture. One way to do this effectively is to write the proposal from the financier's perspective. Strive to convince the financier that the financing provided will produce the cash flows necessary to recapture the financier's investment and generate a rate of return that fairly compensates both you and the lender for the risk assumed.

■ **Know the intended reader.** As is true of the business plan, a good financing proposal is one the intended financier *thinks* is good. To write such a proposal, you must understand the financier's business and his or her perspective on risk and return. Financial institutions are not all the same. They differ in the type of financing offered and in the amount of risk that can be assumed. It is important, therefore, to make sure that the financing request fits the intended financier's business. For example, requesting a short-term working-capital loan from a venture capitalist would be as foolish as approaching a bank for a long-term equity investment. An overview of financial institutions and sources of financing is provided in Chapter 11.

■ **Heed basic financial principles.** As explained in the "Tips For Preparing A Financial Plan" section of Chapter 10, the financing proposal should leave no doubt in the reader's mind that the entrepreneur understands basic financial management principles. Pay special attention to such points as the prudent use of debt financing, having an adequate equity base, and using cash-flow projections to support the financing request.

SAMPLE LOAN PROPOSAL

Figure 3-1 is a financing proposal for the hypothetical firm used in Chapter 1, The Ideal Growth Company. In this case, the proposal is identified as a loan proposal rather than a financing proposal because Ms. George is seeking only conventional debt financing.

FIGURE 3-1 *A Loan Proposal for the Ideal Growth Company*

Amount and Type of Financing Needed

Our loan request, in the amount of $100,000, is structured as follows:

1. **A Line of Credit.** A $30,000 line of credit is needed to support the increase in seasonal working capital.

2. **Three-Year Term Loan.** A three-year installment loan in the amount of $70,000 is needed to purchase additional delivery equipment and the maintenance contracts on this equipment.

FIGURE 3-1 *(continued)*

Use of Proposed Financing

The line of credit will be used to finance the estimated $15,000 increase in accounts receivable, the $12,000 increase in inventory, and the additional operating-cash needs of $3,000 that will accompany the anticipated sales growth next year.

The equipment to be purchased with the term loan is needed to accommodate the increase in customer deliveries that will result from the anticipated 10% growth rate in sales and profits for each of the next three years. The equipment to be purchased at the indicated prices includes:

1. A new flatbed truck purchased from Union Motors, Inc., at a delivered price of $48,000.
2. Delivery equipment, in the form of a large-capacity hydraulic hoist and a self-powered conveyer belt system, purchased from Griner Equipment at a price of $22,000.

Complete sets of manufacturer's specifications for the truck and the delivery equipment, along with a copy of the maintenance plan for each, are contained in the Appendix to the Business Plan (not shown).

Proposed Repayment Schedule

As shown by our cash budget, Cash Flow from Operations will be more than sufficient to repay the $30,000 line of credit within the required 10-month period.

The cash budget also clearly indicates the seasonal nature of the firm's cash flows. The recurring quarterly pattern suggests that quarterly payments on the three-year term loan are in the best interest of both the Bank and Ideal.

Available Collateral

The following assets are available to collateralize the $100,000 of proposed debt financing.

1. All accounts receivable and inventory are available for collateral on the $30,000 line of credit.
2. The new truck and delivery equipment to be purchased with the term loan are available for collateral.
3. A personal guarantee of both notes by Ideal's president, Elizabeth George.

CHAPTER PERSPECTIVE

A financing proposal is included in the presentation package whenever the business plan has been prepared to justify a financing request. It should be a concise, reader friendly summary of the amount of financing needed and of other key points discussed in the financial plan. In some cases, the financing proposal *may* serve as a substitute for the financial plan. The proposal should summarize the amount, type, and maturity of the required financing; describe the intended uses of the funds received; suggest a repayment schedule; identify the proportion of owner's funds invested in the business when equity capital is sought; and identify available collateral when debt financing is sought.

The Business Description

WHAT IS A BUSINESS DESCRIPTION?

As its name suggests, the business description describes the basic nature and purpose of the business. A well-written business description explains what the business is, what it does, how it is done, who gets it done, where it has been, and where it is expected to go in the future. The business description anticipates and provides answers to critical questions such as:

- What is the exact business of the firm or venture?
- What product or service does it sell?
- Where is the market for this product or service?
- To what target market (specific customer group) will the product or service appeal?
- What important events have brought the firm to the current stage of its life cycle?
- How is the business operated?
- Who will manage and lead the business?
- What is the firm's past and/or current financial position?
- Why will it be successful?

A business description that effectively answers these questions meets two important goals. First, it serves as a gauge by which the entrepreneur measures his or her understanding of the business and the factors that lead to its success or failure.

An effective business description also meets the expectations of the intended reader. A busy professional usually does not have the time or inclination to read an entire business plan to determine whether there is sufficient interest to warrant further consideration. He or she expects the business description to provide the information needed to make this judgement. If this information is missing, the entrepreneur runs the risk of not having the business plan read.

After studying the material in this chapter, you will:

- Understand the role of the business description.
- Know what information is needed to prepare the business description.

■ Know the steps to preparing the business description.
■ Understand the business life-cycle concept.
■ Become familiar with the North American Industry Classification System (NAICS).

INFORMATION NEEDED TO PREPARE THE BUSINESS DESCRIPTION

The business description should be the easiest component of the business plan to prepare. Since, as suggested in the "Tips" section of this chapter, the business description should be the last component of the business plan that the entrepreneur prepares, its content is drawn directly from existing material. For example, the summary description of the firm's market and target customer group or its financial profile uses information taken from the market analysis and financial plan components of the business plan.

WHEN TO USE A BUSINESS DESCRIPTION

A business description is normally included when a complete, or essentially complete, business plan is prepared. In some cases, an expanded business description *may* serve as a substitute for a complete business plan. This is true if the description contains sufficient information to answer the essential question of feasibility, and if:
■ The plan is written for a small business that uses a conventional method of operation.
■ The plan is written for a business whose industry, market, and target market are already familiar to the reader.
■ The intended reader is already intimately familiar with the business and its operations.
■ The amount of information needed to adequately expand the description does not make it inordinately large.

STEPS TO PREPARING THE BUSINESS DESCRIPTION

The seven steps identified and discussed here offer a logical sequence for gathering information and preparing the business description. As suggested in the last chapter, the recommended approach is to treat each section as a separate task, and then to complete it before moving to the next. As an additional aid to preparation, guideline questions are included where appropriate to indicate the type of information that should be gathered. Also, a sample business description for a hypothetical retailer is included at the end of this chapter (see Figure 4-1).

   1.   **Identify the firm and location.** The first section of the business description normally consists of the information needed by

the reader to identify the firm and the appropriate contact person. This includes:

- The business name of the firm.
- The legal name of the firm if different from the business name.
- The address, or addresses if there are multiple locations, of the firm.
- The person to contact and his or her office or personal telephone, fax numbers, and e-mail address.

Identifying information, especially that of the contact person, is essential if the entrepreneur is unknown to the intended reader, or if the business plan is not delivered by the entrepreneur. This would be the case, for example, if presentation packages were mailed to a number of prospective financiers.

2. **Trace the firm's history.** If the business description is written for an existing firm, this section should contain a thumbnail sketch of the significant events, episodes, or major milestones of the firm's history. This historical perspective should indicate *why* the firm has been successful to this point or the major obstacles that management has overcome. Significant events or milestones might include:

- The firm's date of origin and the founder(s) name(s).
- The firm's legal ownership form and the date established.
- A profile of the major stages of the life cycle through which the firm has passed.
- The major episodes in the firm's financial history.
- A brief description of any significant changes the business has undergone.
- A brief description of any major crises the firm has encountered and the strategies management used to successfully overcome them.

If the description is written for a new venture, this section should explain the firm's stages of development, what has been accomplished, and what remains to be accomplished before the business is operational.

3. **Identify the business mission statement.** This section should explain the firm's primary purpose or reason for existence, the direction the entrepreneur expects to take the firm, and what he or she expects the firm to accomplish. The expected accomplishments are normally expressed as broad, strategic goals. For example, strategic marketing goals may be set in terms of sales growth or share of the market, and strategic financial goals may be expressed as profit growth or cost-reduction targets.

The following guideline questions are designed to help the entrepreneur focus on the issues that should be considered in formulating the firm's mission statement.

- What broad expression defines the primary business of the firm? For example, since its inception in 1975, Microsoft's mission has been to create software for the personal computer that empowers and enriches people in the workplace, at school, and at home. Today, Microsoft has expanded that early vision to include a strong commitment to Internet-related technologies that expand the power and reach of the PC and its users. Microsoft's broad business expression appears as part of its value statement: "helping customers achieve their goals is the key to Microsoft's long-term success."

- What is the basic purpose of the business? For example, when Sam Walton opened the first Walmart store in 1962, he believed that consumers wanted a discount store that offered a wide variety of merchandise and friendly service. Today that same basic purpose is behind Walmart's continued success. Low prices and wide variety are made possible through the industry's most efficient and sophisticated distribution system, allowing each store to customize the merchandise assortment to match the community's needs.

- Where is the firm expected to be next year, three years from now, and five years from now as measured by growth indicators such as profits, assets, sales, share of the market, etc.?

- What basic business strategy will be used to move the firm toward these targets?

- What are the firm's goals in regard to its owner(s), customers, employees, suppliers, and the general public?

The mission statement should *not* exclude the profit motive. Earning a compensatory return for the firm's owners is the primary reason for starting a business and a necessary condition for staying in business. Failure to express this objective in the mission statement would cause the intended reader to question the entrepreneur's understanding of basic business principles. For example, the reason for starting a restaurant should not be expressed as a fondness for cooking. A more appropriate statement would be "to address a potentially profitable market niche that is not being filled."

4. **Define the firm's industry and market description.** This section should contain a synopsis of the firm's industry, the geographic location of its market(s), and the target market to which it appeals. These external factors are important determinants of the firm's commercial success or failure. The term *industry* refers to the

group of businesses that produce or supply related products or services. *Market location* is the geographic trade area that the firm serves, and *target market* is the distinct segment or group of customers the firm is attempting to reach.

The summary of the firm's industry should consist of information such as the following:

- The North American Industry Classification System (as explained later in this chapter) number and name.
- The primary product or service provided by the industry.
- The major firms in the industry.
- The industry's major competitors.
- The development and current stage of the industry's life cycle.
- The outlook for sales and revenue growth.

Often, the most effective approach to summarizing the firm's market and target market focuses on geographic, demographic, and psychographic characteristics.

- *Geographic* refers to the area, region, country, or continent in which the firm's target market is located. The term is also used to describe the climate conditions that are important to sales of the firm's product or service. For example, "the moderate to semi-tropical climate of the sunbelt states."
- *Demographic* means the specific features that profile either a geographic market area or target customer group. For example, geographic markets are often described using characteristics such as the Standard Metropolitan Statistical Area designation (see Chapter 6), population, number of households, or number of people in a given age group. A target market may also be distinguished from other customer groups by such demographic characteristics as occupation, income level, race, or sex.
- *Psychographic* refers to the psychological makeup of the target market. Psychographics involve needs, motives for buying, lifestyle, tastes, values, beliefs, and interests.

It is important for the industry and market summary to address the issue of commercial feasibility. This will be the intended reader's first major concern. If the firm's target market cannot produce a satisfactory volume of sales, then the firm cannot succeed; nothing else in the business plan matters.

The following questions should help in preparing the industry and market section. Complete discussions of industry analysis, market analysis and sales forecasting, and the marketing plan are provided in Chapters 5, 6, and 7, respectively.

- Is the firm's industry growing or declining relative to competing industries or to broad economic indicators such as gross domestic product (GDP)?
- What strategic opportunity is available in this industry?
- How does the firm's product or service differ from that of competitors?
- Where is the firm's market, and who constitutes its target market?
- What specific characteristics of the firm's geographic market make it attractive?
- What specific feature of the firm's product or service makes it attractive to the target market; or, alternatively, why should this customer group buy from the firm rather than from its competitors?
- Does the target market have sufficient purchasing power to provide the business with a profitable level of sales?
- What is the sales estimate for next year, the next three years, and the next five years?
- What evidence is there to support these sales estimates?

5. **Describe operations.** In a business, the system or set of procedures, processes, and methods used to convert resource inputs (such as raw materials, labor, or an advantageous business location) into a valuable output is known as operations. The summary description of this key function should focus on the flow of activities that identify what the business does and how it gets done. For example, if the business plan is written for a manufacturing firm, the description provides a thumbnail sketch of the product, the work flow that produces this product, and any competitive advantage offered by this particular method of operation. If the firm is a service business, this section consists of a summary of the activities required to perform the service and a brief explanation of the advantage or contribution it provides.

The following guideline questions should help the entrepreneur focus on the important issues to be summarized in this section of the business description. A complete discussion of the operating plan is provided in Chapter 8.

- What product or service does the firm produce or provide, or what product or product line does it merchandise?
- What competitive advantage or contribution does the firm's location offer?
- If the firm is a manufacturer, what are the major steps in the production process?
- What are the keys to success for the production process?

- What competitive advantage or contribution does the production process provide?
- What is the gross profit margin (sales less cost of goods sold) or contribution margin (sales less variable costs) on the major product(s) produced?
- If the firm is a service business, what steps are required to provide that service?
- What competitive advantage or contribution do these operating procedures provide?
- What is the gross profit margin or contribution margin on the service offered?
- To which merchandising category does the business belong and what is its major product or product line?
- What competitive advantage or contribution does this product or product line provide?
- What selling strategy is employed?
- What advantage or contribution is offered by the firm's physical facilities and/or layout?
- What advantage or contribution is offered by the firm's purchasing procedures?
- What advantage or contribution does the firm's inventory management system offer?
- What advantage or contribution do the firm's quality control and customer service system offer?

6. **Develop profiles of top management and other key personnel.** This section should identify the key positions in the firm and summarize the job qualifications and contributions of the individuals in these positions. If the addition of key personnel is part of the long-term plan, a brief description of these positions should be provided as well.

While writing this section of the business description, keep in mind that the intended reader will be keenly interested in the job qualifications of key personnel and how these people contribute to the success of the firm. He or she knows that an organization is only as effective as its employees and the management team that leads them.

The following guideline questions should help the entrepreneur focus on the important organizational issues to be summarized. A complete discussion of the organization plan is provided in Chapter 9.

- What are the top-level management and staff positions in the firm and which ones have already been recruited for and/or retained?
- What are the primary duties and responsibilities associated with the top-level management and staff positions?

- Who holds each management and staff position?
- What are the job qualifications of each position-holder?
- What professional or job-related successes has each position-holder enjoyed?
- What unique contribution does each position-holder make to the success of the firm?
- What salary is paid each position-holder?
- What bonus or incentive plan is provided each position-holder?
- What key positions are planned for the future?
- Why and when are these positions needed, and what contribution will they make to the success of the firm?

7. **Develop a financial profile.** The financial profile should summarize the important points made in the firm's financial plan. Normally this includes information such as the following:

- If the firm is an existing business, a brief review of the firm's past financial performance, as measured by the growth in cash flow and profit, and current financial position.
- The financial goals that have been established for the firm's planning period.
- The financing needed to support planned operations.
- The type and maturity of the needed financing.
- The expected sources of this financing.
- The existing proportions of debt and owner's equity capital used to finance the firm.
- The proportions of debt and equity capital that will exist after the proposed financing.
- Projected cash flow and profit levels or growth rates.
- Projected break-even analysis.
- Any considerations or planned actions that have major financial consequences such as the liability on a pending lawsuit, a change in financial strategy, or the intention to take the firm public.

If a financing proposal is included with the presentation package, summaries of anticipated financing needs should be omitted from this section of the business description. In this case, only summary information on financial performance, financial condition, financing mix, and other important financial considerations should be included.

The following questions should serve as helpful guidelines for preparing the financial profile section of the business description. A complete discussion of the financial plan is provided in Chapter 10.

- What attainable financial goals have been established for the upcoming planning period?

- If the firm is an existing business, what has its financial performance been for the past three years as measured by the trend in key ratio values such as the growth rate of cash flow and profit, or return on investment?
- If the firm is an existing business, what is its current financial position as measured by key indicators such as cash flow from operations, profit margins, and the debt ratio?
- As shown by the cumulative financing figure on the cash budget, what amount of seasonal working-capital financing is needed during the first year of the planning period?
- As shown by the pro forma balance sheet plug figure, how much external financing must be raised to support anticipated growth during the planning period?
- Given the current stage of the firm's development, what category of financing should be used?
- In what form, debt or equity capital, will this financing be raised?
- Given the degree of risk to which the business is exposed, what is the maximum percentage of debt financing that should be used?
- If debt financing is contemplated, would the proportion of debt existing after the financing violate the maximum percentage?

INDUSTRIAL CLASSIFICATION CODING

For years small business marketers relied upon the Standard Industrial Classification (SIC) system to target customers, select mailing lists, and analyze marketing effectiveness. The most descriptive characteristic of an industry is its primary product or product feature. The SIC was created by the federal government to classify business firms according to the specific business activities they engage in. That 60-year-old system, however, was replaced in 1997 by the NAICS system. NAICS, or North American Industry Classification System, increases the number of classifications formerly available under the SIC, providing 358 new industries that the SIC did not identify. The system is purported to be easier to use, more accurate, and more frequently updated. It also provides comparability between the United States, Canada, and Mexico, and was developed jointly by these countries.

NAICS industries are identified by a six-digit code, in contrast to the four-digit SIC code. The longer code accommodates a larger number of sectors and allows more flexibility in designating subsectors. The codes allow for additional detail not necessarily appropriate for all three NAICS countries. The international NAICS agreement fixes only the first five digits of the code. The sixth digit, where used, identifies subdivisions of NAICS industries that accommodate user needs in individual countries. Thus, six-digit U.S. codes may differ from counterparts in Canada or Mexico, but at the five-digit level they are standardized.

The major flaw of the SIC system was that it identified the output of a business, and not the business processes, meaning that the resultant lists were not as clearly defined as marketers might have liked. These broad categorizations made it difficult for marketers to specifically target *segments* within an industry. The NAICS codes, on the other hand, identify processes, making it more specific—and resulting in a 15% increase in the number of classifications formerly available under the SIC. For instance, some of the new classifications that have been added include: bed and breakfast inns, diet and weight-reducing centers, telecommunications resellers, and fiber optic cable manufacturing.

■ The new six-digit NAICS code is more precise than the four-digit SIC for use in target marketing and analysis.

■ NAICS better accommodates new and emerging business activities, especially in the area of technology.

■ NAICS, as the government standard, will be kept up to date. The four-digit SIC will not.

■ NAICS allows for easier cross-border trade because the codes are standardized in Mexico, Canada, and the United States.

The NAICS system provides five levels of classification (compared to four for the SIC). These detailed codes have a maximum of six digits. The changes have required new numbers—so for marketers familiar with certain four-digit SIC classifications, the transition can be, at least initially, a bit confusing.

The highest level of classification is called "sector" (similar to the previous SIC "division" classification). The first two digits of the NAICS code define the sector. Industries are grouped into 20 broad sectors that are, in most cases, similar to familiar SIC divisions:

■ Agriculture, forestry, fishing, and hunting
■ Mining
■ Construction
■ Manufacturing
■ Utilities
■ Transportation and warehousing
■ Wholesale trade
■ Retail trade
■ Accommodation and food services
■ Finance and insurance

- Real estate and rental and leasing
- Information*
- Professional, scientific, and technical services*
- Administrative and support and waste
- Management and remediation services
- Educational services*
- Health care and social assistance*
- Arts, entertainment, and recreation*
- Other services (except public administration)
- Public administration
- Management of companies and enterprises

Digits three through five allow for more specific identification of various sectors processes. The first five digits are fixed for use in the United States, Canada, and Mexico. The sixth digit is optional for each country and may be used to reflect economic and information differences.

New sectors, and more specific identification of processes, added by the NAICS offer greater choice to marketers, but also mean they need to become familiar with these classifications and what they represent.

An example of the NAICS hierarchy is shown below:

NAICS LEVEL	NAICS CODE	DESCRIPTION
Sector	31-33	Manufacturing
Subsector	334	Computer and electronic product manufacturing
Industry group	3346	Manufacturing and reproduction of magnetic and optical media
Industry	33461	Manufacturing and reproduction of magnetic and optical media
U.S. Industry	334611	Reproduction of software

Even though the more specific nature of the NAICS coding system offers definite benefits, some may prefer to stick with the familiar SIC code—particularly if their target market is broad and clearly defined. There are good reasons, though, to begin making the transition to NAICS. Chief among these is that the United States has adopted NAICS for statistical use by all federal agencies. Implementation was

---

* new sectors

completed by 2004. For census purposes, for survey data, for industrial reports and trade surveys, and for a variety of other uses, the NAICS has become the standard.

For those who have been accustomed to using the SIC system, it will be necessary to adjust data sources, methods, analyses, and products to the new coding system. For the United States, 422 previous SIC industries have been continued without substantial change and 38 newly created industries are traceable to SIC counterparts. The NAICS coding system is explained and detailed in a technical manual, which is available from the National Technical Information Service (an agency within the United States Department of Commerce) at 1-800-553-6847 or *www.ntis.gov/naics*. Industry classification experts are also available for assistance and information at 1-888-75NAICS.

Because the NAICS system is widely used by agencies that publish industry and market data, it is an excellent tool for gathering information needed for industry and market research. Information sources using this system are often available in the public library of larger cities and are virtually always available in the reference or government documents section of college and university libraries. An annotated list of such sources, along with a discussion of how they are used, is provided in Chapter 5. Examples illustrating the use of NAICS-coded information sources are provided in Chapters 7 and 8.

TIPS FOR PREPARING THE BUSINESS DESCRIPTION

■ **Draft it first.** It is a good idea to attempt a rough draft of the business description before writing the business plan. Doing so provides an indication of your understanding of the business and the adequacy of your research and planning. It also allows you to see at a glance where you will need to gather more information or do other preliminary planning before going ahead with the business plan.

■ **Write it last.** Since the business description is a synopsis of the entire business plan, the final version of this document should be written after the business plan has been completed. This ensures that important issues are addressed and that the content of both documents is consistent.

■ **Keep it brief.** The business description should be brief and to the point. The intended reader will expect no more information than is necessary to understand the business or business concept and to summarize the crucial points made in the business plan.

■ **Stress commercial and financial success.** The first concern of the reader will be the sales potential of the firm or venture. The business description should identify the intended target market for the firm's product/service, why this customer group should buy it, any competitive advantage, and what level of sales can reasonably be expected. The reader's next concern will be financial success. In this case, the description should focus on key financial indicators such as expected return on investment or profit and cash flow potential.

■ **Experienced management is important.** Another major concern of the reader will be the quality of the management and staff team that leads the firm. The job qualifications and abilities of the entrepreneur and other key personnel should be stressed. If the firm has administrative weaknesses, the description should also indicate the existence of a plan for correcting them.

■ **Be accurate.** Do not diminish the quality of the business description or alienate the reader with hype, misrepresentations, or fabrications. A sophisticated reader is interested in facts, solid evidence, and sound reasoning.

SAMPLE BUSINESS DESCRIPTION

The following business description (Figure 4-1) is for a hypothetical health products company, Ambrosia Health Products, Inc. The business was started in 1987 in a strip mall location with convenient access from a major thoroughfare in a community of 100,000.

Since its inception, ownership and management of the business has remained in the family of Josey Nash, who also serves as the firm's current CEO. She is responsible for designing and implementing major changes in the decor and product line of the store which have taken place since the early 1990s to capitalize on an apparent resurgence in consumer interest in health and health-related products. In addition, she has recently begun exploring the potential for sales of the products via the company's web site and is interested in expanding sales through e-commerce.

To complement the wide variety of healthcare-related products offered, Ambrosia also offers a variety of classes for consumers on various health-related issues and activities and provides massage therapy and other alternative medicine services. She is hoping to expand her reach by implementing a health-related blog and developing podcasts.

Ambrosia employs five full-time and two part-time employees that pride themselves on extensive product knowledge and healthcare trends, delivery service, a 90-day interest-free charge policy, and a no-questions-asked merchandise return policy.

FIGURE 4-1 *Business Description of Ambrosia Health Products, Inc.*

Business Name and Location

Business Name: Ambrosia Health Products, Inc.
Legal Name: same
Location: 576 Marshfield Ave.
                     Luther, MS 20000
Telephone: (100)555-1000
Fax: (100)555-2333
E-mail: jnash@ambrosia.com
Web site: www.ambrosiahealth.com
Contact Person: Ms. Josey Nash

Business History

Ambrosia Health Products Inc., an independently owned, new-age retailer of health products, has been in business since 1987. The firm was legally incorporated in 1988 and currently has S Corporation tax status. It is operated by its major stockholder, Josey Nash. Ms. Nash is responsible for a number of innovations over the years the store has been in business, including the addition of health-related courses and activities, mail order delivery of products, and, most recently, entry into online commerce.

Business Concept and Mission Statement

Ambrosia's business strength and profitability stems from its rigid adherence to carrying only those products that can be supported through credible, clinical reports and by maintaining a staff of highly skilled and very knowledgeable individuals who form and maintain relationships with customers. The firm's basic philosophy is to profitably meet the needs of discriminating health-care customers by providing quality products, meticulous personal service, and total shopping satisfaction.

Ambrosia's management realizes that, in order to maintain the 25% growth in sales and 12% profits the firm has enjoyed over the past ten years, management must be sensitive to new opportunities and to changing customer needs, attitudes, and preferences. It is the ongoing goal of Ambrosia's management and employees to continually search for new profit opportunities as well as new ways to meet the health-care needs of its target market.

FIGURE 4-1 *(continued)*

Market and Target Customer Group

Currently, Ambrosia serves consumers within a 60-mile radius of Luther. The primary target market is women age 35+, representing 30% of the total adult population in the current market area. A primary focus for future expansion, however, will be to extend the market radius of 60 miles exponentially by developing an existing web site into a major e-commerce distribution network. One way Ambrosia plans to expand its reach is through creating a blog and delivering podcasts to its mailing list, keeping them updated on current health trends, research, and new products.

Description of Operations

A combination of somewhat unique, but highly successful, marketing and operating strategies have been crucial to Ambrosia's growth. The most important among these is the decision to carry only high-quality product lines that are backed by credible clinical information.

Ambrosia's sales policy complements its product line. The firm has well-trained and knowledgeable sales personnel who pay particular attention to product attributes, health trends, and the individual needs of customers. Classes and services are offered to support product sales, including massage therapy and other alternative healthcare services. Ambrosia also provides a no-questions-asked merchandise return policy, a delivery and mail order service, and a 90-day interest-free charge policy.

An important part of Ambrosia's sales strategy is maintaining a store atmosphere that supports its upscale image. The plush surroundings, amenities, availability of skilled staff, and specialized courses and activities make shopping at Ambrosia a comfortable social outing for its customers.

Management Profile and Needs Assessment

Ambrosia's management team consists of the CEO, Ms. Josey Nash, the Store Manager, Mrs. Elizabeth Gray, and the Buyer, Mrs. Lisa Marie. Ms. Nash holds a B.S. degree in Marketing from Valdosta State University and an M.B.A. from Indiana University. She has 19 years experience in health-care product retailing. Ms. Nash owns 87% of the firm's outstanding shares.

FIGURE 4-1 *(continued)*

Mrs. Marie holds a B.S. degree in Marketing and Retailing from the University of Georgia, has successfully completed numerous administrative seminars and workshops, and has 5 years of experience with Ambrosia. During this time she has held positions as junior buyer, senior buyer, and buying manager. Mrs. Gray has 10 years of experience with Ambrosia and has also successfully completed numerous administrative seminars and workshops. She has also held positions as part-time summer employee, full-time sales trainee, and sales representative with Ambrosia. Mrs. Gray has held the store manager position for the past 4 years.

The planned addition of an e-commerce distribution channel during the next year will create the need for additional management and staff personnel. Included are a webmaster, an online products sales manager, and a vice president of e-commerce.

Financial Profile

Since the implementation of Ambrosia's current marketing and operating strategies in 1998, sales have grown at an average annual compounded rate of 25%, profits at a 12% rate of growth, and cash flow from operations at a 15% growth rate. It is estimated that e-commerce will cause sales, cash flow, and profits to quadruple over the next six years.

Ambrosia owns all its assets, and there currently is no long-term debt outstanding. There are short-term working-capital loans outstanding in the amount of $187,000. These loans are drawn against the $500,000 line of credit granted by First National Bank of Luther. As required by bank policy, outstanding loans against the line will be repaid by the end of November of this year.

The move into e-commerce will create the need for approximately $500,000 in new capital. Management feels this amount can be raised through debt financing in the form of a five-year term loan.

CHAPTER PERSPECTIVE

The business description is a summary (snapshot) of the key points or conclusions contained in the business plan. It is included in the presentation package when a complete plan has been prepared for the intended reader. The sections typically included in the business description are the firm name and location, business history, mission statement, industry and market description, description of operations, management and key personnel profile, and financial profile. Since the intended reader will look to the business description to determine whether further reading is warranted, it is important that this document pique his or her interest. To do so, the focus of this writing should be commercial and financial feasibility.

PREPARING OPERATING PLANS

The Industry Analysis

WHAT IS AN INDUSTRY ANALYSIS?

To effectively plan, forecast, and project success for an existing business or new venture, you must first identify the factors in your firm's external and internal environment that determine its ability to generate sales (commercial success) and positive cash flows (financial success). The *internal environment* refers to those activities in your business, such as production or cash-flow management, that are under management's direct control. The *external environment* refers to the variables that affect the firm's performance but are outside the direct control of management. Included in this category are such influences as:

- The industry, market, and competitive environment.
- The economic environment.
- The technological environment.
- The social, legal, and political environment.
- The demographic environment.

While all these factors affect the firm, the performance of the firm's industry is one of the stronger influences. An *industry* is defined as a group of businesses producing or supplying related products or services and the complementary firms that support them. Complementary firms include indirectly related businesses such as industry suppliers and distributors. An *industry analysis* is a study of the characteristics that define and influence the primary and secondary businesses that supply a related product or service. When prepared for a business plan, an effective industry analysis provides the following information:

- A discussion of the characteristics that define the industry, including the products or services provided, the scope and geography of its markets, the major competitors, and the demographics of the industry's major customers.
- A description of the economic, competitive, social, legal, and political factors that drive the industry, and that directly impact the firm's performance.

■ An indication of the historical trends of sales and profits in the industry, an explanation of the factors responsible for this performance, the outlook for future industry sales and profits, and the reasons for these projections.

■ A description of the strategic opportunity that exists for the firm in this industry, why this opportunity exists, how the firm plans to exploit it, and why this opportunity should result in success for the firm.

After studying the material in this chapter, you will:

■ Understand the role of the industry analysis.

■ Know the information needed to prepare an industry analysis.

■ Know the major sources of information available for performing an industry analysis.

■ Know the steps to performing the industry analysis.

WHEN TO USE AN INDUSTRY ANALYSIS

The information provided by the industry analysis is usually required in any well-prepared business plan. This is true whether the business plan is used internally, whether the presentation package is limited to a loan proposal and summary updates from selected business plan components, or whether a complete business plan is presented to the intended reader.

The industry analysis provides you with the understanding and insights needed to begin to answer the questions of *why* commercial success can be achieved and *how* this success will occur. An analysis of the conditions of your firm's industry and the factors affecting your industry, such as governmental regulation, also provides essential information for internal planning. Realistic operating, marketing, and financial strategies cannot be developed without an understanding of the industry factors that directly affect the firm.

THE INFORMATION NEEDED TO PREPARE AN INDUSTRY ANALYSIS

The information collected for the industry analysis should include what is necessary to describe the product or service the industry provides, its most important customers and suppliers, the dominant firms in the industry, its major competitors, and its past performance and future outlook. These information needs are described in the guideline questions and in the subsequent sections of the following chapter.

The chapter also contains an annotated bibliography of the principal sources of published information used in industry and market analyses. A sample industry analysis at the end of this chapter illustrates how NAICS codes can be used in conjunction with these published sources to gather industry and market information. The sample market analysis in Chapter 6 contains an example of how published information sources are used to prepare a market analysis and a sales forecast for a proposed new venture.

STEPS TO PREPARING AN INDUSTRY ANALYSIS

While preparation of an industry analysis may appear daunting when viewed in its entirety, it is not difficult if properly approached. The key is to divide the analysis into a series of small, sequential tasks, completing each step before beginning the next. Following is one logical approach for accomplishing this.

1. **Industry analysis summary.** This optional section *may* be used when the analysis is prepared for outside presentation. The summary is a convenience for the reader and should be no longer than what is needed to provide a basic understanding of the industry and the major factors that affect it. This is the only section that should be completed out of order. Because this section is a top view summary of all the information you have researched and gathered and your resulting analysis, it is best to write this section last. After going through the whole research process, you will be better able to capture the key findings and conclusions that will be most pertinent to the reader.

2. **Industry description.** A discussion of the firm's industry should begin with an identification of the economic sector and industry classification or segment to which it belongs. The term *economic sector* refers to a primary business area such as manufacturing, merchandising, service, transportation, or construction. An *industry classification* identifies the various segments into which an economic sector is divided. For example, retailing is one classification under the merchandising sector, and industrial chemicals is a segment of the manufacturing sector. Industry classifications are further divided into a wide variety of subcomponents. For example, the classification for retailing contains many subcomponents such as sporting goods, women's apparel, and hardware. As indicated in Chapter 4, the most widely used system for classifying industries used to be the SIC system, but this system has been replaced by the NAICS system.

The industry description should further identify the geographical boundaries of the industry and the products or services supplied to its markets. For example, basic steel manufacturers operate primarily in the national market supplying such products as steel plate, cold-rolled sheet steel, and tin plate. Commercial banks, on the other hand, tend to confine their various financial service operations to either regional markets (e.g., the Southeast) or local markets (e.g., Atlanta).

This section should provide answers to questions like:
- What is the economic sector and sector classification for this industry?
- What is the NAICS code number and name for this industry?

3.   **Industry suppliers, customers, and distributors.** The industry characteristics that should be described next are those relating to the primary suppliers of the industry, the products or services they supply, the major customers of the industry's product or service, and the channels of distribution used by the industry to move the product or service from producer to ultimate consumer. Each description should include a discussion of the factors that materially affect them. For example, the key concerns regarding suppliers are normally the cost of the product or service they provide, the extent to which it is available when needed, and the reliability for on-time delivery. If access to industry supplies or suppliers is limited or unreliable or supply costs are prohibitive, it will be difficult, if not impossible, to convince a knowledgeable reader that a strategic opportunity exists for the firm in this industry.

The discussion of the industry's major customers should include considerations such as why they buy the industry's product or service; why, as a member of this industry, the firm is able to reach them; whether the customer base is stable or changing; and what future industry changes are anticipated. Likewise, the discussion of distribution channels should include key considerations such as whether existing channels maximize customer exposure, whether they are cost-effective, and how the firm will be able to use or modify them to its advantage.

This section should provide answers to questions like:
- Who are the industry's primary suppliers and how reliable are these supply lines?
- What are the primary distribution channels used to move the industry's product to its consumers?
- What is the scope of the market for the industry's products or services?
- Who are the industry's primary customers and what common buying characteristics do they share?
- What factors influence the purchases of these customers?

4.   **Competition.** Since commercial feasibility is critical to the success of any business, the intended reader of a business plan will be keenly interested in both direct and indirect competition. *Direct competition* refers to products or services that consumers treat as acceptable alternatives, such as McDonald's and Burger King, Kmart and Walmart, and plastic and aluminum. *Indirect competition* refers

to products or services that can be easily substituted for one another, such as automobile travel for air travel, video movie rentals for attendance at a movie theater, and yogurt for ice cream.

It is unrealistic to indicate an absence of competition for your product or service. Statements suggesting that you believe you have no competitors will be viewed as naïve or uninformed. Unless the industry has an absolute monopoly on a life-essential item such as water or insulin, varying degrees of alternatives or substitutes are always available. For example, the local electric utility may have a monopoly on the sale of electricity in a particular city, but residents can use an alternative energy source such as natural gas or propane or, given the right incentives, resort to generating their own electric power. Or, while the prospects of being without an automobile may be troublesome, other means of transportation are available.

Strategic opportunity or competitive advantage does not exist because of the absence of competition. It results from having a product or service that is, in the mind of the consumer, a better choice than available alternatives or substitutes. The industry analysis must, therefore, make a convincing case for why the product or service represents a *better choice.*

This section should provide answers to questions like:
- What are the primary products or services supplied by this industry?
- Which products or services compete directly and indirectly with those of the industry?
- Who are the major firms in the industry and which firms compete directly with the entrepreneur's business or new venture?
- What are the strengths and weaknesses of the top competitors?
- How many new firms have entered this industry in the past three years, and what have been their successes or failures?

5. **Historical performance.** This section of the industry analysis should describe and illustrate industry performance to date. Typical performance indicators are sales revenue, units shipped, operating profits, workers employed, the number of customers served, and geographic areas covered. To highlight trends, industry performance data should be compared to the same data series for competing industries or to indicators of aggregate economic activity such as gross domestic product (GDP) or personal disposable income (PDI).

The discussion of industry performance should include reference to any cyclical and seasonal patterns shown in the data. *Cyclical patterns* are those recurring swings in business activity that move production, sales, cash flow, profits, and employment through a recessionary phase to the peak of an upswing. Industry cycles should be compared to those of the overall economy as measured by key indicators of activity such as GDP. These comparisons indicate the extent to which industry sales and profits are sensitive to economic change. For example, sales and profits of consumer durables such as autos and appliances are highly sensitive to changes in PDI. When the economy is in a general recession, sales of consumer durables decline as the level of PDI declines. Other industries, such as health care, are more recession-proof.

Seasonal patterns refer to pronounced changes in activity within a calendar year. For example, the retail apparel industry normally does a large percentage of its business during the fall holiday season. On the other hand, the largest portion of the winter holiday season output of toy manufacturers is produced and shipped by the preceding August. Seasonal peaks and valleys affect a number of business variables such as cash flows, working capital build-up, and financing needs.

An essential component of this section is an explanation of the factors that determine and drive industry performance. For example, the widespread use of computers in business, government, education, and the home are an important reason for the existence of a large-scale software industry. By identifying factors responsible for industry performance and relating these to the performance of the firm, the entrepreneur effectively addresses the implicit question of *why* success is anticipated.

This section should provide answers to questions like:
- How is this product/service affected by economic changes and/or seasonal patterns?
- What new products/services or innovations have been introduced in this industry in the past three years?
- What is the average rate of technological obsolescence for products in this industry?
- What major technological changes have taken place in this industry in the past three years?

6.   **Future outlook.** The outlook for industry growth is an important indicator of both the extent to which strategic opportunities exist and the degree of risk associated with entry into the industry. For example, because developing industries have not gained wide-scale product/service acceptance, they typically offer the opportunity for large-scale profits, represent the least competition, and have the highest risk of failure. On the other hand, industries in the rapid-growth stage have gained product/service acceptance, enjoy a rapidly expanding customer base, experience increasing sales and profits, represent lower investment risk, but experience more formidable competition.

Again, it is essential that the discussion of growth prospects includes a convincing explanation of *why* expectations are realistic. A forecast or projection is meaningless unless its underlying assumptions are clearly identified and convincingly supported. Without justification, a forecast is nothing more than a guess, which will be quickly dismissed by an experienced reader.

This section should provide answers to questions like:

- What are the major economic, competitive, and demographic factors that drive this industry?
- What are the trends and outlooks for these key factors?
- Is there any evidence that the key industry factors are changing?
- What have been the growth trends of industry sales, profits, and other key indicators of industry performance over the past three to five years?
- How do these trends relate to those of broad-based indicators of the economy and to those of competing industries?
- What is the outlook for industry sales and profits over the next three to five years?
- What key assumptions underlie these forecasts and what data or evidence substantiates this outlook?
- Why should these forecasts materialize?

7. **Strategic opportunity.** The primary reason for preparing the industry analysis is to determine whether a commercially and financially successful industry niche exists. Fortunately, there is no one formula that defines a successful strategic opportunity. A successful strategic opportunity may be achieved in a variety of ways, including:

- Creating a marketable new product or innovative service.
- Finding a market niche in a rapidly growing industry.
- Meeting an unfilled need or unsatisfied market demand.
- Developing or accessing a new or untapped market for an existing product.
- Developing a lower-cost method of doing business.
- Providing better service than what is currently available.

Regardless of the opportunity envisioned, a convincing case must be made for *why* the firm can capitalize on it. The factors that should lead to success must be identified and the reasons the firm is or will be in position to take advantage of them must be carefully explained. It is also advisable to include in this section a discussion of the pitfalls that can result in failure and, to the extent possible, the entrepreneur's plans for protecting against them.

An informed reader of the business plan knows there are risks associated with any business opportunity. It is as important, therefore, to identify what can go wrong and what precautions will be taken to minimize risk as it is to explain what factors lead to success. If the entrepreneur fails to address this issue, the reader may conclude the analysis is unreliable. Risks can include both internal and external factors. Internal risks are those considered within the company's control, such as personnel issues, negative cash flow, or the need for additional research and development. External risks, or threats, are considered outside the company's control, such as economic fluctuations, natural disasters, or the entrance of new competitors into the marketplace. Both types of risks should be evaluated and plans developed in an attempt to resolve, or mitigate, these risks.

This section should provide answers to questions like:

- What strategic opportunity exists in this industry for the business or new venture?
- Why should this strategic opportunity be successful for the business or new venture?
- What are the major threats to the industry?
- What strategies do the major firms in the industry use to protect against these threats?
- What strategies would the firm use to protect against these threats?

SOURCES OF INDUSTRY INFORMATION

The information needed to conduct a diligent industry analysis may come from primary sources, secondary sources, or some combination of the two.

Primary information is information that you have gathered directly. For instance, you might personally contact other firms in your industry to gather information or you might conduct interviews with consumers to identify their buying habits. In addition, any research that you would do yourself or that you would contract with a research firm to do for you, would be considered a primary source of information.

There are several ways primary information can be gathered. One effective way to reach many key players in the industry, including suppliers, customers, and competitors, is to visit conventions, trade shows, and conferences that are targeted to the industry. There you will not only get a chance to meet and network with many people in a short amount of time, but you will also hear about some of the needs of your target market which can be valuable for conducting your market analysis (see Chapter 6). You will obtain an understanding of the products and services that are already serving this industry, as well as hear about future projections, challenges, and the competitive environment. If your business is regionally focused, you may even gain valuable insight from competitors in other geographical areas that are willing to advise you since you do not pose a threat, serving a different market.

Another source for contacts are associations and trade groups. Most of these organizations hold regular meetings that the public can often attend for a nominal fee. In addition, there are a plethora of online forums, discussion boards, and blogs that can reach your target market, suppliers, distributors, and competitors, and give you information on how purchasing decisions are made in your industry.

Finally, some firms have had success in gathering industry information through creating and distributing surveys that reach appropriate players in the industry. Contact lists for appropriate industry segments that can be sorted by function, geographic area, size of firm, among others, can be found in some of the sources listed in Table 5-1.

Secondary information is information that you have not gathered directly, but that is pertinent to your area of research. A study conducted by another firm in your industry would be a secondary source of information. Articles or books published on the industry you are addressing would be secondary sources. Groups such as the federal government, state governments, industry trade associations, specialized research agencies, security analysts, and financial investment services routinely gather both numerical data and qualitative industry information. Much of this information is published and made available through secondary sources.

Table 5-1 identifies the most widely used government and privately published sources of secondary information for conducting industry and market analyses. Many of these sources are now available via the Internet and if not, they are in city libraries, and nearly all are available in college and university libraries which provide much of this data in electronic format.

The sample industry analysis at the end of this chapter explains how the NAICS/SIC systems can be used to identify and obtain industry information from secondary sources. In addition, the sample market analysis in Chapter 6 illustrates how secondary sources can be used to do a market analysis and sales forecast for a new venture. Because of the large number of secondary sources available, finding information for the industry and market analysis components of the business plan is not a problem. The real challenge is becoming familiar with available sources and then narrowing down the choices to those that are most relevant to the needs of the particular analysis.

TABLE 5-1

Industry and Market Information Sources

The Internet has had a profound impact on the availability of statistics and data that can help the entrepreneur prepare a well-researched business plan. The sheer volume of resources can be staggering. Sorting through the clutter to select those which are most appropriate can present a challenge. Fortunately, the federal government provides a tremendous amount of readily accessible and reliable information on-line. In addition, many other popular sources of information that have traditionally been available in book or journal format are now also easily accessible on-line. By using an on-line search engine you can quickly determine if the material you're looking for might be available in this format.

The FedStats web site at *www.fedstats.gov* provides information from more than 100 agencies in the United States Federal Government that produce statistics of interest to the public. The Federal Interagency Council on Statistical Policy maintains this site to provide easy access to the full range of statistics and information produced by these agencies for public use. FedStats provides access to information from agencies including the Bureau of Economic Analysis, the Bureau of Labor Statistics, the Bureau of the Census, the Environmental Protection Agency, the Consumer Product Safety Commission, the United States Customs Service, the Federal Reserve Board, the International Trade Administration, the Small Business Administration, Stat-USA, and many more. The site also offers the option to profile your state and county using MapStats. MapStats provides information, at a county level, on population, immigration, and demographics; census; crime; energy and environment. An initial stop at the FedStats site can save you a great deal of time and yield reliable results for the preparation of your industry analysis.

The remainder of the resources in this listing are provided in alphabetical order, by category. Information on Internet access is provided within each listing.

Federal Government Sources

American Statistics Index (ASI) (published by the Congressional Information Service).

The ASI is a comprehensive index of U.S. government statistical publications. Accompanying the index is an abstract volume which contains descriptions of the content and format of each publication.

The purpose of the *American Statistics Index (ASI)* is to identify statistical data published by all branches and agencies of the Federal Government. The ASI is a guide to federal statistical publications that relate primarily to social, economic, demographic,

TABLE 5-1 *(continued)*

and environmental topics. It includes references to periodicals, annual reports, special studies, and irregular publications. The ASI is issued in two parts: index and abstract sections and is supplemented bimonthly.

Bureau of Economic Analysis (BEA). BEA, an agency of the U.S. Department of Commerce, is the nation's economic accountant, preparing estimates that illuminate key national, international, and regional aspects of the U.S. economy. The BEA's web site (*http://www.bea.gov*) provides GDP and related data from the national accounts programs of the U.S. Department of Commerce's Bureau of Economy and includes regional, national, and international data, as well as news releases and articles.

Census of Population: General Population Characteristics: U.S. Summary (published by the U.S. Department of Commerce, Bureau of Census).

The U.S. population census, which is taken every ten years, provides a wealth of comprehensive demographic data. This data is organized by Metropolitan Statistical Area (MSA) and includes key demographic characteristics such as age and income distributions, number of households, and ethnic group concentrations. Business firms use this data in a variety of applications. For example, market analysis, sales forecasting and numerous business decisions such as where to locate the business, mapping sales territories, and choosing advertising and promotion strategies require demographic information.

The U.S. Census Bureau web site, *www.census.gov*, contains a wealth of information including census data, publications, facts by state and country, and population projections.

County Business Patterns (published by the U.S. Department of Commerce, Bureau of Census).

This annual publication provides data on employment, total payroll, and number of business establishments classified by employment size, by county, and by NAICS codes. Data is also available online at *www.census.gov*.

Current Population Reports (Published by the U.S. Department of Commerce, Bureau of Census).

The *Reports* are published monthly and include information on eight demographic subject areas. Data is also available online at *www.census.gov*.

TABLE 5-1 *(continued)*

Economic Census (published by the U.S. Department of Commerce, Bureau of Census).

The Census Bureau conducts an economic census every five years and publishes the statistical information that has been gathered. The data, which is organized by industry classification, appears in the following Bureau publications: *Census of Construction Businesses, Census of Manufactures, Census of Mineral Industries, Census of Minority-Owned Businesses, Census of Retail Trade, Census of Selected Service Industries, Census of Transportation Businesses,* and *Census of Women-Owned Businesses.* Data is also available online at *www.census.gov.*

The *Federal Reserve Bulletin* is a monthly journal published by the Federal Reserve Board containing reports and analysis of economic developments, regulatory issues, and new data. It features articles on selected topics in economics, domestic and international business activity, and recent developments in the banking community. The *Bulletin* also contains statistical tables that detail activity in various sectors of the economy. It is available online at *http://www.federalreserve.gov/pubs.*

The GPO Monthly Catalog (formerly the U.S. Government Printing Office Monthly Catalog of Publications) is available as a database consisting of citations to documents published by the GPO since July 1976. The catalog includes references to congressional committee reports and hearings, debates, documents from executive departments, and more, and is updated monthly. It can be accessed by subject, author, or title and contains a current list of publications issued by departments and bureaus of the U.S. government. Information is available through *www.gpoaccess.gov.*

The 2012 U.S. NAICS Manual *North American Industry Classification System—United States, 2012* includes definitions for each industry, tables showing correspondence between 2012 NAICS and 2007 NAICS for codes that changed, and a comprehensive index.

The *Statistical Abstract of the United States* is a basic source of national statistics that includes hundreds of charts and tables on the political, social, economic, educational, judicial, geographical, and scientific aspects of the United States. Data is supplied by the U.S. government as well as private agencies. The abstract can be accessed at *www.census.gov.*

The *U.S. Industry and Trade Outlook* provides a sector-by-sector review and an outlook of the U.S. industrial economy. It includes projections for economic growth and trade over a five-year period,

TABLE 5-1 *(continued)*

assessments of major industrial and developing country markets for U.S. exports, and analysis of the prospects for major sectors of the economy.

The U.S. Patent and Trademark Office, *www.uspto.gov*, allows users to search for patents, trademarks, and copyrights, and offers a variety of reports and statistics.

State and Local Sources

Area Industrial Information (published by county and city planning commissions and industrial authorities).

Various municipal agencies responsible for the promotion of new business and economic growth in their areas typically publish information on businesses by industry classification and by individual plant or office location. While publication dates for these sources vary, most are published annually or biannually. Much of this information is available on-line. To find out what information on your area is available, visit your local city or county government's web site.

State Industrial Directories (published by state agencies).

All state industrial agencies publish, either annually or semi-annually, some form of state business or industrial directory. While these directories vary in scope and content, they usually provide information on company names and addresses, employment size, product or industry classification, and names of key executives. Some states do, however, limit their data and listings to manufacturing firms in the state. Much of this information is available on-line. To find out what information for your state might be accessible in this format, visit your state government's web site.

Private Sources

The Almanac of Business and Industrial Financial Ratios (published by CCH Tax and Accounting).

This annual publication contains financial statement data and selected financial ratios for a large sample of businesses. The data is organized by SIC industry classification and asset-size categories and is especially useful for sales forecasting and for preparing pro forma financial statements for a new business. The Almanac provides comparative financial data and benchmarks (including 50 performance indicators) for 179 Standard Industrial Classifications based on the latest IRS data for more than 3.7 million U.S. corporations, as well as ten-year trends for 13 key indicators for each SIC. The book includes fully interactive software.

TABLE 5-1 *(continued)*

Hoover's, *www.hoovers.com*, provides histories and current status of American public companies, industry overviews, forecasts, and industry updates.

The International Directory of Company Histories is a collection of major companies' histories by industry group.

The Market Share Reporter is an annual compilation of published market share data on companies and products that is taken from periodicals and brokerage reports.

Million Dollar Directory (published by Dun & Bradstreet, Inc.).
This database provides information on more than 1.6 million public and private companies (across all industries) with sales of one million dollars or more, or 20+ employees, or branches with 50+ employees. It includes companies in the U.S. and Canada. The company data is updated every 60 days.

Predicasts Forecasts (published by Predicasts, Inc.).
This two-volume publication provides a comprehensive index of published articles from a wide variety of secondary information sources. These sources include business and trade association magazines, newspapers, financial publications, and special reports that provide industry and market analysis information. The publication is divided into the "Industries and Products" issue and the "Companies" issue.

RMA Annual Statement Studies (published by Risk Management Associates).
These studies are used as a source of detailed industry financial data for comparing businesses to industry in valuation reports, company/industry ratio analyses, and credit decisions. The industry data is derived from 150,000 small and medium-sized U.S. businesses and is especially useful for sales forecasting and for preparing pro forma financial statements for a new business.

Standard & Poor's Industry Surveys (published by Standard & Poor's Investor Services).
This valuable resource provides historical data, qualitative information, and predictions for the industries that comprise the S&P 500. It is particularly useful for the novice analyst because each analysis is essentially a tutorial on how to perform an industry analysis.

TABLE 5-1 *(continued)*

ThomasNet, www.ThomasNet.com, is a wholly owned subsidiary of Thomas Publishing Company. The site helps industrial sellers target their marketing investment to reach the most qualified industrial buyers on-line. *ThomasNet.com* is where many buyers and engineers from Fortune 500 companies, the government, the military, and others go to find suppliers. Users can link to company web pages and search 155,000 U.S. and Canadian companies to find industrial products or services.

Trade and Industry Journals (published by various trade and industry associations).

There are a large number of associations representing various industry and trade groups that publish periodicals containing industry data, qualitative information, descriptions of trends and analyses, and growth expectations. An excellent reference for identifying national and international trade associations is *Gale's Encyclopedia of Associations* published by Gale Research. *Gale's Encyclopedia* is carried by most public, college, and university libraries. An excellent reference to trade association information such as trade and industry publications, trade shows, venture capitalists, and consultants is the *Small Business Sourcebook,* also published by Gale Research.

The Value Line Investment Survey provides descriptions of industries followed by reports on major, publicly-held companies within the industry.

A frequently overlooked source of data and information on industries and markets located within state boundaries are various research bureaus and academic departments housed in schools of business administration of state colleges and universities. Business research bureaus typically gather and evaluate industry and market data and publish periodicals or newsletters containing updates of economic data series and forecasts of activity in state and local industries and markets. Various academic departments within schools of business have highly qualified faculty that often do research and consulting in specialized areas that directly or indirectly involve industry and market analysis.

TIPS FOR PREPARING AN INDUSTRY ANALYSIS

■ **Don't slight this component.** The industry analysis is critical to the overall business plan. Your industry analysis should include the nature and scope of the industry as provided in the description section of the industry analysis, data on historical performance, industry growth prospects, and strategic opportunity; the assumptions underlying all projections and conclusions. Finally, the documentation used to support your assumptions, projections, and conclusions should be included. Preparing an industry analysis that satisfies both the concerns of a knowledgeable reader as well as the needs of the entrepreneur is a valuable learning experience. The required effort forces the entrepreneur to develop industry expertise and to identify and evaluate those factors critical to the success of the business.

■ **Reference the life-cycle stage where appropriate.** The industry analysis is often more effective when presented within the context of the current stage of the industry's life cycle (see Chapter 6). For example, the description of the industry's historical performance is more effective when incorporated within a discussion of its development and growth stages. Or, the arguments for strategic opportunity are usually more persuasive when coupled with a description of the factors responsible for rapid industry growth. Explicit reference to the life-cycle stage of an industry is often found in secondary information sources.

■ **Emphasize opportunity.** Since strategic opportunity is critical to the success of any business, it is important that the industry analysis leave no doubt in the reader's mind about the existence of a commercially and financially attractive opportunity.

■ **Use graphics.** Some portion of the industry analysis will include quantitative data such as sales revenue, units shipped, and growth rates. These data are often delivered more effectively when accompanied by tables, graphs, and charts.

■ **Take advantage of available help.** There are two major sources of this help: state Small Business Development Centers (SBDC) and the U.S. Small Business Administration (SBA). Both agencies offer management education programs, business management literature, and consulting assistance. The SBDC is a state-sponsored agency. It is structured as a statewide network of satellite centers that serve local small-firm entrepreneurs. As noted on the SBA web site, the SBDC provides a "vast array" of technical assistance to small businesses and aspiring entrepreneurs. The SBA has regional offices located throughout the country. Both agencies offer consulting assistance at no charge to the small-business entrepreneur and management education programs and literature at nominal prices.

■ **Don't be intimidated.** There is a natural tendency, especially for those unfamiliar with using library or Internet references or collecting data, to be apprehensive about performing an industry or market analysis. Don't be! The task can be done effectively by the typical entrepreneur willing to put forth the necessary effort. As previously discussed, the trick is to take the analysis one small step at a time.

■ **Industry analysis is an ongoing process.** Preparing the industry and market analyses for the firm's business plan should only be the start of an information-gathering process that is never completed. The essence of operating and managing a business is planning and decision-making, and a necessary part of these critical management functions is gathering, analyzing, and evaluating timely information on the firm's industry and market(s). Unless this information is updated to reflect the changes that are continually taking place in the firm's rapidly changing environment, the business will quickly become passé.

SAMPLE INDUSTRY ANALYSIS

The following sample illustrates how the North American Industrial Classification System (NAICS) (see Chapter 4) can be used with secondary information sources to gather industry and market information. To illustrate, assume a small legal publishing firm, Legal Information Systems (LIS), has developed an on-demand source of on-line information for attorneys. To develop an effective marketing strategy for the new software, management must estimate its market potential by identifying the number of potential customers as well as sales volume. This requires data and qualitative information on the legal industry.

The LIS marketing director begins by identifying the NAICS code number for law firms—541110. But the code is just a starting point—a reference that allows the marketing director to find information in a variety of sources—all pertinent to the legal industry. The marketing director begins gathering information by first determining how many U.S. law firms are included in the 541110 industry classification. By surveying the sources listed in Table 5-2, he discovers that this information is readily available in the *U.S. Census of Manufacturers.* This reference provides information like:

■ The number of firms with this NAICS code by state
■ The number of employees used by these firms
■ The total annual capital expenditures made by these firms

TABLE 5-2
Leading NAICS Coded Data Sources

NAICS Source	Possible Applications
NAICS Manual	Obtaining the NAICS code number for industry classifications.
Statistical Abstract of the United States	Obtaining national statistics, including charts and tables, on the political, social, economic, educational, judicial, geographical, and scientific aspects of the United States.
FedStats (*www.fedstats.gov*)	Obtaining on-line information from more than 70 agencies in the U.S. Federal Government.
MapStats (*www.fedstats.gov*)	Obtaining a profile by state and/or county, including population, immigration and demographics, census, crime, energy, and environment.
Predicasts Forecasts	Obtaining information and data on a wide variety of industry and market topics including size, growth rates, performance indicators, and forecasts through the index of publications.
Dun's Census of American Business	Obtaining descriptive business firm data such as state and county location, number of firms, sales volume, and number of employees.

The marketing director is also interested in knowing whether the legal industry has been growing over the past five years and how this growth rate compares to the growth rates of the economy and other industries. Since the legal industry is a service industry, the *U.S. Census of Manufacturers* will not be a pertinent resource. Fortunately, a wealth of information from a variety of sources is available on the Internet. The FedStats Internet site at *www.fedstats.gov* provides information from more than 70 agencies in the United States Federal Government, which produce statistics of interest to the public. FedStats provides access to information from agencies including the Bureau of Economic Analysis, the Bureau of Labor Statistics, the Bureau of the Census, the Environmental Protection Agency, the Consumer Product Safety Commission, the United States Customs Service, the Federal Reserve Board, the International Trade Administration, the Small Business Administration, Stat-USA—and many more. The LIS marketing director may also choose to profile his state and county using MapStats. MapStats provides information, at a county level, on population, immigration, and demographics; census; crime; energy and environment. Other sources the director finds useful are Standard & Poor's *Industry Surveys,* from periodicals published by the legal industry and made available through trade associations and from a variety of articles on the legal industry indexed by *Predicasts.*

Once the historical perspective is complete, the next step is to make an educated estimate of the sales volume that might be expected from this industry. This is a challenging task and, obviously, a combination of both art and science. To help in developing a realistic sales forecast, the LIS marketing director turns to a variety of sources including the *Statistical Abstract of the United States,* a basic source of national statistics that includes hundreds of charts and tables on the political, social, economic, educational, judicial, geographical, and scientific aspects of the United States. Data is supplied by the U.S. government as well as private agencies. The abstract can be accessed on-line at *http://www.census.gov.* Dun & Bradstreet's *Census of American Business* and national and state legal associations are also consulted.

As the wealth of information becomes visible, the LIS marketing director quickly realizes that only a few of the many resources available have been reviewed. Still the effort provides a very detailed picture of the legal industry and serves as a valuable resource for management to allow a realistic projection of the market potential available for the on-line information service. The marketing director's next steps will involve getting an even clearer picture of the market potential for the service, by identifying and reaching out to their target market, conducting an informal survey of potential customers, and networking with key players in the legal industry. This will allow LIS to achieve an effective understanding of how the firm can meet their customers' needs and ensure that they develop and promote the service in a way to minimize risk and ensure strong sales.

CHAPTER PERSPECTIVE

Because industry performance is one of the more important determinants of a firm's commercial success, an industry analysis is an essential component of the business plan. An industry analysis is a study of the factors that define and influence the group of primary and secondary businesses that make up the firm's industry. It usually consists of a description of the economic sector and classification to which the industry belongs; the product or service it provides; geographical boundaries of its markets; its major suppliers, customers, and distributors; the major firms in the industry; the product or service that directly or indirectly competes with the industry's product or service; the historical performance of sales and profits; the future outlook for industry performance; and the strategic opportunity the industry offers for the firm.

The Market Analysis and Sales Forecast

CHAPTER

6

WHAT IS A MARKET ANALYSIS AND A SALES FORECAST?

The market analysis and sales forecast are companions to the industry analysis and related steps in supporting commercial success. If the firm is to attain commercial success, its industry must provide a strategic opportunity and its market must provide a profitable niche. The sales forecast, which provides a measure of commercial feasibility, converts market potential into numerical targets that become the driving force for all planned activity in the firm.

As commonly used in business, the term *market* refers to the geographical boundaries encompassing the firm's target market and the competition it faces. Its geographical boundaries may be as limited as a specific district within a metropolitan area or as large as a domestic or international market. The firm's *target market* is the group of potential customers with characteristics, needs, and expectations to which the firm's product or service should appeal.

Market competition refers to the direct and indirect competitive threats faced by the firm. As discussed in Chapter 5, *direct competition* refers to substitute products or services, such as accommodations offered by major motel chains. *Indirect competition* refers to the alternative choices available to consumers, such as eating chicken instead of beef.

A *market analysis* is a study of the basic factors that define the market for the firm's product or service and how the firm must position itself to take advantage of the opportunity that is available. These factors include:

■ The geographic boundaries of the market.
■ The economic, competitive, social factors, and trends that influence activity in this market.
■ The specific market niche in which the firm does business.
■ The specific characteristics that define the target market for the firm's product or service.
■ The sales potential for the identified target market.

■ The businesses and products or services that directly and indirectly compete with that of the firm.

The sales forecast is an estimate, based on a given set of assumptions about the firm's environment and market, of expected sales volume for specific future time periods. This estimate is an important indication of a new firm's potential for commercial success and is the criterion by which the venture's feasibility is assessed. Also, since all activity in a business is ultimately predicated on sales volume, the sales forecast provides critical data for other components of the business plan.

After studying the material in this chapter, you will:

■ Understand the role of the market analysis and sales forecast.

■ Know the information needed to do a market analysis and a sales forecast and the major sources of this information.

■ Know the steps to preparing a market analysis.

■ Understand the basics of the Metropolitan Category System, which is used by the Census Bureau to classify market segments by population density.

■ Know the major sales forecasting techniques.

WHEN TO INCLUDE THESE COMPONENTS IN THE BUSINESS PLAN

As with the industry analysis, the market analysis and sales forecast are required in any well-prepared business plan. This is true whether the business plan is used internally, whether the presentation package is limited to a loan proposal and summary updates from selected business plan components, or whether a complete business plan is presented to the intended reader. Market information, when combined with information on the firm's industry, is critical to both an assessment of commercial feasibility and to the internal management process.

Without comprehensive information on the forces that drive its market and a realistic estimate of the sales potential this market offers, neither the entrepreneur nor the intended reader of the business plan can effectively evaluate the firm's potential for commercial success. Equally important, the entrepreneur needs a continuous supply of market information to develop the firm's marketing strategy and to make the many day-to-day marketing decisions that are an essential part of planning and operating the business.

INFORMATION NEEDED TO PREPARE THESE COMPONENTS

To prepare a convincing marketing analysis, a variety of information on the firm's external environment, its industry, its target market, and its competition are needed. The questions listed below provide guidelines for identifying what information is required.

- Where is the market for the product or service located; how large is this market in terms of potential sales?
- What demographic factors characterize this market?
- What are the key economic, social, and legal factors that influence business activity in this market; what are the historical and future trends of these factors?
- What is the outlook for this market in terms of sales, profits, and growth potential?
- What market niche does the firm seek to fill or exploit?
- What marketing strategy will be used to exploit the intended market niche?
- What demographic, psychographic, and behavioral characteristics describe the firm's target customer group?
- How will the firm reach its target market, and what messages will be used to do so?
- Why will the target customer group buy from the firm rather than from its competitors?
- What sales volume should this market niche and target customer group generate for the firm?
- Which products or services and which businesses represent the strongest competitive threat to the firm?
- On what basis (price, quality, service, etc.) does the firm's product or service compete?
- What competitive advantage does the firm hold over its competition?

The rapid expansion of the Internet has had a dramatic impact on the concept of "market." With the ability to sell products and services on-line (e-commerce), even the smallest company can have a national or international market base. Just because this wide distribution is possible, however, does not mean that the entrepreneur should automatically choose the broadest market available. Segmentation is still the name of the game, whether operating from a traditional bricks-and-mortar storefront or through an e-commerce web site.

STEPS TO PREPARING THE MARKET ANALYSIS

Chapter 5 indicated that a complex process is simplified when viewed and treated as a series of small tasks performed in logical sequence. This approach is also recommended for preparing the market analysis. The ordering of the seven steps discussed below offers a logical approach for doing so.

1. **Market analysis and sales forecast summary.** This optional section *may* be used when the analysis and forecast are pre-

pared for outside presentation. The summary is a convenience for the reader and should be no longer than necessary to provide a basic understanding of the firm's market, the factors that affect it, and the sales outlook.

2. **Define the firm's market location.** *Market location* refers to the geographic boundaries within which the firm does business. While the ultimate focus of the market analysis is the firm's target market, a clear understanding of the geographical limits of the market in which the firm operates is important for the following reasons.

- The aggregate forces that influence the broad market area will, to varying degrees, affect the firm's target customer group as well. For example, the rapid increase in the sale of products on-line has had a dramatic influence on related products such as packing materials, boxes, and shipping companies (UPS initiated an IPO in 1999, as a way to raise funds to finance a heavy expansion in services due to Internet commerce.)
- The physical size of a given market area sets the upper limit for the potential number of customers the firm may attract.
- Geographic boundaries may be an important basis for market segmentation. *Market segmentation* refers to subdividing a larger market into smaller segments according to shared consumer attributes or characteristics. When markets are divided by geographical boundaries, the process is referred to as *geographic market segmentation.*

Geographic market segmentation is most often done on the basis of population concentrations. For example, the greater Atlanta metropolitan area, the Pacific Northwest region, or the sunbelt states are typical examples of markets defined by population concentrations. Metropolitan statistical areas (MSAs) are defined for federal statistical use by the Office of Management and Budget (OMB), with assistance from the Bureau of the Census. Most individual metropolitan areas with populations over one million may be subdivided into Primary Metropolitan Statistical Areas (PMSAs). An MSA or PMSA is a geographic territory consisting of a large population center and adjacent communities that have social and economic ties with that center. The Bureau of the Census identifies three basic metropolitan categories:

- **Standard Metropolitan Statistical Areas (SMSAs):** These are free-standing areas that are not closely associated with other SMSAs. Most often, SMSAs are surrounded by nonmetropolitan counties. For an area to qualify for recognition as an SMSA it must be either (a) a city or urbanized area with a population of at least 50,000 or (b) a total metropolitan area with a population of at least 100,000. For example, Albany, Georgia, and Tallahassee, Florida, are SMSAs.

- **Primary Metropolitan Statistical Areas (PMSAs):** A PMSA is a population area of more than 1,000,000 that consists of either (a) a large urbanized county or (b) a cluster of counties with strong economic and social links. PMSAs often have close ties to neighboring CMSAs or PMSAs. For example, the cities of Gary/Hammond, Indiana, constitute a PSMA with close ties to the Chicago, Illinois, CMSA.
- **Consolidated Metropolitan Statistical Areas (CMSAs):** These are large areas that include several PMSAs as components. For example, under the SMSA classification scheme, Anaheim/Santa Ana, Los Angeles/Long Beach, Oxnard/ Ventura, and Riverside/San Bernardino are the PMSAs that make up the Los Angeles CMSA.

The Metropolitan Category System designations are used in many secondary information sources to identify specific geographic areas. For example, the wide array of consumer and business statistics published in the "Survey of Industrial & Commercial Buying Power" are organized using the Metropolitan Category System classification system.

Other commonly used bases for geographical segmentation are political boundaries, such as countries, states, or cities; regions, such as the Pacific Northwest; and climate differences, such as cold or hot climate zones.

3. **Understand market forces.** One major goal of market analysis is to identify the forces that influence the firm's market and understand how these forces do so. To gain this insight, the entrepreneur must gather the information necessary to answer questions such as:

- What is the primary source of business activity in the market area? For example, is the main driving force agriculture, commercial and financial, manufacturing, tourism?
- What is the total volume of business activity in the market area as measured by such indicators as retail sales, sales tax revenue, total payroll, or number of people employed? What is the outlook for these indicators?
- What are the major business firms, governmental agencies, or organizations that account for the largest percentages of business activity in the market area? What are the sales and/or employment projections for these entities?
- What is the average unemployment rate in the market area, and how does this rate compare to the national average? What is the current outlook for this indicator?

- How does the average price level and living standard for this market area compare to the national average for these statistics?
- How sensitive is business activity in the market area to changes in overall economic activity? Which major economic indicators have the largest impact on business activity in the market area?
- Is the tax and regulatory environment in the market area favorable to business?
- What are the key demographic factors that characterize the market? For example: What is the current population of the market area? Is the population trend growing or declining? What is per capita income, and how does it compare with the national average or the averages of other market areas? What are consumer expenditures by retail category in this market area? What is the gender, age, and ethnic makeup of the population in the market area?
- What are the major social or cultural factors that shape or influence buying habits in the market? Is there evidence that these trends are changing? What are the most dominant social goals in the market area? What are the prominent attitudes on religion, family, and education in the market area? What social value system is most dominant in the market area? What is the breakdown of major social classes (e.g., upper class, middle class, or working class) in the market area?

4. **Identify the firm's market niche.** A *market niche* is a specific segment of a larger consumer or business market that the firm can profitably exploit. It is identified by a target customer group (target market) having needs and expectations to which the firm can appeal. If the niche is to be commercially successful, the firm must establish a competitive position through careful matching of its strengths and capabilities with the needs and wants of its identified target market. An effective market segment is measurable, accessible, substantial, and responsive. Examples of successful market-niche positioning abound. For instance, sales of BMW automobiles have been successfully directed toward the elite segments of the retail automobile market; Pepsi-Cola has been successful in targeting its marketing effort at the youth segment of the soft drink market; and Porsche obtains a premium price for its cars by appealing to a loyal group of aficionados who feel no other automobile offers the desired bundle of product/service/membership benefits.

A market niche can be segmented in terms of various combinations of possible attributes or characteristics. The major categories of segmenting variables used to partition consumer markets are shown on Table 6-1; those used for business markets are shown on Table 6-2.

Market segmentation involves dividing the total market for any given product or service into groups of buyers that have common characteristics based on needs, attributes, or behaviors. Market segmentation is important because consumers have diverse needs that cannot be satisfied by one firm. This is to a firm's advantage—market segmentation is a process of identifying the specific niche within a market that the firm may target through unique strengths and market advantages.

Fortunately, there is no one best strategy or approach to successful market-niche segmentation. A commercially successful market niche can be established with such diverse strategies as offering a new or technologically more efficient product or service, having a convenient location, selling at lower prices or providing better service than competitors, maintaining a superior product image, or tapping a market segment that has been ignored by other businesses.

While the vast array of domestic and international markets offers countless opportunities for developing a market niche, not all are realistic for a given firm. Identifying a potential market opportunity is only one-half the equation for commercial success. The other is the firm's capacity for capitalizing on the opportunity. Before attempting to enter and develop a market niche, the entrepreneur should have satisfactory answers to questions such as:

- Is the market opportunity consistent with the firm's basic strategy?
- Are the sales and profit potential of this opportunity sufficient to provide a compensatory rate of return?
- What clearly defined competitive advantage does the firm have to justify entry into this market?
- Does the firm have the ability to make the opportunity successful? Does it have the necessary technical know-how, production capacity, management and staff expertise, employee skills, and financial resources?
- Does the firm have any weaknesses that affect its chance for commercial success? If so, how can the weaknesses be overcome?
- What pitfalls or risks are associated with this market opportunity, and can precautions be taken to minimize their impact?

5. **Define the firm's target market.** A target market or target customer group is that segment of the market having defined characteristics, needs, and expectations to which the firm's product or service is expected to appeal and toward which its marketing effort is

TABLE 6-1

Major Categories of Segmenting Variables for Consumer Markets

Geographic	Demographic	Socioeconomic	Psychographic
• Political boundaries • Climatic regions • Population boundaries	• Age • Gender • Race • Ethnicity • Marital status • Family size • Family life cycle	• Occupation • Education • Income • Social Class	• Lifestyle • Activities • Interests • Hobbies • Opinions • Values • Religion

Behavior Patterns	Consumption Patterns	Consumer Predispositions
• Online shopper • Type of store • Shopping location • Shopping frequency • Time of purchase • Size of purchase • Media habits	• Occasion or season for use (birthday, Christmas, etc.) • Frequency of use (heavy vs. light) • Types of products owned or services used • Product or service price level • Brand loyalty	• Product knowledge • Benefits sought • Reasons for purchase • Beliefs about products and brands

aimed. The reasons for identifying the characteristics that distinguish the firm's target market from other consumers are:

- **To capitalize on these differences.** Consumers buy a specific product or brand name or use a particular service because it satisfies some perceived want, need, or expectation. The key to identifying a potentially successful market niche is, therefore, understanding these motives and how the firm can take advantage of them.
- **To provide justification for commercial success.** By demonstrating an understanding of the factors influencing purchases of the target customer group and how the firm's product or ser-

TABLE 6-2
Major Categories of Segmenting Variables for Business Markets

Purchasing Characteristics	Financial Characteristics	Operating Characteristics
• Order frequency • Order size • Centralized or decentralized purchasing • Purchasing criteria—cost, quality, reliability, service • Purchasing attitude—see product as routine purchase, moderately important, critical	• Account size • Credit rating • Payment practices • Likelihood of default • Profitability of account	• Type of technology employed (labor-intensive or capital-intensive) • Frequency of use • Operating capacity • Continuous or seasonal operations • Delivery lead time required

Geographic Characteristics	Demographic Characteristics
• Geographic regions • Political boundaries • National boundaries • Climatic regions	• Industry classification • Type of business • Company size • Location

vice can meet their needs, the entrepreneur provides the evidence needed to make the business plan convincing.

- **To provide evidence of managerial ability.** By demonstrating marketing knowledge, the entrepreneur provides evidence of managerial ability.
- **To develop the marketing plan.** As discussed in Chapter 7, one important purpose of the firm's marketing plan is to decide how the firm will reach and motivate its target customer group. Unless the wants, needs, and expectations of the target market are clearly understood, it is impossible to create an effective plan for reaching them.

The most effective method for presenting the entrepreneur's characterization of the firm's target market is the *customer profile*. A customer profile identifies the geographic, demographic, psychographic, and behavioral characteristics that distinguish the target market from other consumers. These characteristics are explained below, and two examples of customer profiles are shown on Tables 6-3 and 6-4. The first profile, shown on Table 6-3, reflects the findings from a segmentation study of coffee drinkers. The data reveal three distinct segments in this category of consumer: those drinking decaffeinated, caffeinated, and ground coffee. The customer profile shown on Table 6-4 identifies the breakdown of the two primary demographic variables, age and income level, used by a bank to segment its retail customers.

Companies use market segmentation as a means of identifying potential buyers because no company can possibly serve all of the customers in any single large market. There are four primary ways to segment a market:

1) Geographic segmentation
2) Demographic segmentation
3) Psychographic segmentation
4) Behavioral segmentation

As previously discussed, *geographic segmentation* involves the subdivision of a market into distinct geographical units such as national, state, regional, county, city, or neighborhood boundaries.

Demographic Characteristics are the general-population characteristics that distinguish the target market from other consumers. Included here are commonly used segmenting variables such as age, gender, race, ethnic background, income level, occupation, education level, and religious preference. Marketing experts suggest that demographic characteristics are the primary set of influences driving the purchase of consumer goods and services and the easiest of the segmenting variables to measure. There are numerous examples of how demographic variables are used by marketers to reach specific market segments. For instance, much of the marketing efforts of major breweries are aimed at the blue-collar worker because this group accounts for the largest percentage of total beer sales. General Foods has effectively used a segmentation strategy based on the age and life-cycle stage of a typical dog to market its Cycle 1 through Cycle 4 dog foods to concerned pet owners. Segmentation based on gender has long been applied to the marketing of such products and services as clothing, hairdressing, cosmetics, and magazines.

Psychographic characteristics are the segmenting variables that identify the consumer's social class, lifestyle, or personality makeup. Experienced marketers agree that what consumers buy and the reasons for their purchases are strongly affected by their psychological makeup. For example, marketers have discovered that social class has a strong influence on consumer preferences in cars, clothing,

TABLE 6-3
Coffee Market Segment Profiles

Attribute	Decaffeinated	Caffeinated	Ground
Percentage of Total Users	35%	33%	32%
Frequency of Use	Light user	Medium user	Heavy user
Distinguishing Benefits Desired	Does not cause nervousness or lost sleep, concentrated form, prepared quickly	Helps people to wake up, provides lift, easy to prepare, convenient packaging, brand name	Non-concentrated form, taste, aroma indifferent on preparation requirements, indifferent on equipment requirements, indifferent on packaging
Form Desired	Instant	Both instant and ground	Ground
Demographics	Older, widowed, low income, more minorities	Average age, divorced, average income, more minorities	Younger, married, higher income, fewer minorities

TABLE 6-4
Bank Customers Segmented by Age and Income Level

	AGE		
	Under 39	40-65	Over 65
Below $16,000	Young, Low Income	Middle-Aged, Low Income	Retired, Low Income
Income $16,000–44,000	Young, Middle Income	Middle-Aged, Middle Income	Retired, Middle Income
Above $44,000	Young, High Income	Middle-Aged, High Income	Retired, High Income

home furnishings, leisure activities, and reading activities. Publishers and marketers of magazines rely heavily on lifestyle segmentation to reach identified target markets. Likewise, marketers rely heavily on identifying the values, attitudes, and beliefs that identify consumer personality. This knowledge allows them to endow their products or services with brand personalities that correspond to the personalities of their target markets.

Behavioral variables refer to consumers' attitudes, habits, or responses to a product or service. For example, automobile buyers can be segmented by the perceived benefits provided by ownership, such as the degree of functional utility received, how well the vehicle fits the buyer's lifestyle or self-image, or the degree of brand loyalty demonstrated by consumers. Consumers can also be categorized by the occasions that prompt a purchase, such as Christmas presents or wedding gifts; by user status, such as first-time user, regular user, or potential user; or by usage rate, such as light, medium, or heavy. Many marketing experts believe that behavioral characteristics are the most logical starting point for identifying a market segment or niche.

As this overview of segmentation suggests, there are numerous ways to segment a market. Not all, however, are practical. For example, the customers of a commercial print shop could be segmented by hair color, race, or age. Yet none of these characteristics are useful for identifying who uses the service and why or how often it is used. However, these characteristics could have a direct relation to the amount of units sold of a hair care product manufacturer, for example. To be effective, a market segment or niche should exhibit three characteristics. A market niche or segment should be:

- **Measurable.** It must be possible to identify and measure the characteristics, size, and purchasing power of the target market if this customer group is to be distinguished from others.
- **Significant.** The segment or niche must be sufficiently large and profitable to warrant the marketing effort.
- **Accessible.** It must be possible to effectively reach and serve the segment or niche.

For the typical entrepreneur, the information needed to define a target market may come from secondary information sources, personal observation, personally or professionally conducted market research, or some combination of these. Market segmentation, target market analysis, and consumer behavior are widely discussed marketing topics, and there are numerous sources of secondary information available on these subjects—in industry or trade journals and on the Internet.

Entrepreneurs from smaller firms can often conduct their own marketing research to segment a market by target customer group. This effort can take a variety of forms ranging from something as simple as observing traffic patterns at various city intersections to conducting face-to-face or mail-out customer-opinion surveys. Often, deciding on a target market starts with some assumptions and educated guesses that are then verified through conducting focus groups, analyzing consumer behavior, researching secondary information sources, or simply going out into the public and asking questions of individuals in the potential target market.

Target market information can also be obtained through the services of a professional market research firm.

6. **Identify the competition.** The degree of competition faced by the firm and the extent to which the entrepreneur can effectively combat competitive forces are important determinants of commercial success. Since the intended reader of the business plan will carefully evaluate the section describing the firm's competition, it should detail:

- The substitute products or services that pose competitive threats to the firm's sales and how the entrepreneur will counter these threats.
- The major businesses that compete directly with the firm and their relative strengths and weaknesses.
- The competitive advantage the firm holds over its rivals.

Some information on the firm's competition may be obtained online or from trade journals. For many businesses, however, the most effective method of assessing competition is by direct observation. In these cases, the entrepreneur can assess a competitor's strengths and weaknesses by visiting that business web site or physical location; observing its method of operation (by using its products or services, for example); and speaking with customers, suppliers, and others that deal with it. The competitor assessment should focus on characteristics such as the following:

- Product or service differentiation.
- Product or service quality.
- Selling price.
- The type and quality of customer service.
- Customer relations.
- Credit policy.
- Reputation and image.
- Location and appearance.
- Advertising effectiveness.

- Quality of employees.
- Financial strength.

So, for example, if a business owner operates a golf course, he or she not only needs to evaluate other golf courses or country clubs, but also other businesses that might be competing for the same target market's dollar, such as gyms, fitness centers, tennis clubs, and other social organizations.

7. **Forecast sales and prepare the marketing plan.** Sales forecasting is discussed in the next section of this chapter. Preparation of the marketing plan is the subject of Chapter 7.

SAMPLE COMPETITIVE ANALYSIS FOR ZUPERMAIL, INC.*

Zupermail, Inc. offers on-line marketers the ability to reach highly targeted consumers who have requested, or given permission to receive, information via direct e-mails. Advertisers (Zupermail "Partners") are able to send personalized messages to Zupermail members who have provided demographic and psychographic information to the company. In return for "opting in" to the program, Zupermail members receive incentive Zuperpoints, redeemable for merchandise and/or gift certificates. Though not the first entrant into the permission e-mail marketing arena, Zupermail offers a unique proposition to potential partners, investors, and members.

Analysis

The competition requests from its "members" little more than a name, postal address, and e-mail address. It does not request, in most cases, detailed demographic or psychographic information. Nor does it seem to screen for duplicate addresses of its members. By relying on list brokers and network partners, the competitors build lists with quantities of names, but do not claim to have unique members in their databases.

Rather than representing individuals who have specifically chosen to participate in a membership program, the competition, in purporting to have at least 5 million names each, are in all probability maintaining names that are identical across companies. Adding the number of "members," each of the competitors claims to have totals of 147 million individuals, representing more than 68.5% of the 215 million 2007 "active" Internet users in the United States. This dupli-

---

* Sample provided by Jamie Hait, Partner, NextLevelPlan.com, a strategic business planning firm that specializes in creating comprehensive business plans for small to mid-sized ventures.

Competitive Analysis

	Description	Sample Clients	Membership Acquisition	Membership
My Points	Members earn points by submitting demographic, attitudinal, & behavioral data. Points supplemented by transactional data for life of membership. Private label point-reward loyalty programs, in addition to general public program. Loyalty points redeemable in gift certificates, cruises, merchandise, etc. Alliances with airline mileage programs for point redemption. Average 20% click-through, 10% conversion. Entering into point redemption for off-line purchases	Target Blockbuster Barnes and Noble Eddie Bauer The Sports Authority 224 advertisers total	True opt-in and list purchases from outside companies	15.1 million
YesMail	Public company Technology "One-to-one architecture": personalized messages, deliver campaigns, track and analyze results, customize responses, generate reports in real time Partners with Email Service Providers High-tech product delivered No incentive for adding name to list	AT&T Interactive Buy.com eMarketer Flowerbud.com Fingerhut Flycast GoTo.com HP OfficeMax.com ShopGuide.com	Opt-in and list purchases from brokers and outside companies	28 million

Competitive Analysis, cont.

	Description	Sample Clients	Membership Acquisition	Membership
TargitMail	Offers targeted e-mail campaigns to individuals Provides ad-serving system to clients and web-based e-mail service. Message architecture designed to leverage convergence of e-mail, voice and fax messages. Multimedia e-mail products. Streaming video content Demographic/psychographic search, automated accounting, online account tracking, regressive modeling, dynamic response querying	Boston Gas John Hancock Charles Schwab Ziff-Davis Disney Conde Nast Staples Parke-Davis Pfizer American Express Paramount IBM Sony	Purchase of lists only	27 million
BulletMail	Targeted e-mail marketing Targeted data and ease of direct mailing 100+ targeted "lists" of recipients Unlimited hotlinks "Ten free gifts" offered to new members upon sign-up	Dell Talkcity BMG Music Etoys.com The Gap American Express AT&T CD Now	Purchases lists Opt-in member database from web site	27 million

Competitive Analysis, cont.

	Description	Sample Clients	Membership Acquisition	Membership
NetCentives	Public Company Currently offers customized incentive programs for corporate clients (ClickRewards) Entering permission direct e-mail marketing sector 1500 direct marketing clients	Barnes & Noble FTD eTrade 10 major Airlines Novell Cicso	opt-in email addresses Lists from client databases	25 million + 13 million ClickRewards members
NetCreations	Public Company PostmasterDirect.com delivers e-mails to members who have given permission Partners with 200 affiliate web sites No incentive program	Dell Compaq J Crew Cybershop Tech Republic Ziff Davis Haines U.S. Web	Direct opt-in addresses— "Double opt-in" system for individuals 200 3rd-party web sites including internet.com, AltaVista, NetZero, Entrepreneur Magazine	25+ million

cated effort indicates that competitors' lists are high on quantity: a costly proposition with less than optimum results. Clearly, a significant percentage of the names that each competitor claims to "own" are duplicates from purchased lists.

The clientele of the largest competitors in this industry tend to be large-sized national retailers, most frequently in the computer or general retail arenas. There appears to be no competitor focusing on the high-end consumer goods marketplace.

PREPARING THE SALES FORECAST

The ultimate aim of researching the firm's industry and its market is to gather the information necessary to make a realistic sales forecast. This forecast is the single most critical piece of information contained in the business plan. It is important to both the intended reader of the plan and to the entrepreneur for the following reasons:

■ Since sales volume is the most obvious indicator of commercial success, the sales forecast and its underlying assumptions will be carefully evaluated by the reader of the plan. A questionable sales forecast creates suspicion about the enterpreneur's claim of commercial success.

■ For the new business, sales potential is the ultimate criterion for judging the feasibility of the venture. If the target market cannot be expected to produce a profitable sales volume, then the venture is doomed from the outset.

■ The sales forecast is essential information for other components of the business plan. For example, expected sales volume is the starting point in the financial plan for estimating asset needs and period-by-period cash flow. Likewise, the planned level of operations as developed in the operating plan, the planned level of promotion and advertising as indicated in the marketing plan, and the estimated number of employees needed to produce and sell planned output as shown in the organization plan, are all dependent on the sales estimate.

■ Since virtually all business planning and operating activity in the firm are predicated on sales or the expectation of sales, the sales forecast is essential information for the internal planning, goal setting, and decision-making required to operate the business.

Forecasting is the art of estimating what is likely to happen given some assumed set of conditions. A sales forecast, then, is an informed estimate, based on a given set of assumptions about the future, of sales volume for a specific market, a target market, a firm, a group of firms, or an entire industry. The forecast may be stated in terms of either sales revenue or units, and the time period covered by the forecast may be short, such as the monthly or weekly forecasts used in preparing a cash budget, or the planning horizon may extend to as much as five years.

Both the term "art" and the phrase "assumed set of conditions" are critical to the sales forecasting process. Forecasting, unfortunately, is not a precise science. Rather, good forecasting is a blend of relevant information about the past and future, sound forecasting tools, the judgment of an experienced entrepreneur, and the learning and expertise that comes from preparing forecasts.

Since a forecast deals with an unknown future, any forecast is subject to varying degrees of uncertainty or forecasting error. The extent of the error inherent in a sales forecast depends on the type of business for which the forecast is prepared, its age, and the circumstances under which it operates. In general, the degree of accuracy in a sales forecast increases, or forecasting error declines, if the firm and/or industry is established, operates in a relatively stable market, has experienced management, and has an experienced and informed person making the forecast. Conversely, if the firm is new, if the entrepreneur or the forecaster has limited experience, or if the product is unique or the market volatile, forecasts are subject to much greater uncertainty.

In order for the sales forecast to be viewed as credible by the reader of the business plan, the assumptions on which the forecast is built must be sound and carefully detailed. As discussed in the previous sections, the firm's sales are affected by a variety of external and internal influences. The value of the sales forecast—and the business plan—will be diminished unless specific assumptions about the impact and future status of these influences are clearly spelled out.

THE LIFE-CYCLE CONCEPT

The life-cycle concept is widely used in business to describe the state of development of a business firm, a product, or an entire industry. The business life cycle, like that of living organisms, has four distinct phases: birth, growth, maturity, and death. These periods are generally referred to as the development stage, the growth stage, the maturity stage, and the decline stage.

The Development Stage

This stage covers the period from the formulation of the business concept to start-up. It is the period before market acceptance has been established. For entrepreneurs able to develop a new product or service or to get in on the ground floor of a new industry, this stage often offers the opportunity for large-scale profits. Unfortunately, this profit potential is accompanied by high risk. Since there is no hard evidence during this stage of wide-scale consumer acceptance, especially for a new product or service or in a new industry, there is no accurate gauge for measuring success.

The effort required to move the venture from birth to actual operation will challenge the most determined entrepreneur. This stage of the firm's life cycle is full of frustrations that range from searching for qualified employees to dealing with unsympathetic financiers.

The Growth Stage

This phase of the life cycle is a period of accelerating market acceptance and rapid expansion of sales and profits. As is true of the development stage, the growth phase may offer excellent profit opportunities for the alert entrepreneur. Equally important, the risk exposure at this time is less than during the developmental stage.

The growth phase of a typical business can involve both satisfaction and frustration for the entrepreneur. The profits that replace start-up losses are rewards for the time, effort, and financing invested in the business. Unfortunately, growth often involves management problems, such as inadequate staffing, production bottlenecks, inadequate cost control, or the chronic need for financing. This is why, even though this stage poses less risk to investors, they will nonetheless be looking closely at cost projections and operational strategies to ensure that the business will not grow too fast. They will be evaluating whether the entrepreneur has a concrete strategy in place to make sound financial decisions in keeping up with demand.

The Maturity Stage

This stage of the life cycle refers to the period of successful stability for the firm, a product or service, or an industry. Weaker firms or less competitive products or services have been eliminated by competition, and growth has declined to levels that leave industry or market survivors profitable and financially secure. A product in the maturity stage of its life cycle is usually in the enviable position of a cash cow. Sales are strong and profit margins are healthy because fixed overhead costs, such as R&D (research and development) expenditures, have usually been recaptured by this time.

When applied to the individual firm, the maturity stage usually means the time when the entrepreneur is able to enjoy the fruits of his or her labor. Cash flow and profits from the business are rewarding, and the disruptive problems encountered in the earlier stages of the firm's existence are only vague memories.

The Decline Stage

In this last stage in the life cycle disruptive changes have reduced product/service demand to a point where profit and cash flow are declining. Unless a strategic overhaul is possible, this stage signals the ultimate demise for the product/service or the industry. The same is true for the individual firm in the decline stage of its life cycle. To counteract the forces of decline and avoid liquidation of the firm, a new strategy that rekindles consumer demand or creates a new direction for the business must be devised.

THE SALES FORECASTING PROCESS

Preparing the firm's sales forecast is typically a four-stage process. A forecast is prepared for the following:

- The national economy.
- The firm's industry.
- The firm's market or target customer group.
- The firm and its individual products.

Since general economic conditions and industry sales affect the firm and its market, the sales forecasting process should begin with assumptions about these two important external variables. The forecast for the economy, the firm's industry, and possibly its market will usually not have to be made personally. Acceptable projections are readily available in numerous business, trade, and government publications as well as on-line. The information gleaned from these sources can be used to make the assumptions that serve as the backdrop for the sales forecast.

SALES FORECASTING TECHNIQUES

A sales forecast for the firm is made using information about what buyers have done in the past and what potential buyers are likely to do in the future. The data and other information gleaned from these sources can be used with virtually any forecasting technique.

Forecasting methods can be grouped into two basic categories: (a) the quantitative tools used to extend past behavior and (b) the qualitative or quantitative tools used to predict future behavior. For an existing business, either or both types of forecasting methods can be used. The new venture is, by necessity, limited to techniques for predicting future behavior.

Forecasts themselves fall into three general categories: qualitative or judgmental forecasts, which depend heavily on the informed judgment and intuition of the forecaster; quantitative forecasts, which apply mathematics to historical or estimated data; or some combination of the two. *A qualitative sales forecast* is an estimate based on research and the expertise and experience of an informed forecaster. Where possible, qualitative forecasts should be enhanced by the quantitative analysis of historical or projected sales data.

There are essentially two types of *quantitative forecasts:* (a) projections produced by extending or projecting trends and patterns found in historical sales data and (b) projections produced by predicting future sales using the relationship between sales and an influencing variable or group of variables. The more commonly used methods in each category are described below.

Extrapolating Past Sales

The sales forecasting process for an existing business typically starts with a detailed analysis of past sales. This review helps management understand why sales behaved as they did and assists the forecaster in predicting future sales.

The quantitative forecasting methods used with historical data are generally referred to as *time-series methods.* A time series is a collection of data that occurred, or was measured, in regular time intervals such as months, quarters, or years. Time-series patterns can be separated into the following components:

■ **Basic trend:** A trend represents the long-term movement of sales through time. It is represented as a smooth, mathematically or graphically fitted line of historical or projected sales. For example, if sales have grown at the long-term trend rate of 10% per year, sales for each of the forecast years are assumed to grow at this same 10% rate.

■ **Cyclical movements:** Cyclical patterns are the intermediate-term, periodic, wave-like movements of sales. These waves have clearly defined peaks and valleys and usually reflect the strong influence of general swings in overall economic activity (business cycles). Since the typical business cycle lasts from one to three years, identifying cyclical patterns in sales is important for intermediate-range forecasting.

■ **Seasonal patterns:** Seasonal patterns refer to the consistent, periodic movement of sales within the year. The term *seasonal* describes any recurring hourly, daily, weekly, monthly, or quarterly sales pattern. Seasonal patterns are usually related to holidays, trade practices, weather, or the influence of predominant social customs. The recognition of seasonal patterns in sales data is essential to the accuracy of short-term sales forecasts.

Extrapolating historical data by relating sales to time periods is a common method of sales forecasting. It can work well for mature firms selling products or services in markets that are relatively free from dynamic change. In these cases, the method is especially effective when used to make the monthly sales estimates needed for cash budgeting and for projecting the firm's long-term sales trend.

Before leaving this section, two important points should be noted. First, it is clear that any time-series forecast, regardless of the level of technical sophistication employed, implicitly assumes that the conditions causing historical sales patterns will continue into the future. Since any forecast is only as good as its underlying assumptions, a sales projection based on time-series analysis can be realistic only if the past is a good indicator of the future. Where circumstances are changing, any mechanical projection of sales should be considered no more than a starting point for the sales forecast. Projected sales values should be adjusted for the impact of what management expects to occur.

Second, while a detailed discussion of time-series techniques is beyond the scope of this book, the topic is covered in books on forecasting or statistics. Also, and of more importance to the entrepreneur preparing a business plan, there are numerous user-friendly software packages available that feature forecasting techniques. Many of these packages require neither prior knowledge of forecasting techniques nor computer sophistication.

Estimating Market Potential and Market Share

Obtaining a sales projection from historical data is not the end of the forecasting process. Rather, it is usually the starting point. As indicated above, even when historical data is available, it is desirable to tie the sales forecast to a variable or variables other than time. A common method for doing so involves estimating the sales potential of a market segment, a geographic target area, or a target customer group, and then estimating the share of that total to be captured by the firm. The forecast values produced by this approach can stand alone or they can be used as checks on, or refinements of, the results produced by other forecasting techniques.

The most common approaches to estimating market potential and market share are the *market build-up method* and the *market factor method.* The former approach is most often used to estimate sales of business-related products or services, and the latter is most often used to estimate sales of consumer-related goods and services.

Market Build-up Method: Forecasting sales using the market build-up method involves identifying the potential business buyers of the firm's product/service in each market and then estimating the purchase potential of each. The estimates for individual markets are totaled to arrive at the sales forecast for the firm.

One variation of this approach is explained in the following example. It uses North American Industry Classification System (NAICS) codes to identify potential purchasers and Standard Metropolitan Statistical Area (SMSA) to identify market areas.

To illustrate, assume the management of XYZ Company, a hypothetical manufacturer of packaging material, is considering expanding into the southeast market. Their first goal is to estimate sales potential for this regional market. They begin by dividing the southeast region into sub-markets according to SMSA designations. The contrived sales and employment data for product-user-groups (NAICS codes) in one hypothetical SMSA are shown in the first three columns of Table 6-5.

The first calculation is average packaging sales per worker in each user group. These values are shown in Column 4 and are calculated by dividing the Column 2 value by that of Column 3. For example, the Food group purchased $586,164,000 of packing material and employs 1,587,305 workers nationwide. Average sales per employee in the Food group is, therefore, $371.

Estimated packaging material sales for each user group in the SMSA are obtained by multiplying Sales Per Worker by the number of workers employed in that industry group. For example, the $1,845,000 sales estimate for the Food group, Column 6, is calculated as the Sales Per Worker of $371 times the 4,973 Food group workers employed in the SMSA (Column 5). Total estimated sales for the SMSA, $2,387,000, is obtained by summing the estimated sales for each industry group. This process would be repeated for each SMSA in the southeast region. The sales of individual SMSAs are then totaled to obtain the sales estimate for the southeast market. Given this estimate, management's next task would be to estimate the share of this market they believe the firm could capture.

Alternative Methods: One alternative method of forecasting business sales involves calculating the historical percentage relationship between the firm's sales and total industry sales (firm sales/industry sales). This percentage, which represents the firm's share of the industry, is then applied to an industry sales forecast to obtain estimated sales for the firm. Industry sales forecasts are available from a number of secondary sources of published information, such as those identified in Chapter 5.

Another alternative for estimating business sales would be to purchase total sales and brand sales reports from marketing research firms such as the A. C. Nielsen Company. This data can be used to calculate the firm's historical share of the market. For example,

TABLE 6-5

Estimated Sales of Packaging Materials in a Hypothetical Market

(1) Product Users By NAICS Group Code	(2) Value Of Product Used ($000)	(3) Number Of Workers By User Group	(4) Sales Per Worker By User Group	(5) Workers By User Group In SMSA	(6) Est. SMSA Sales By User ($000)
311 Food	$586,164	1,587,305	371	4,973	$1,845
312 Tobacco	17,432	74,557	233	None	None
313 Textile	91,520	874,677	104	250	26
315 Apparel	34,865	1,252,443	27	1,974	53
321 Lumber	19,611	526,622	37	690	26
442 Furniture	89,341	364,166	245	616	151
322 Paper	211,368	587,882	359	190	68
511 Printing & Publishing	32,686	904,208	36	2,876	104
325 Chemicals	128,564	772,169	166	488	81
324 Petroleum	28,328	161,367	175	None	None
326 Rubber & Plastics	67,551	387,997	174	190	33
Total					$2,387

Nielsen audits retail sales in supermarkets and drug stores for various product categories. The percentage of this total captured by the firm can be applied to published estimates of industry sales to obtain forecast sales for the firm.

Market Factor Method:
When the factor method is used to estimate sales of consumer goods, the forecast is made by relating sales behavior to the behavior of a factor or a set of factors that is highly correlated with sales. A factor is simply a variable that relates the behavior of one item to that of the item being forecast.

Assume, for example, that the management of a wholesale bakery company in Jacksonville, Florida, has determined from historical records that the firm's sales average one-half of one percent (.005) of the total retail sales in the Jacksonville SMSA. Management can forecast sales for the firm by multiplying .005 by an estimate of retail sales for the Jacksonville SMSA. For instance, if total retail sales for Jacksonville are estimated to be $120,000,000 next year, the sales forecast for the bakery is $600,000 (.005 × $120,000,000).

Other Forecasting Methods
Other forecasting methods fall into either of two broad categories: (a) forecasts designed to measure consumer response to a product or service and (b) expert or judgmental forecasts.

Consumer surveys can be used to gather sales information for existing businesses or new ventures and for either business or consumer products or services. These vary from simple direct questioning to intricately designed consumer interviews, panels, or questionnaires. The more sophisticated approaches are usually conducted by marketing research firms or other marketing experts. Surveys are especially valuable if consumers have clearly formulated intentions and are able to describe them. For example, a former client of the authors was interested in opening a neighborhood fresh-seafood market. To determine the number of potential customers in the area and their purchasing habits, he conducted personal-contact interviews with residents in an eight-block radius of the intended site. The data gathered provided a clear indication of potential target market sales and an estimate of the likelihood for the success of his proposed venture.

Test marketing is often used to measure potential sales when the product is new or expert or judgmental forecasts are not reliable. The technique involves selling the product or service in a representative market area or to a sample of targeted customers using the same marketing program that is intended for the broad-scale campaign. Test marketing is useful for measuring consumer reaction to the product, the extent to which the product is repurchased after the initial trial, and the effectiveness of various advertising and promotion techniques.

Forecasting the level of sales required to ensure commercial success for a new business venture or a new product or service is often done using the judgmental estimate of a marketing expert or an informed entrepreneur. Experts include such diverse groups as sales personnel, distributors, suppliers, retailers, wholesalers, marketing consultants, marketing research firms, trade associations, and firms that specialize in making industry and market forecasts, such as Data Resources, Chase Econometric, and Wharton Econometric. The estimates can be obtained using various information-gathering techniques such as interviews, questionnaires, or panel discussions. Again, expert opinion is an effective form of documenting the entrepreneur's claim of commercial success.

TIPS FOR PREPARING THE MARKET ANALYSIS AND SALES FORECAST

■ **Don't assume a market exists.** There is a natural tendency for an entrepreneur excited about the firm's product or service to assume consumers will be equally enthusiastic. The reader of the business plan will expect to see solid supporting documentation and not unsupported claims. Communicate with your target market. Even though it is still more effective to back up any qualitative information with quantitative statistics, it is nevertheless beneficial to not get lost only in the numbers. To find out if there is a market for your product or service, particularly for a new venture, personally go out into the marketplace and ask. Ask questions about buying habits, unfilled needs, concerns, and challenges. Even if your representative sampling is not large enough to be classified as a thorough and statistically sound research study, it can still steer you in the right direction and prompt you to further research the opportunity—prior to investing a lot of time, money, and energy into the venture.

■ **Don't slight this component.** Along with the industry analysis, the market analysis and sales forecast are critical to the question of commercial success. The intended reader will carefully evaluate the quantity and quality of information presented in this section, and it is important that the entrepreneur do his or her homework before it is prepared.

■ **Do this analysis second for new ventures.** Before committing time and energy to preparing a complete business plan for a new venture, do a quick market feasibility study after completing the preliminary industry analysis. This will provide a clear indication of whether the venture has sufficient merit to justify preparing a complete business plan.

■ **Make multiple sales forecasts.** Since a forecast is only as accurate as the assumptions upon which it is built, it is wise to create three variations of the sales forecast: a worst-case scenario, a best-case scenario, and one based on the most likely set of conditions. There are two basic advantages to this "what if" approach to forecasting and planning. First, multiple sales forecasts clarify the distinction between what is deemed most likely to occur and what is possible. Second, the entrepreneur sends another strong message about management ability. Using the "what if" forecasting and planning indicates that he or she understands and prepares for the uncertainty associated with projecting the future.

■ **Contact suppliers for information.** The potential suppliers of a new business have a vested interest in its success. In many cases, they have information that can help estimate sales volume. Some suppliers also have sophisticated models for estimating sales for a given type of business. This is true, for example, with suppliers of restaurants, feed stores, department stores, automobile dealerships, and many fast-food franchise operations.

■ **Contact industry trade associations for information.** Most industry trade associations have a wealth of data that are useful for developing a sales forecast. Some trade associations also have sophisticated sales forecasting models that can assist the entrepreneur.

■ **Study similar sales experiences.** It is often possible to estimate sales potential by evaluating the sales experiences of others, including competitors, other new firms in the industry, or similar products or services. For example, assume XYZ Software Company develops a totally new and revolutionary computer program. Since the program is unique, there are no direct sales comparisons available. Yet, valuable insights for estimating sales of the new program can be gained by examining the sales history of other successful software.

■ **Use graphics.** Some portions of the market analysis and sales forecast will necessarily deal with quantitative data. The message in this data is delivered more effectively when verbal explanations are supplemented with tables, graphs, and charts.

SAMPLE MARKET ANALYSIS AND SALES FORECAST

John King intends to open a facilities management services firm—"Dial a Janitor"—to serve small and mid-size businesses in the Phoenix area. He expects that his 19 years of industry experience and "one-stop-shopping" service contract will appeal to businesses in the

Phoenix metropolitan area. Services will include commercial cleaning, window cleaning, handyman, HVAC, and plumbing services, in addition to janitorial supplies sales, landscape management, and aluminum and paper recycling.

Since this is a new business, he wants to (a) determine whether sufficient market potential exists to support the business and (b) make a realistic sales estimate that can be used in his business plan. To do this, Mr. King first conducts an industry and market analysis. The key points from these studies are summarized as part of the following six-step process.

1. **Identify the firm's industry.** Realizing that the facilities management industry includes a number of different NAICS codes, Mr. King begins the analysis by reviewing the description of the business and its intended operations as explained in the business summary component of his business plan. He then explores the various descriptions on-line at *www.census.gov/epcd/www/naics.html,* and finds the following options:

- 541513 computer facilities management services
- 561210 facilities support services

He selects 561210 as the appropriate code for his business.

Using this code, Mr. King begins his investigation of the facilities management industry by researching secondary information sources selected from those listed in Chapter 5. His research provides a wealth of information, including the following key facts:

- There is a new direction to head in the industry of managing buildings. Most small to mid-sized business owners contract out janitorial services to one company, plumbing maintenance to another, landscape management to yet another, and call still another company for recycling. There is substantial opportunity for one competent company to fulfill all of these needs for smaller business owners in the Phoenix area.
- The Phoenix janitorial market can be divided into two types of services: services provided for large sites (over 100,000 square feet) and those provided for the smaller to mid-sized sites (20,000 to 100,000 square feet).
- The demand for facilities services is closely linked to general economic conditions. This demand rises during economic upswings as DPI and GDP increase, and declines during downswings.
- Phoenix has been growing at the rate of 1 to 2mm ft^2 of office space since 2000, with an average of 1.5mm ft^2 per year. As of August 15, 2007, the year has realized the greatest gross growth to date with 1.79 million ft^2 of office space, with an

additional 1.55mm ft^2 expected by year end (this is double the average growth of previous years). The total space in the greater Phoenix area is 43,691,000 ft^2 with 2.9mm ft^2 under construction. Approximately 75% of total office space is located in the 20,000 ft^2 to 100,000 ft^2 building range.

This information gives Mr. King a working knowledge of the industry. He now understands the industry's nature, sensitivity to changes in economic activity, primary factors influencing industry performance and the major indicators of industry success. His research also produces a realistic forecast of the industry's long-term growth rate and industry sales and profits for each of the next three years. Of greatest importance, Mr. King has identified which secondary information sources should be monitored in the future to keep abreast of industry developments.

2. **Identify the firm's market area.** Mr. King's next task is to define the specific geographic area that his facilities management company will serve. Based on personal observation, market demographics, the expected rates of economic and demographic growth, the recommendations from published market research, and readings from other selected secondary information, he has selected Phoenix as his primary market area.

3. **Define the firm's target market.** Mr. King's 19 years of experience in the facilities industry has led him to identify a new and unmet need: that of bundling all building services for the smaller and mid-sized corporation—those with square footage between 20,000 and 100,000 square ft. These smaller business owners rely upon a multitude of service contractors to maintain their offices, oftentimes necessitating up to eight separate calls.

4. **Identify and evaluate the firm's competition.** Useful information on competition may be found in a variety of secondary sources such as industry and trade association publications or at various online professional, trade, and government sites. Many competitors may also have web sites and these sites can be a rich source of information. With a clearly defined and geographically contained target market, such as Mr. King's market of Phoenix, the most reliable source of competition can readily be based on personal experience. He identifies two primary competitors in his market area and outlines strengths and weaknesses for each:

- **CLEAN STUFF** provides office janitorial, industrial, clean rooms, windows, carpet cleaning, fire damage restoration, and handyman services.

Strengths:

- An established firm with more than 35mm sq. ft. of office space under contract.
- Prides itself on training program and customized work schedules to meet clientele needs.
- Owner-operator system seems to work well, with managers having a vested interest in their business.

Weaknesses:

- While successful in its core business, has had its head in the sand regarding the growing trend of offering the full facility care management package.
- Seems to take on clientele of all sizes: from small (38,000 sq. ft.) to very large (210,000 sq. ft.).
- Claims no market niche and the specialization and service this affords.

- **THE TOP CLEANERS** provides cleaning and janitorial, windows, medical, and dental facility services.

  Strengths:

  - In business for more than 26 years, the Top Cleaners is competitive on price and has solid customer service.
  - Specialized service offerings available (i.e. carpet cleaning, wall washing, light bulb replacement).

  Weaknesses:

  - Limited offerings beyond standard janitorial service.
  - Market niche encompasses small-sized structures with little focus on growing service base beyond smaller structures.

5. **Estimate market sales potential.** Through his extensive network of contacts both professionally and personally, Mr. King will take on most of the initial sales responsibilities himself, soliciting businesses and business owners in the Phoenix metropolitan area. Revenue will be generated through various channels that include:

- Direct employment of in-house cleaning staffs and aluminum/paper recycling services.
- Commissions received on subcontracted employment of specialized services.
- Membership fees from subcontractors groups joining Dial-a-Janitor.
- Premiums placed on janitorial supplies (20%) ordered through the company.

Dial-a-Janitor will capitalize on its vast network of subcontractor relationships and its understanding of the janitorial/facilities management needs of smaller and mid-sized businesses in the Phoenix metropolitan area. Because the Phoenix metropolitan area is estimated to continue growing exponentially, Dial-a-Janitor will be able to target more than 32,000,000 sq. ft. of office space by the year 2012. Revenues are projected to begin at approximately $3500 per month in the first four months of business, growing to $10,000 per month and over from month five, generating over $1.5 million in net profit by 2015.

CHAPTER PERSPECTIVE

The market analysis and sales forecast are an extension of the industry analysis. A market analysis provides the information needed to convert an assessment of market potential into a realistic sales forecast. It is a study of the basic factors that define and affect the market for the firm's product or service and what the firm must do to effectively position itself to take advantage of the opportunity that is available. A market analysis usually consists of a description of its geographic location, the firm's market niche, the target market the firm expects to reach, the firm's competition, and an estimate of the sales potential the market should provide, factoring in any market trends. The sales forecast is a gauge of the firm's ability to achieve commercial success and, because all activity in the firm is ultimately related to sales, it is the basis for all other plans and projections. Before marketing commences, be sure to test market the product or service, which simply entails an experiment conducted in the field without the buyers knowing they are participating in an evaluation exercise.

The Marketing Plan

MARKETING AND PLANNING

This chapter is the first in the series that applies planning to one of the basic functions of a business firm—marketing. This is where all the prior research is utilized to develop concise strategies that will enable the entrepreneur to reach the target market in the most effective way possible. Planning takes into consideration questions of what, how, when, and who. The marketing function is responsible for establishing the plans, policies, and procedures that will get the right goods or services to the right people, at the right time and price, using the right promotion and distribution techniques. The marketing plan, which combines these functions, is the basic strategy for satisfying the needs and wants of the firm's target customer group.

After studying the material in this chapter you will:

- Understand what planning is and the basic steps in the planning process.
- Understand the role of the marketing plan.
- Know the information needed to prepare the marketing plan.
- Understand the steps to preparing the marketing plan.
- Understand what a marketing-mix strategy is and the role it plays in the marketing plan.

WHAT IS PLANNING?

Planning is the cornerstone of the management process and the most important function any manager performs. Planning is the art and science of deciding what course of action the firm will take to meet established objectives. Through planning, a manager:

- Gathers the information needed to evaluate the firm's strengths, weaknesses, opportunities and threats.
- Sets realistic long-term objectives and short-term operating goals.
- Develops long-term strategies that capitalize on the firm's strengths and opportunities and minimize its threats and weaknesses.

■ Develops the short-term operating plans that identify the resources and activities that will be employed to meet strategic aims.

The necessary corollary to planning is the management function of control. It involves monitoring activity to ensure that actual results are consistent with planned expectations and, when necessary, that corrective action is taken.

A MODEL OF THE PLANNING PROCESS

Planning is not a single act, but a process consisting of interrelated steps. These steps and their interrelationships are shown in Figure 7-1. The process starts with the entrepreneur's statement of the firm's business philosophy and its intended mission. These basics form the personality and character of the firm, identify the image to be projected, determine the general direction the business will take, and establish the foundation from which the firm's strategic and operating plans are determined.

To develop operating plans that effectively carry out adopted strategies, the entrepreneur must have reliable information on the firm and its environment. This information is used to prepare the forecast on which detailed operating plans and budgets are developed.

Figure 7-1 also indicates the importance of the control function. Plans are developed using assumptions and forecasts about the future. Since the future is uncertain, it is necessary to monitor actual results and compare these outcomes to what has been anticipated. Doing so puts the entrepreneur in a position to take corrective action before problems become crises. Corrective actions can range from a simple fine-tuning of operations to a complete remake of assumptions, forecasts, and plans.

WHAT IS A MARKETING PLAN?

A marketing plan describes how the firm's target customer group will be motivated to purchase its product/service. The plan details the marketing goals to be achieved, the marketing-mix strategy that will position the firm's product/service in its market, and the marketing and selling programs required to achieve marketing goals. A well-prepared marketing plan serves two important purposes:

■ Validating commercial success and convincing the intended reader of the merits of the business plan.

■ Driving the firm's internal planning and decision-making process.

FIGURE 7-1 *The flow of activities in the planning process*

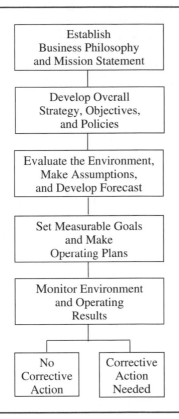

INFORMATION NEEDED TO PREPARE THE MARKETING PLAN

A variety of information on the firm's external environment, its industry, markets, competition, and target market are needed to develop a convincing marketing plan. The questions below provide guidelines for identifying that information.

▬ What is the firm's basic business philosophy and basic mission statement?

▬ What market opportunity exists for the firm's product or service?

▬ What key factors influence sales in this market?

- What opportunity exists to establish a niche in this market?
- Who are the consumers of the type of product or service the firm sells and why and how much do they buy?
- How do consumers perceive the product or service in terms of value, quality, benefits, and price?
- From whom does the target market now buy the product or service, and why do they buy from these firms?
- What are customers' attitudes toward the firm's competitors?
- What advertising and promotion techniques are used by competitors, which have been least and most effective?
- At what price does the competition sell its product or service?
- What advantages or disadvantages do the firm's competitors have?
- What competitive advantage does the firm have?
- What current channels of distribution are used by competitors to supply customers; how effectively do these channels function?
- What channels of distribution does the firm use; what advantages, if any, do they offer over competition?
- How will the target market be made aware of the firm and the product or service it offers?
- What marketing-mix strategy can be used to reach the target market and to motivate them to buy the firm's product or service?
- What marketing program will be used to carry out the marketing-mix strategy?
- What are historical sales for the firm (if it is an existing business) and what factors have influenced these sales?
- What are the firm's sales and profit goals?
- What are forecast sales for the firm for each of the next twelve months? For each of the next three years?

The information needed to prepare the marketing plan should come from the market analysis and sales component of the business plan.

WHEN TO INCLUDE A MARKETING PLAN WITH THE BUSINESS PLAN

Since the marketing plan is an essential component of a convincing business plan, the information it provides is a required part of the document. This is true whether a complete business plan is prepared for outside presentation, whether the presentation package is limited to select business plan information, or whether the marketing plan is used internally. The intended use of the marketing plan does, however, determine the amount and detail of its content. If the marketing plan is used as part of an outside financing request, only the information needed to explain the adopted marketing strategy should be included. On the other hand, a highly detailed marketing plan is needed for internal planning and decision-making.

STEPS TO PREPARING A MARKETING PLAN

Marketing planning is predicated on the firm's market and target customer group. Without an understanding of what constitutes the market for the firm's product or service and the characteristics, perceptions, and motivations of the target customer group, it is impossible to devise an effective plan for satisfying customer needs and expectations. Following are six steps to preparing a marketing plan.

1. **Consider a marketing plan summary.** This optional section of the marketing plan *may* be used when the plan is prepared for outside presentation. It serves as a convenience for the reader and, if included, should be no longer than what is needed by the reader to gain a quick grasp of the plan's major thrust. Like most other summaries mentioned thus far, it is more effective to write this section last, to ensure that all major points of the marketing plan are covered.

2. **Prepare a situational review.** The situational review establishes the groundwork for the key components of the marketing plan. This section should summarize the important findings and conclusions from the industry analysis, market analysis and sales forecast components of the business plan. It should include a synopsis of the the firm's market, the market niche that is available, the competitive advantage held by the firm, the target market, the competition, and the outlook for sales. If the firm has major competitive weaknesses these should be identified along with an explanation of plans to combat them. If the business plan is prepared for an existing business, this section should also include historical sales data for the past three to five years and a brief summary of the key factors that influenced this sales performance.

3. **Identify marketing goals.** A marketing plan, as is true of all business plans, cannot be effective without clearly defined, realistic, measurable goals. Goals serve several important purposes.

- They define objectives toward which all activity is coordinated and directed.
- They provide incentives for motivating management and employee efforts.
- They serve as standards or targets for measuring progress toward planned outcomes.
- They are the criteria used to identify deviations from the plan that require remedial action.

Marketing goals should be established with careful consideration of the firm's business philosophy and mission statement, the needs and expectations of its target market, the firm and product images management wishes to project, and the sales and financial goals to which marketing activity will contribute. Marketing goal statements can be expressed in the form of quantitative targets, such as expected sales volume or percentage share of the market, or as qualitative objectives, such as increasing the consumer product-awareness level or establishing an ongoing sales training program.

Regardless of the form in which marketing goals are expressed, goal statements should be sufficiently specific and detailed to allow progress to be measured. For example, note the difference between the following goal statements:

- **Poor goal statement:** We expect to increase sales for our product by lowering price.
- **Effective goal statement:** We expect sales to increase at a compound growth rate of 10% per year over the next five years. This target growth rate will be accomplished by (a) opening a branch location in the rapidly growing northeast section of the county; (b) doubling the size of our mailout promotion list; (c) increasing mailout promotions to four per year; and (d) increasing attendance and displays at industry trade shows to three per year.

It is crucial for all parts of the business plan—marketing, operations, and financial—to be streamlined, and so it is also important that marketing plans be coordinated with and contribute to the firm's overall financial goals. Financial goals set the ultimate performance standards the entrepreneur wishes the firm to achieve. Marketing goals, in turn, should convert financial goals into specific marketing accomplishments. For example, assume the XYZ Company has established a net profit goal of $1,000,000 and a minimum net profit margin goal of 10% of sales as two of its overall financial goals. In order to meet the profit goal and maintain a 10% net profit margin, sales revenue of $10,000,000 would have to be generated ($1,000,000/10%) and, if the intended selling price for their product is $369, then 27,100 units must be sold ($10,000,000/$369). Quantifying goals in this manner allows the entrepreneur to visualize specific short-term goals and decide on appropriate marketing methods to help meet those goals.

4. **Explain the intended marketing strategy.** *Marketing strategy* is the firm's broad-scaled plan for reaching and motivating targeted consumers and for positioning the firm's product/service relative to the firm's identified competition. The focal point of the marketing strategy should be the firm's marketing mix. *Marketing mix* is the combination of controllable marketing variables identified as best able to meet the needs and expectations of the target market.

These marketing variables, or decision areas, include what is traditionally referred to in marketing as the "Four P's": *product/service, price, place,* and *promotion.*

The *product/service decision* involves identifying the product/service or product/service mix that meets the defined needs and expectations of the target market and, at the same time, is consistent with the firm's adopted philosophy, mission, and strategic objectives. For example, if the entrepreneur has decided the firm will be a high-quality, high-price operation and this combination meets the expectations of the target market, the product/service offered must be consistent with this image.

As shown on Tables 7-1 and 7-2, there are various product classes within the basic consumer goods and industrial (business) goods categories that are an important part of this decision. The consumer goods product classes identified on Table 7-1 are defined as follows:

- **Convenience products** are goods the consumer needs but is unwilling to spend much time, effort, or planning to shop for or purchase. These products are purchased frequently, require little or no selling effort, are often inexpensive, and are often purchased out of habit. Included in this category are such commonplace items as table salt, soft drinks, and magazines.
- **Shopping products** are goods the consumer feels are worth spending the time and effort needed for careful planning and comparison shopping. These include products such as furniture, stereo equipment, and appliances.
- **Specialty products** are goods the consumer wants and is willing to make a special effort to find. While specialty products are not necessarily expensive products, they are often brand name items that serve as status symbols or fit the consumer's self-image. Specialty products include recognizable items such as Tommy Hilfiger jeans, ethnic foods, or automobiles.
- **Unsought products** are goods unknown to the consumer.
- **Services** are specialized assistance provided for a fee.

The industrial goods product classes identified on Table 7-2 are defined as follows:

- **Installations** are major capital expenditures that have a long economic life, such as land or standard or custom-made heavy equipment, machinery, buildings.
- **Accessory equipment** includes short-lived capital expenditure items such as tools, equipment, computers, and vehicles.
- **Raw materials** are unprocessed expense items such as iron ore, crude oil, and cotton that are used in the firm's finished product.

- **Components** are preprocessed, custom-made, or standardized items that are used in and become part of the finished product such as disk drives for a computer or motors for appliances.
- **Supplies** are routine maintenance and repair items such as paint or lubricating oil.
- **Professional services** are specialized skills that support the operations of a business, such as accounting, legal, or engineering services.

Attention to differences between product classes is important. Consumers and industrial users view, shop for, and buy products/services differently. These differences affect how a product/service should be marketed. Examples of the considerations associated with the various product classes and types are shown in the last columns of Tables 7-1 and 7-2.

The last column also shows that the considerations for offering a service to targeted customers differs from those for a product. Services are intangible, inseparable, and perishable. Since a service must be performed anew on each occasion, it is virtually impossible to separate the quality of the service from the supplier. Service firms live or die by their reputations. The marketing of a service must focus on the firm's good name, expertise, and quality of work provided.

The decision on an appropriate marketing mix should reflect the entrepreneur's understanding of the target market. Without this knowledge it is impossible to develop a realistic, consumer-oriented marketing strategy that is tied directly to the needs, expectations, and perceptions of targeted customers. Where the firm's selling efforts are concentrated, how a product/service is positioned, and where and to whom it is promoted and advertised depends, to a large extent, on demographic characteristics. Table 7-3 lists examples of some of the many possible marketing-mix decisions that are related to and affected by target market characteristics.

The *pricing decision* is important to the marketing-mix strategy for two reasons. First is the issue of product/service image and how the established price is perceived by the target market. Selling price should be consistent with the consumer perceptions the entrepreneur is attempting to influence. If, for example, the goal is to have consumers view the firm as a low-cost, high-volume seller, the selling price of the product/service must be lower than that of competitive products/services. If the product is aimed at the upscale, image-conscious consumer, the product would not be priced low nor marketed through discount stores.

TABLE 7-1
Consumer Product Classification and Marketing-Mix Decisions

Product Class	Product Type Included	Marketing Considerations
Convenience Goods	Staples Impulse products Emergency products	In general, these goods require widespread distribution and maximum exposure. Staples require low selling price and impulse and emergency goods need preferred display and counter positions.
Shopping Goods	Homogeneous Heterogeneous	Both product types need enough exposure to facilitate price comparison and should have adequate representation in major shopping districts or large shopping centers near other, similar shopping products.
Specialty Goods	N/A	This product may have limited exposure, but in general should be treated as a convenience or shopping good in order to reach persons not yet sold on its specialty status.
Unsought Goods	N/A	These products need attention directed to their existence and aggressive promotion in outlets, or in places where similar products are sought.
Services	Personal Professional	Effective selling requires widespread availability and aggressive and widespread promotion through technically competent contact personnel.

TABLE 7-2
Industrial Product Classification and Marketing-Mix Decisions

Product Class	Product Type Included	Marketing Considerations
Installations	Long-lived capital expenditures	Effective selling requires widespread, knowledgeable, technically competent contact and selling effort by well-trained personnel.
Accessories	Short-lived capital expenditures	Effective selling requires fairly widespread and numerous contacts and selling effort by knowledgeable, well-trained, and sometimes technically competent personnel.
Raw Materials	Unprocessed items used in product production or service rendering	Effective selling requires widespread contacts, reliable distribution channels, uniform quality and grading, and competitive pricing.
Components	Preprocessed, custom-made, or standardized items used in product production or service rendering	Effective selling requires widespread contacts by knowledgeable, well-trained, technically competent personnel, reliable distribution channels, uniform quality, and competitive pricing.
Supplies	Low cost, routine maintenance and repair items	Effective selling requires widespread contacts and distribution and prompt, reliable delivery, at competitive prices.
Services	Out-of-house specialized skills	Effective selling requires widespread availability, sales and contact efforts conducted by well-trained, technically competent personnel, and reputation for expertise and reliability.

TABLE 7-3
Relationship Between Target Market Characteristics and Marketing-Mix Decisions

Target Market Characteristics	Decision Variables Affected
1. Geographic location and other demographic characteristics.	Affects *size* and economic potential of target market; the *place* where products should be made available; and where and to whom the product is *promoted*.
2. Behavioral needs and attitudes, and how present and potential products/services fit into customers' consumption patterns.	Affects *product* image, design, packaging, and depth of product line; and the information conveyed and appeals used in *promoting* the product/service.
3. Product expectations and perceived value and benefits.	Affects *product* image, design, packaging, and depth of product/ service line; the product/service selling *price;* and the information conveyed and appeals used in *promotion*.
4. Consumers' urgency to get need satisfied and their desire to compare and shop.	Affects *place*—how directly products are distributed from producer to consumer, how extensively they are made available, and the level of service needed—and *price,* or how much potential customers are willing to pay for product or service.

The second major consideration in pricing strategy is profit margin. The selling price must be sufficient to cover the cost of both producing/rendering the product/service and other directly related cost elements. For example, cost considerations such as discounts offered, credit extended, and the degree of service provided after the sale must be factored into the pricing decision.

While there are no mechanical formulas for making pricing decisions, the following basic guidelines will help establish a rational pricing strategy.

- **Know your full costs.** Research indicates that new entrepreneurs rarely understand the full cost of operating their businesses. The most effective method for understanding cost is to perform a breakeven analysis (see Chapter 10) for the business as a whole and for individual products/services or product lines.
- **Price, image, and goals are interrelated.** Pricing policy cannot be established in a vacuum. The selling price of the product/service should be consistent with the entrepreneur's marketing goals, the image he or she is attempting to project, and the perceptions and expectations of the target market.
- **Price, product differentiation, and market power.** The ability to set price independent of competition depends on the degree of differentiation the product/service commands and the market power of the firm. The more difficult it is to differentiate the product/service from that of the competition, the more likely it is the firm will have to accept the going market price. The same is true of market power. Larger firms and industry leaders with more brand awareness have more flexibility in setting selling price than smaller firms and industry followers.
- **Price and non-price perceptions.** While selling price is an important influence on consumer purchases, it is not the main reason consumers buy. More important is how price and non-price considerations are perceived by consumers. In general, price, quality, value, and service are closely interrelated in the mind of consumers.

The *place* component of the firm's marketing-mix strategy involves deciding which channels of distribution will be used to get the product in the right place at the right time. *Distribution channels* are the interconnecting steps used to move the product from producer to the ultimate user. A channel may consist of one or more marketing middlemen, such as selling representatives, brokers, wholesalers, and retailers, or the product may move directly from producer to consumer.

The Internet has become a major distribution channel, with e-commerce (electronic commerce, or business conducted online). The Internet has leveled the playing field in a lot of cases, where a small firm can now conduct business on a worldwide basis and compete with bigger industry leaders. Online commerce has both expanded the distribution methods and a firm's potential consumer market, while minimizing the need for overhead such as a store front and additional labor. This has allowed even a small proprietorship to compete at all levels, from convenience goods to specialty items.

Distribution channels play an important role in the marketing process. As shown on Table 7-4, they perform three basic functions that benefit manufacturers, suppliers, and consumers: physical distribution, communication, and facilitation.

TABLE 7-4
Services Performed by Intermediaries for Suppliers and Customers

Marketing Function	Performed for Suppliers	Performed for Buyers
Physical Distribution	Breaking bulk Accumulating bulk Creating assortments Transportation Storage	Sorting by quantity Sorting by type Storage Delivery

Communication	Impart product
	  information
	Gather market
	  information
	Gather consumer
	  information
		Identify needs
		Buy based on needs
		Advise
		Impart information

Facilitation	Take product risk
	  through ownership
	Provide personalized
	  services
	Finance customer
	  purchases
		Business management
		  assistance
		Extend credit
		Provide repair and
		  maintenance services

The following factors should be considered by the entrepreneur when selecting a distribution channel.

- **Cost.** Marketing intermediaries through which goods are moved are specialists that perform functions essential to the marketing process. For example, it may be cost-effective to use sales representatives to sell the product or service. The trade-off is the risk of having less selling interest and motivation than that of the firm's sales force. One major benefit the Internet has to offer small businesses is, in effect, "eliminating the middle man." Companies are able to sell directly to consumers via web sites at distribution costs that are a fraction of more traditional routes.

- **Product class.** As discussed above and shown in Tables 7-1 and 7-2, the type of product or service offered the buyer or consumer often dictates the channel of distribution. For example, effective selling of consumer convenience goods or industrial supplies dictates widespread distribution. Therefore, these products have traditionally been marketed through a large number of wholesalers and retailers.

- **Degree of exposure required.** Ideally, the appropriate goal for deciding the number of intermediaries used in the distribution channel and/or the number of outlets for a given intermediary is just enough product availability to satisfy the target market. Too much exposure needlessly increases marketing costs and too little results in lost sales.

- **Other marketing-mix considerations.** As true with other components of the marketing-mix strategy, a decision on the appropriate distribution channel cannot be made in a vacuum. The choice of a distribution channel is interrelated with product image, selling price, and promotion and advertising strategy. For example, a high-quality, high-priced status product would not be distributed through discount retailers.

- **Market characteristics.** The nature and characteristics of the firm's market and targeted customer group often influence the distribution channel. For example, the number of customers in a given market and the size of the average purchase influence the number of intermediaries in the distribution channel. In general, the fewer the number of large-scale purchasers, the shorter and more direct the channel.

- **Service marketing.** A service is defined as a bundle of benefits provided the user and is, essentially, a product. Because it is intangible and usually rendered directly to the end user by the supplier, it often appears that no distribution channel exists. While there is normally no intermediary involved in the delivery of a service, the marketing-mix functions necessary to render a service for the end user are still required. As is true of tangible goods, the type of service provided must be consistent with the image and business philosophy of the firm; a price consistent with market forces and firm image must be established; information regarding the existence and nature of the service must be communicated; and the service must be promoted and advertised.

Promotion involves a decision on the strategy and techniques that are used to communicate product/service information between seller and prospective buyer. The ultimate goal is influencing consumer attitudes and behavior. Promotion is communication with a purpose: telling and selling the customer. It includes the mix of activities surrounding sales promotion, sales strategy, advertising, and public relations.

- **Sales promotion** involves the methods used to communicate information about the firm and its product/service and to provide out-of-the-ordinary incentives to purchase. Non-routine purchase incentives are inducements such as coupon deals, offers for free goods or extended services, point-of-purchase displays, or free in-house or video tape demonstrations.

- **Sales strategy** involves the procedures used to make sales. The appropriate goal for this strategy is to use cost-effective selling methods that make it easy for the customer to buy from the firm. These methods can range from highly personal selling using trained, knowledgeable personnel to contact the customer either in-house or on-site to mass selling through the use of telemarketing or the Internet.

- **Advertising and public relations** is any form of nonpersonal, persuasive message delivered through mass media either through the form of paid advertisements or through free press such as press releases, articles, or speaking opportunities. The primary purpose of advertising and public relations is to maximize brand awareness, thereby influencing purchaser behavior.

Promotion should detail how, given the image and message to be projected, the entrepreneur will zero in on targeted customers. The strategy should focus on how targeted customers will be influenced to think of the firm when they want to buy the type of product/service it sells; how they are motivated to buy from the firm; and what selling approach will be used to close the sale. As is true of the other components of the firm's marketing mix, developing the appropriate promotion strategy begins with a clear understanding of the target market. The defined characteristics of the customer group should determine the specific methods used to accomplish promotional goals.

Common examples of promotion activities often used for each of the four basic target market groups are shown on Table 7-5. The important point made by these examples is that different blends of promotion mix are needed for different target markets. By identifying its target market, the entrepreneur not only establishes the primary area of marketing emphasis but is able to concentrate scarce marketing dollars into a mix of promotion methods, time, and media combinations that most directly hit the target audience.

TABLE 7-5
Promotion Activities by Target Market Group

Group	Objective	Strategy	Methods
Final consumer	Reach, inform, persuade, and motivate numerous customers	Mass promotion and selling	Area media advertising Internet Mailouts 800 number Catalogs Free merchandise Samples & coupons Contests Aisle displays Point-of-purchase displays Sponsor special events
Industrial user	Reach and inform limited number of customers	Personalized promotion and selling	Trained contact & sales personnel Trade publication ads Trade shows National media advertising Product information mailouts
Middlemen	Reach, inform, and persuade limited number of intermediaries	Personalized promotion and selling	Trained contact & sales personnel Trade shows Trade publication ads Promotion deals Price deals Gifts Sales contests Provide sales training Provide technical liaison personnel

TABLE 7-5 *(continued)*

Group	Objective	Strategy	Methods
Retailer	Reach numerous outlets Transmit product information, persuade and motivate	Personalized promotion and selling	Trained contact & sales personnel Trade shows Trade publication ads Price deals Promotion deals Sales contests Financing or credit extension Provide market & customer advice Sponsor special events

The following questions can be used as a guide to developing the promotion strategy.

- What are the perceived needs, wants, and expectations of the target customer group?
- Does the target market know the firm is in business, and what evidence is there to this effect? If not, how will they be informed?
- Is the target market aware of what the firm sells, and what evidence is there to this effect?
- If the target group must be educated as to what the firm sells, how will this be done?
- What promotional methods will be used to reach the target market?
- What message will be used to persuade the target customer group that the firm can meet their needs?
- What selling strategy and techniques will be used to achieve sales?

5. **Prepare the marketing budget.** Effective planning must also consider the cost of implementing what is to be done. A *budget* is simply a plan expressed in quantitative terms such as estimated dollars of expense, expected sales revenue, sales in units, the number of services performed, or dollars of expected profit. These budgeted figures are the results of decisions on how scarce dollars will be allocated and, as such, serve as standards against which the efficiency and effectiveness of actual operations is measured.

The marketing budget should detail both estimated revenues and expenditures. The revenue estimates consist of forecast sales in units (or number of service units performed) and the selling price per unit. On the expense side, the budget should detail the dollar amount and timing of all marketing-related expenditures. The difference between forecast revenue and expenses is the projected marketing profit goal.

The commonly used approaches to budgeting marketing programs are the *percent-of-sales, matching, default or affordable,* and *objective and task* methods. The first three budgeting methods, while offering the advantage of simplicity, suffer from flawed logic. Each contradicts the rationale behind business planning. The percent-of-sales method establishes the amount to be spent on marketing by assigning an arbitrarily established percentage-of-sales value to the forecast sales figure for the period. For example, if 5% of sales is judged a reasonable amount to spend on marketing activities and forecast sales total $100,000, the budget allocation for marketing would be $5,000. The matching method uses the same procedure but bases the percent-of-sales figure on what competitors or other firms in the industry are using.

Both the percent-of-sales and matching methods imply that marketing activities are the consequence of sales. That is, sales occur without any marketing effort. The reality is, however, that sales are the result of effective marketing. What's more, either method produces marketing expenditures in amounts that often run counter to what is needed. When sales decline, marketing expenditures decline as well. Yet, this may be the time when increased marketing activity is needed to boost lagging sales.

With the default or affordable approach, the amount spent on marketing activities is determined by the cash flow remaining after the firm's mandatory obligations and management priorities are met. This approach also defies sound business logic. The funds spent on marketing activities are an investment. As is true of the investment in any business asset, planned marketing expenditures should generate a return on investment (ROI) that justifies the funds used.

The expected rate of return on the dollars that could be invested in the marketing program should determine the amount actually spent and not how much money remains after spending priorities have been satisfied. In theory, dollars should be committed to an investment as long as the expected return is greater than the cost of the funds invested.

The objective and task method involves the application of planning principles to the budgeting process. With this method, the dollars to be allocated are determined by the task(s) that must be completed to achieve an established marketing objective. Application of this method involves (a) setting marketing goals according to what can realistically be accomplished, (b) identifying the marketing activities that must be performed to achieve the objectives, and (c) estimating the cost of performing each task. The estimated costs of each task are totaled to arrive at the total marketing budget.

6. **Establish marketing controls.** Any experienced entrepreneur, manager, or reader of a business plan knows that the planning process does not end with the finished document. Planning is not complete, nor can it be effective, until the control procedures are put in place and used on a regular basis. Control is as essential to successful marketing planning as the plan itself, and the control procedures that will be used should be clearly spelled out in the last section of the marketing plan.

Control involves the monitoring and evaluation of actual and planned results in order to keep operations on course. The performance standards used in the control process are budgeted goals and activities. Through the periodic comparison of actual and planned results, the entrepreneur ensures that plans are executed, that changing conditions have not invalidated planning assumptions, that the firm is on course to meet planned objectives or, if these are not the case, that remedial actions are taken.

Marketing controls take three basic forms: sales standards, cost standards, and profit standards. The tools used to compare actual performance against these standards are sales analysis, cost analysis, and profit analysis. Sales analysis is the breakdown and evaluation of sales data in order to determine the effectiveness of the marketing effort. The manner in which sales data are disaggregated for analysis depends on the nature of the business, the product/service, the market(s), the customer, and the information needed to accurately assess performance. The four most common methods of disaggregating sales data are shown on Table 7-6, along with examples of control variables used in the monitoring and control process.

Cost analysis is similar to sales analysis. It involves the breakdown and restructuring of marketing costs in order to evaluate the efficiency of the marketing effort. The process of restructuring costs begins with the breakdown of the marketing costs shown on the traditional accounting income statement into two cost categories: direct costs and indirect or common costs. The restructured direct costs are then assigned to the activity being analyzed. This activity may be a

TABLE 7-6

Types of Sales Breakdowns and Control Variables

General Sales Analysis	Analysis By Customer	Geographic Sales Analysis	Analysis By Product
Annual sales dollars	Customer classes	By state, city, county	Product class
Annual unit sales	Customer SIC code	By zip code or area code	Product line
Monthly sales dollars	Percentage cash versus credit purchase	By sales territory	Product
Monthly unit sales	Percentage old versus new customer	By salesperson	Product defect
Seasonal sales	Average purchase size	By product type	Product return
Sales by product life cycle	Frequency of purchase	Sales per call	Price
Comparative sales by year, month, or season		Percent of quota	Packaging
Average sale size		Promotion dollars	Promotion dollars
Average order size		Advertising dollars	Advertising dollars
Average sales per sales call			

specific sales category, a particular marketing activity, or a given marketing segment of the business. Indirect costs are allocated to a common overhead category.

Direct costs are those that can be directly traced to or associated with a given activity. They are easily identified by answering the following question: Would this cost be incurred if the activity under analysis were no longer performed? If the answer to the question is no, then the cost item is directly related to that activity. If the answer is that the cost would not disappear if the activity were discontinued, it is an indirect cost and would be assigned to a common pool of marketing overhead costs.

For example, assume XYZ Company has a multi-product product line and the sales force is paid a monthly base salary plus a bonus in the form of sales commissions. Sales commissions are structured by individual product. If management were considering dropping a poorly performing product from the product line, the sales commissions on that product would no longer be paid (they would disappear),

TABLE 7-7

Examples of Direct and Indirect Marketing Costs

Direct Cost Items	Indirect Cost Items
Sales commissions	Marketing manager's salary
Shipping costs	Marketing clerical salaries
Packaging costs	Sales salaries
Purchase discounts	Travel allowance expense
Product promotion	Vehicle expense
Product advertising	Company-wide promotion
Product liability	Company-wide advertising
	Depreciation expense on selling equipment

but the base salary expense would still be incurred. For this particular analysis, sales commissions are a direct cost item and sales salaries are an indirect cost. The first column of Table 7-7 contains examples of commonly incurred direct and indirect marketing costs.

Profit analysis is the breakdown and evaluation of sales revenue and cost charges by activity. The focus of the analysis may be the profitability of a product or geographical territory, a particular marketing activity such as advertising, or the marketing department itself. The most effective tool for this purpose is a *contribution format income statement.* An example of a contribution format statement prepared for each of the products in the XYZ Company's product line is shown in Table 7-8. As indicated there, when the contribution format is used for marketing analysis and control, direct costs are assigned to the sales revenue items to which they are related. Indirect costs are assigned to the common marketing-overhead-cost pool. Profitability is measured at two levels: the contribution margin of individual products and the contribution of the total marketing effort to overall company profits. The former item measures the direct or incremental profit produced by each product. It is the additional dollars of profit that remain after the direct cost associated with the sale of a given product are deducted. The total product contribution ($9,330) is the sum of the individual product contributions ($4,510 + $2,620 + $2,200). The total marketing contribution indicates the contribution to overall company profits that remains after the deduction of both direct and indirect marketing costs.

TABLE 7-8
The XYZ Company
By-Product Sales Breakdown and Marketing Cost Analysis
(000 omitted)

Item	Product A	Product B	Product C
Sales Revenue	$ 6,000	$ 3,500	$ 4,000
Direct Costs:			
Product promotion	100	-0-	300
Product advertising	450	500	760
Sales commissions	600	200	440
Packaging costs	65	55	100
Shipping costs	155	75	120
Purchase discounts	120	50	80
Total Direct Cost	$ 1,490	$ 880	$ 1,800
Product Contribution	$ 4,510	$ 2,620	$ 2,200

Indirect Marketing Costs

Total Product Contribution	$ 9,330
Indirect Marketing Costs:	
Marketing management salaries	400
Marketing clerical salaries	70
Sales salaries	525
Travel allowance	65
Vehicle expense	130
Company-wide promotion	235
Company-wide advertising	1,000
Selling equipment depreciation	75
Total Indirect Marketing Costs	$ 2,500
Total Marketing Profit Contribution	$ 6,830

WHY MARKETING PLANS FAIL

Marketing plans can fail for a variety of reasons. Some of the more common causes that can be avoided or controlled are identified below.

- **The plan is prepared for the wrong purpose.** When the entrepreneur is not convinced of the value of sound planning, preparation of the marketing plan will be viewed as a one-time, necessary evil. This attitude virtually ensures that marketing planning and control will not become a routine part of the management process. The result is a business whose success is dependent on good luck rather than good management.

- **The plan is poorly prepared.** When the effort put into planning is inadequate, the plan will be shallow and lack the substance and detail necessary to make it an effective guide for decision-making.
- **The plan is a one-time task.** Much like a business plan, a marketing plan should continually evolve with the firm. Some business owners at best create a marketing plan and follow it to the letter, despite factors changing in the firm or the economic business climate. At worst, they create a plan only to stick it on a shelf and never look at it again. The marketing plan should be reviewed and updated on a regular basis, to ensure that current marketing activities are continuing to meet the needs of the firm.
- **The environmental analysis is deficient.** When the firm's external and internal environment are not sufficiently analyzed or understood, the entrepreneur lacks the background necessary to prepare a marketing plan that will be viewed as realistic.
- **Goals and objectives are unrealistic.** When the entrepreneur does not have a clear understanding of the realities of the firm's market, target market, or competitive environment, established marketing goals will be seen as impractical or unattainable.
- **There is a failure to understand the limitations of planning.** While planning is a powerful tool capable of providing positive results for the firm, it is not a panacea. It is not a substitute for sound judgment developed from experience; it will not endow management with the ability to predict the future with certainty; it will not prevent mistakes from being made in the future; and plans, once developed, are not permanently and immutably fixed. Planning does, however, force the entrepreneur to understand the environment in which the firm operates and to identify the factors that lead to success or failure.
- **There is a failure to monitor results.** Diligent monitoring of actual results and periodic comparison of these results to planned expectations is critical to effective planning. The firm's environment is constantly changing. Monitoring allows the entrepreneur to identify and prepare for change.

TIPS FOR PREPARING THE MARKETING PLAN
▬ Use help in developing the marketing plan. In addition to using primary and secondary sources of information to prepare the marketing plan, the entrepreneur should take advantage of available

assistance. Agencies such as chambers of commerce, area planning and development commissions, small business development centers, the U.S. Small Business Administration, and college and university schools of business administration often provide planning information and/or assistance at little or no cost. The entrepreneur may also consider using a professional marketing consultant to assist with the marketing plan. While this alternative may be costly, the cost may be justified, if, for example, the plan is to be presented outside the firm as part of a critical financing proposal.

■ **Planning is not a one-time job.** Planning is a basic function of management, and the entrepreneur's planning effort should not end when the business plan is completed. Rather, planning should be a continuous process that includes monitoring the firm's internal and external environment, gathering information, preparing strategic and operating plans, and comparing the results of actual operations against planned expectations. Since an outside reader will expect to find evidence of the entrepreneur's understanding of the importance of sound planning, the business plan should indicate how planning will become an integral part of the entrepreneur's management process.

■ **Good plans are based on good information.** Plans are only as good as their underlying assumptions. While creativity, insight, experience, and intuition play an important part in the planning process, sound plans cannot be developed without sound information.

■ **Documentation is critical.** Plans are, by necessity, built on assumptions about the future environment in which they will be implemented and conducted. In order for plans to be accepted as realistic and to serve as effective guides for operating the business, these assumptions must be clearly stated and periodically reviewed. If underlying assumptions are not made clear or they are unrealistic, plans will be considered nothing more than pipe dreams.

■ **Reach the target market one step at a time.** Marketing experts suggest that promotion and advertising should be designed to move customers toward the purchase in a series of steps. This means the entrepreneur should make certain the marketing plan clearly indicates the steps to be followed in the adopted promoting and advertising scheme. For example, first identify what image will be projected. Next indicate how targeted customers will be made aware of the firm and its product or service. Third, discuss how the firm will attempt to convince targeted customers that the firm's product or service can meet their needs. Fourth, make clear how targeted customers will be motivated to buy the firm's product or service. And last, have a process in place that not only retains current customers but capitalizes on their loyalty through referrals and cross-selling.

■ **Use multiple "touches."** Although there are specific steps to follow, from creating brand awareness to closing a sale, professional marketers agree that reaching their target market on multiple levels tends to be the most effective. For example, instead of just placing one advertisement in one publication for six months, hit your target market with a direct mail piece, followed up with a phone call, as well as participating in a trade show geared toward your target market. Experts say a consumer can see a brand more than ten times before it registers; therefore, you want to ensure that your potential customer group is exposed to your brand as much as possible, and in as many venues as possible.

■ **Avoid advertising myths.** There are three popular advertising misconceptions to which new entrepreneurs often fall prey. The first suggests that only creative, clever advertising can be effective. In reality, advertising is most effective when it sends the appropriate message, when the message is properly directed, and when it is done consistently rather than haphazardly. The second myth suggests that the firm can rely on word of mouth rather than media advertising to send the message. While the praises sung by satisfied customers are important, this vehicle is not a substitute for effective advertising. Available research indicates that ten satisfied customers tell an average of only about eight other people about the positive experience. Third, it is often suggested that the entrepreneur can save money by doing his or her own advertising. Again, research indicates that unless the entrepreneur is an experienced marketer, do-it-yourself advertising is usually ineffective and proves to be a costly mistake.

■ **More money does not necessarily mean better.** Depending on the type of business and the characteristics of the target market, expensive advertising may not only be unnecessary, but even non-effective. By having conducted preliminary research beforehand and knowing your target market, you should be able to determine what the best marketing mix will be, whether it is advertising, direct mail, telemarketing, networking, or a combination of activities.

■ **Focus on the customer.** There is a natural tendency for new entrepreneurs to feel that the business and its product or service are the most important elements in the profit equation. In reality, there is nothing more important to the success of the business than its customers. Without customers there is no business. The entrepreneur's understanding of this basic fact should be clearly conveyed in the marketing plan and, even more important, should be the foundation of the entrepreneur's business philosophy.

■ **Be specific.** The more specific you can be with your marketing activities, timing, and goals, the more you will be able to track progress and follow the strategy. Instead of simply indicating where and how you will market your product or service, be specific with dates, timing, costs, and details of the various resources to be used. For example, if you plan to advertise in a trade publication, indicate the size of the ad, the cost, where it will be placed in the magazine, for how long, the circulation of the magazine, and the demographics of the readership.

SAMPLE MARKETING PLAN*

Zupermail, Inc. offers on-line marketers the ability to reach highly targeted consumers who have requested, or given permission to receive, information via direct e-mails. Advertisers *(Zupermail "Partners")* are able to send personalized messages to Zupermail members who have provided demographic and psychographic information to the company. In return for "opting in" to the program, Zupermail members receive incentive Zuperpoints, redeemable for merchandise and/or gift certificates.

Zupermail, Inc.'s mission is to become a leading e-mail permission-based marketing concern on the Internet by facilitating transactions between specific and targeted customer groups, building quality databases and reducing customer acquisition and retention costs.

SALES AND MARKETING
Sales Objective

Zupermail Inc., will strive to achieve over $3.5 million in revenue in year one of operations. Revenue will be generated from both domestic (USA) operations and from international licenses and distribution. The company plans to increase revenues by over 233% during year three of operations, over 190% in year four, and 166% in year five.

The Internet Commerce Marketplace

▬ The number of businesses with one or more owners but no paid employees grew nationwide from 17.0 million in 2001 to more than 17.6 million in 2002, a growth rate of 3.9%. Nationally, these small businesses make up more than 70% of all businesses.[1]

▬ Small and mid-sized businesses point to the Internet as a primary driver of growth and 83% strongly agree that the Internet helps them run their companies.

---

* Sample provided by Jamie Hait, Partner, NextLevelPlan.com, a strategic business planning firm that specializes in creating comprehensive business plans for small to mid-sized ventures.

[1] U.S. Census

■ Close to one quarter (22%) of small and mid-sized businesses make use of the Web as a marketing tool using e-mail marketing (62%); search engine optimization (56%); banner advertising (36%); and pay-per-click advertising (25%).[2]

■ Among small and mid-sized business' net marketers, 74% plan to increase their investments in on-line marketing over the next six months and their peers seem to recognize the benefits they are receiving as an additional 43% percent intend to begin on-line marketing within the next six months.

Online Users

■ By end 2004, online e-commerce reached $6.8 trillion for both B-to-B and B-to-C transactions.[3]

■ By end 2007, 215 million Americans were online, representing about 17% of all users in the world.[4]

■ 29 million U.S. households are online, up from 21 million in 1998.

■ By 2005, the average consumer received about 308 e-mail messages per week.[5]

■ International growth: English is the mother tongue of 35.8% of all web sites.[6]

■ Europe represents 27.2% (343 million users) of worldwide users as of 2007. Asia: 461 million users; South America: 122 million users.[7]

SALES AND REVENUE GENERATION

As all industries begin to recognize the value of deeper, more sophisticated knowledge of their potential customer base, the value of Zupermail lists will increase. Zupermail member lists will develop a "personality" that is appealing to a wide range of advertisers. Zupermail will assist its "partners" in identifying the tastes and purchasing behaviors of specific target groups. The deep level of information gathered from Zupermail opt-in members will enable companies to successfully market their services and products to specific career groups, affinity groups, and other consumers.

---

[2] Frank N. Magid Associates
[3] Forrester Research
[4] Internet World Stats
[5] Double Click
[6] Global Reach
[7] Internet World Stats

SALES AND MARKETING STRATEGY
List Generation Strategy

As Zupermail is not the first mover in the permission e-mail marketing industry, the company has taken an approach that is different from its competitors: Zupermail plans to cultivate its own lists of highly targeted segments of the United States and international markets. Zupermail will not commission list brokers or a network to build its database of member names. Instead, Zupermail, Inc, will utilize targeted media to obtain members and their deep demographic, psychographic, and behavioral data that will be most valuable to the company's partners. The cultivation of quality traffic and data gathering will appeal to partners wishing to target highly defined groups within the membership database.

Revenue Generation Strategy

Management has determined that the strategy of *quality of data* rather than merely the quantity of names will build its reputation as a trusted brand name in permission-based e-mail marketing and will create significant demand for the product, generating significant return for investors. The ability to communicate to highly targeted audiences and the receipt of relevant advertisements will appeal to both the partners and to the members. This, in turn, will prove a higher conversion rate of members into purchasers of advertised products.

This strategy and subsequent success of the company may prove to bring the company to an initial public offering, which may change the direction of the company during or after the first year of operations.

TARGET MARKETS

Members. Zupermail, Inc. is currently building lists of members by attracting targeted segments of the U.S. population. The first audience that the company will target is defined as "affluent." With more than 212 million Americans on-line in 2007, it is widely accepted that these households are in the upper income brackets. The Mendelsohn Affluent Survey of 2007 identified more than 29 million households as "affluent," and that affluent household expenditures on personal computers ranks second only to home furnishings. More than 90% of these households own a personal computer, with 97% of these having Internet access. Furthermore, while the percentage of affluent households in the United States remains relatively steady, eMarketer projects that the number of affluent Internet users will grow from 43.7 million in 2006 to 57.1 million in 2011.[8]

The company has determined that the 26.1 million affluent households with Internet access from their personal computers to be the most responsive and therefore the most profitable segment to target utilizing Zupermail's "narrow and deep" strategy of permission e-mail marketing. The affluent population will most value money saving offers in specific areas of interest, including travel, gourmet foods, financial services, and computer and wireless devices, for example, and will be responsive to Zupermail's point redemption plan.

The company plans to expand its membership base to other specifically targeted groups, leveraging its brand equity to attract new members and partners over time.

The company has determined that acquiring the fully opt-in members will require approximately $5 per name. Budgets have been defined to include new member acquisition at achievable growth rates of: .5 million members by year one, one million members by end year two, and 2.5 million members by end year three.

Methods used to attract new members to the Zupermail website and subsequently opt in to the lists will include the following, with approximate percentages of total marketing costs dedicated to each medium:

Marketing Method	Budgetary expenditures
Print Media	25%
Public Relations	10%
Direct Marketing	15%
Viral marketing*	
Affiliate Marketing**	25%
Other Net marketing	
Event Partnerships	5%
Electronic	10%
Incentive Marketing	10%

Estimated 8% of all names in Zupermail database in Alpha testing
**Affiliate marketing proved to be successful for Zupermail in Alpha testing, at a cost of $1 "commission" per name*

---

[8] "Household Expenditure Variations within Affluent Income Segments," Mendelsohn Media Research, 2007.

Sample Marketing Budget

The Pegasus Electronics Company is a hypothetical medium-sized manufacturer of sophisticated electronic components. Until recently, approximately 80% of total company sales were to defense industry firms and only 20% were made to the private sector. Given the government's recent large cutbacks in defense spending, Pegasus's management has changed the firm's basic strategy. Its goal is to reverse the proportions of defense and private sector sales over the next three years.

The marketing budget consists of annual pro forma, contribution format income statements for each year of the planning horizon. The annual pro forma statement for the first year is partitioned into 12 monthly statements. This breakdown allows more frequent and detailed monitoring of key budgeted amounts.

To ensure that planning and budgeting at Pegasus is done on a continuous basis, a rolling-budget procedure is used. As each month or year of actual operations is completed, the statement for that period is dropped from the planning horizon and a new monthly or annual projection is added. By so doing, management always has current 12-month and 3-year annual budgets to guide and control operations.

The annual pro forma statement for the first year of the planning horizon is shown below on Table 7-9. Although the 12-month statement for the first year and the annual statements for the remaining two years of the planning horizon are not shown, they are prepared using the identical format.

TABLE 7-9
Pegasus Electronics
The Paragon System Annual Budget[1] for Pro Forma 20X1

	Budgeted	% Of Sales	Actual	Variance
Unit Sales[2]	24,932			
Price	$ 369			
Sales Revenue[3]	$9,200,000	100.0%		
Direct Costs:				
Production[4]	$5,360,610	58.3%		
Packaging Costs	99,729	1.1		
Shipping Costs	124,661	1.4		
Product Promotion	1,000,000	10.9		
Product Advertising	500,000	5.4		
Sales Commissions	230,000	2.5		
Total Direct Costs	$7,315,000	79.5%		
Gross Contribution Margin	$1,885,000	20.5%		

TABLE 7-9 *(continued)*

Indirect Marketing Costs:		
Marketing Mgmt Salaries	$ 400,000	4.3%
Sales Salaries	800,000	8.7
Clerical Salaries	35,000	0.4
Travel Expense	150,000	1.6
Company-wide Promotion	400,000	4.3
Company-wide Advertising	100,000	1.1
Total Indirect Costs	$1,885,000	20.5%
Net Contribution Margin	$ –0–	0.0%

Notes:

1. The Budget has been prepared under the primary assumptions that no major recession will occur over the three-year planning horizon and the economy's expansion phase of the current business cycle will continue over the planning horizon.

2. Unit sales forecasts are based on the assumption that the strong competitive advantages of the Paragon system will allow 10% of target market sales to be captured the first year and up to 65% over the next two years.

3. Since current sales by all manufacturers to the compact stereo market total about $80,000,000 and these sales are expected to grow at a rate of 15% per year, the estimate of a 10% market share generates first-year revenues of approximately $9,200,000 ($80,000,000 × 1.15 × 10%).

4. While total production costs of the Paragon system are not under the direct control of the marketing department and technically are not a marketing budget item, the figure has been included here in order to accurately portray contribution margin goals.

CHAPTER PERSPECTIVE

Planning is a process consisting of interrelated steps that begin with the firm's mission statement and a forecast of its external and internal environment and end with control and feedback. The marketing plan describes how the firm's target customer group will be motivated to purchase its product/service. It details the marketing goals to be achieved, the marketing-mix strategy that will position the firm's product/service in its market, and the marketing and selling programs required to achieve established marketing goals. The heart of the firm's marketing strategy is its marketing mix, or the Four P's of marketing, directly under management's control. They are product/service, price, place, and promotion.

The Operating Plan

WHAT IS AN OPERATING PLAN?

The term *operations* is usually associated with a production process or a manufacturing firm. While production is one form of operations, it is not the only one. Operations is an essential function of every business, whether the firm produces a product or service, or merchandises (retails or wholesales) consumer or industrial goods. As the noted management expert Peter Drucker has suggested, operations is simply the application of logic to work.

Operations can be defined as the process or system through which resource inputs such as raw materials, creative talent, labor, selling skills, or a convenient location are converted to useful outputs. Outputs may take the form of products, services, information, or the consumer satisfaction that results from effective merchandising. In short, the operating function determines how the firm creates value for its customers and the operating plan describes the planned procedures and flow of activities required to do so, namely, what steps the firm will go through to achieve its goals and fulfill its mission.

After studying the material in this chapter, you will:
- Understand the role of the operating plan.
- Know what information is needed to prepare the operating plan.
- Know the steps to preparing the operating plan.
- Understand the basic differences between operations for a manufacturing, service, and merchandising business.

INFORMATION NEEDED TO PREPARE AN OPERATING PLAN

As is true of each component of the business plan, the operating plan should be written as a miniature feasibility study. It is the vehicle that provides the intended reader with an understanding of the process that creates value and how this process contributes to the success of the firm. To accomplish these objectives, the operating plan should provide information for the following key questions:

■ **What value does the firm create?** This means identifying the firm's primary output: the product that is produced, the service that is performed, or the goods that are merchandised.

■ **How is value created?** This question is answered by determining the essential functions that make up the firm's normal operating activities.

■ **What resources are used in creating value?** This means identifying the primary physical, human, informational, and financial assets that are required to conduct normal operations.

■ **Where is value created?** This means identifying both the physical location(s) of the business and the boundaries of its market(s).

■ **How does operations contribute to the firm's success?** In other words, what unique advantage or benefit does the operating function provide? This contribution may take a variety of forms such as lower production costs, a good location, a new product or service, or more efficient distribution.

■ **What factors influence operations?** This means identifying the variables that determine the success or failure of the firm's operations.

WHEN TO INCLUDE AN OPERATING PLAN WITH THE BUSINESS PLAN

In general, an operating plan is included as a separate component of a business plan when one or more of the following conditions exist.

■ When operations, or an important part of operations, is unique, highly technical, or complicated.

■ When operations is critical to the firm's success.

■ When a major change in operations is intended.

■ When the reader is unfamiliar with the operations of the business and needs details in order to make an educated funding decision.

If none of these conditions is present, the extent to which operating procedures are discussed is a matter of judgment. For example, if the firm's method of operations is uncomplicated or self-evident, reference to operations may be omitted entirely. Or, if some mention of operations is warranted, a summarization could be included in the business description section of the business plan.

STEPS TO PREPARING AN OPERATING PLAN

The eight steps identified and discussed here offer a logical sequence for gathering information and preparing an operating plan. However, since operations differ among different types of businesses, each step may not be included in every operating plan. Some steps may be omitted because they are inappropriate, some may be combined under one title for clarity or convenience, or some may be renamed to make them more descriptive of the situation. For example, if the operating plan is prepared for a traditional retailing business, it is unlikely that such topics as distribution and quality control will be discussed. On the other hand, these sections are usually critical to the description of operations in a manufacturing firm.

As an aid to gathering information and preparing the operating plan, guideline questions are included, where appropriate, with a given step. Also, a sample operating plan appears at the end of this chapter as Figure 8-1.

1. **Consider an operating plan summary.** This optional section *may* be used when the operating plan is prepared for outside presentation. The summary is a convenience for the reader and should be no longer than what is needed for him or her to gain an understanding of the plan's major thrust. This can usually be accomplished in a paragraph that summarizes the essential functions that make up the firm's operations. As a matter of course, prepare the summary after the other sections of the operations plan have been thoroughly considered and completed. This will help you determine what to focus on in the summary.

2. **Prepare a situational review.** Normally, this section serves either of two purposes. It may be used to describe a major change that has occurred or is intended to occur in the operations of an existing firm. Or, in the case of a new venture, the review may be used to describe how operating procedures were developed and the current stage of that development, and what the final operations plan will look like, as well as a basic timeline for when development is to be completed.

3. **Identify the firm's location.** Location is a factor that can mean the difference between success and failure of a business. This is especially true for the new venture and for firms that are highly dependent on proximity to either its resource needs or its target market.

Note that as e-commerce has become more prevalent, the concept of "location" is no longer restricted to geography. An Internet retailer, for example, has the opportunity to define its market far beyond the limited scope that may have been possible in the past.

The underlying theme for this section of the operating plan should be providing answers to the implicit questions of *where* and *why*. *Where* refers to the site of operations and *why* refers to the reason(s) this site was selected. In the case of the e-commerce (or partly e-commerce) business, the entrepreneur should include a discussion of why the Internet is the most (or one of the most) appropriate "locations" for the business. As indicated in both the following discussion and the guideline questions for this section, these reasons may include such considerations as competitive advantage, favorable traffic patterns, accessibility to shipping and distribution facilities, or a plentiful labor supply.

The six location factors discussed below are, to varying degrees, a consideration for all businesses. Table 8-1 lists the major factors that should be considered in selecting a city, an area within a city, and a site within an area. Note that service businesses are combined with merchandising and production firms on Table 8-1 because the location needs of these businesses often overlap both categories.

TABLE 8-1
Major Location Factors

A City	Factors Affecting The Selection Of: An Area In A City	A Specific Site
Retail & Service:		
Size of Trade Area	Area Potential	Cost of Site
Potential of Area	Access Routes	Auto Traffic Volume
Population Trends	Zoning Regulations	Pedestrian Volume
Purchasing Power	Appearance	Appearance
Competition	Competition	Competition
Related Shopping	Amenities	Related Shopping
	Related Shopping	Customer Convenience
		Parking
Production & Service:		
Cost	Cost	Cost
Market Location	Zoning	Zoning
Vendor Location	Transportation	Utilities
Labor Supply	Compatible	Transportation
Transportation	Businesses	Employee Convenience
Utilities	Competition	Waste Disposal
Taxes		
Government Regulations		
Government Incentives		
Community Amenities		
Competition		

- **Location of customers:** To virtually all merchandising firms and many consumer service firms, a location that is accessible to the target customer group is critical to success. Such firms depend heavily on customers who are drawn into the place of business, and their location is influenced by such considerations as population clusters, traffic or pedestrian movement patterns, and customer needs. Service firms that are able to take the service to customer locations have somewhat more flexibility than retailers, but even in these cases population clusters are important to having cost-effective operations.

Producers are typically more concerned with proximity or access to suppliers than customers. Yet, customer location is often critical to manufacturers that sell to firms using a just-in-time inventory system or whose products are perishable or expensive to ship. In these cases, a convenient location is an important consideration in measuring the cost of operations.

E-commerce businesses also must consider this point. Why is the firm's target market most likely to access the firm's products or services on-line? For example, an e-commerce firm selling posters to college students could easily provide evidence that the target market (college students) is a high-volume user of the Internet. A firm selling durable medical equipment directly to a senior population may not be able to make that same claim.

- **Location of suppliers:** For many businesses the cost, time, or certainty of supplying its inventory needs mandates a location close to its suppliers. For example, producers of foodstuffs, such as canneries, locate near the source of the perishables on which they rely. Likewise, manufacturers that use just-in-time production systems are concerned with proximity to major suppliers.

- **Location of competitors:** Proximity to competitors is not a negative factor in all cases. In some synergistic situations, having customers drawn to one business will often create awareness of, and traffic to, surrounding businesses. For example, a small independent used book store located near a major national book store chain retailer can benefit from customer traffic already visiting the major chain if the store can differentiate itself enough with either its offerings and/or price to entice customers.

  Alternatively, being aware of the location of competitors that are nonsynergistic is just as important, and differentiating from closely placed competition is crucial in this situation.

- **Location of labor supply:** The availability of human resources having appropriate, cost-effective skills is a consideration for most businesses. For example, producers of high-tech products that rely on a well-educated labor force tend to concentrate near major educational centers. On the other hand, firms that use predominately unskilled labor often seek areas characterized by low standards of living and a minimum threat of unionization.

- **Access to transportation:** The cost and availability of different modes of transportation influence the location of many businesses. Manufacturing firms often rely heavily on controlling the cost and time involved in shipping the raw materials used. For example, manufacturers using low-unit-cost, bulky raw materials such as coal or basic steel locate near low-cost transportation. Or the producers of some perishable goods such as greenhouses typically locate near fast or specialized modes of transportation.

  The availability of appropriate transportation is also a location requirement for many merchandising and service firms. Retailers and service firms whose success depends on heavy automobile traffic such as manufacturers' outlet stores, restaurants, and motels, locate near major highway systems. Firms dependent on local, high-flow automobile or pedestrian traffic would choose locations having negotiable city streets and safe, pleasant access walks.

- **Services, taxes, and regulations:** A firm's location is often heavily influenced by governmental considerations such as the rates and types of taxes levied or the tax incentives granted. Other considerations such as zoning requirements; building codes; and restrictions on pollution, waste disposal, and industrial growth can make a location more or less desirable. In many cases, state or local governments, governmental agencies, or industrial authorities may provide a number of valuable services as an inducement to locating in a given area. For example, municipalities may raise the capital necessary for the construction of production facilities, assist firms in raising low-cost capital, or provide long term, rent-free leases on land.

- **Community features:** An important location requirement for many businesses is the quality of life the community can provide for the firm and its workers. Living conditions and community amenities such as educational facilities, cultural and recreational activities, and climate may make the difference when deciding between locations.

The following guideline questions should help the entrepreneur identify the type of information needed to develop an effective plan for locating the firm.

- Where is the business located?
- How and why does this site contribute to the success of the business?
- What competitive advantage(s) does this site offer?

- Are rental costs, lease costs, or purchase prices for land and buildings reasonable for this location?
- Do local authorities offer benefits such as tax breaks or financial assistance for locating businesses?
- Does this area provide an adequate supply of trained or trainable labor?
- Does this area have adequate educational facilities for the firm's labor force and their dependents?
- Is the location convenient to cost-effective transportation?
- Is there an adequate supply of cost-effective energy available to this location?
- Are city, county, and state taxes reasonable for this location?
- How much time and cost are involved in delivering to customers from this location?
- Does this location minimize the risk of product perishability?
- Is the location suitable to major customers using just-in-time inventory systems?
- Is the location conveniently accessible for the firm's suppliers?
- Is the location suitable given the firm's inventory needs?
- Is the location convenient to the firm's target customer group?
- Is there sufficient customer demand for the product or service in this area to support the business?
- Is there sufficient customer purchasing power in this area to support the business?
- Is the location suited to customer needs such as parking, transportation, and pleasant, safe surroundings?
- Is the volume of automobile and/or pedestrian traffic adequate at this location?
- Is the business clearly visible to automobile and pedestrian traffic at this location?
- Are adequate, cost-effective facilities available in the area of highest population cluster and people flow?

4. **Exploring operating procedures.** Once the issue of location has been decided, the policies and procedures that determine how value is created and how day-to-day operating procedures are conducted must be developed. If the operating plan is prepared for internal use, policies and procedures must be described in sufficient detail to guide employee and supervisory work efforts. If the plan is prepared for outside presentation, it is important that the operating process is made clear for the reader. In general, the more technical, the more complicated, or the more unique the firm's operations, the more descriptive this section of the plan must be. If a financier cannot understand the firm's operations, financing will not be forthcoming.

It is also important that this section of the operating plan include a discussion of how the entrepreneur will balance the critical trade-off between creating value and the cost of doing so. The ability to effectively maximize difficult cost/benefit trade-offs such as those associated with operations is a management quality for which the intended reader will be searching.

The questions on the next few pages should serve as guidelines for identifying the type of information that is needed to prepare the operating plan. Since operations differ for different types of businesses, the guideline questions are divided into manufacturing, service, and merchandising (retail, wholesale, or distribution) categories.

The following guideline questions should help the entrepreneur identify the type of information needed to develop an operations plan for a manufacturing firm.

- What product(s) does the firm produce?
- What is the planned level of product output per unit of time (hour, day, week, etc.)?
- What major pieces of machinery and equipment are needed to produce the anticipated level of output?
- What is the maximum output per unit of time the facilities can accommodate?
- What are the major steps or stages in the firm's production process?
- How does work flow from the beginning to the end of the production process?
- Why is this work flow efficient and cost-effective?
- What transformations take place at each stage in the production process?
- Which raw materials are required to produce the product?
- What is the per-unit cost of raw materials?
- How stable are raw material prices?
- What is the minimum number of employees required for the production process and in which capacities?
- Which labor skills are required to produce the product?
- What wage levels will these labor skills command?
- What is the materials and labor cost per unit of output?
- What is the expected level of productivity (output per man-hour) of the manufacturing process?
- What unique or competitive advantage (lower cost, better quality, etc.) does the firm's production process provide?
- What is the key to success for the production process?
- How does the production process contribute to the overall success of the business?

- What new technologies or unique production techniques are employed, and why do they provide an advantage for the firm?
- Are the subcomponents used in the firm's product manufactured in-house, or are they sourced outside the firm?
- If the subcomponents are sourced outside the firm, what lead times are required in order to have them in inventory when needed?
- How is production volume planned and scheduled?
- What cost savings or other production advantages does this scheduling procedure provide?
- Is the production process more dependent on labor (labor-intensive) or on machinery and equipment (capital-intensive)?
- What are the direct labor, direct materials, and overhead costs of producing the firm's product(s)?
- What percentage of the firm's total production costs represents variable costs (those costs that change as production and sales levels change), and what percentage represents fixed costs (those costs that remain unchanged over longer time periods or over a reasonable range of production volume)?
- What is the contribution margin (selling price minus variable production cost) of the firm's product(s) or product lines?
- What is the firm's breakeven volume of production or sales?
- What is the gross profit margin (selling price minus cost of goods sold) of the firm's product(s) or product lines?
- What measures are used to monitor and control production costs?
- What measures are planned to ensure quality control?

The following guideline questions should help the entrepreneur identify the type of information needed to develop an operations plan for a service firm.

- What service does the firm provide?
- How is the service performed?
- What steps are involved at each stage of providing the service?
- What unique or competitive advantage does the service provide?
- What is the key to success for the service process?
- What in-house manufacturing is associated with rendering the service?
- Which components used in providing the service are subcontracted?
- What portion of the total cost of providing the service does in-house manufacturing or subcontracting represent?

- How many service representatives are required to provide the service?
- What guarantees, warranties, or maintenance agreements, if any, accompany the service provided?
- What is the cost per man-hour or per employee to provide the service?
- What percentages of the total cost of providing the service do variable and fixed costs represent?
- What is the contribution margin of the service provided?
- What is the breakeven level of service revenue for the firm?
- What measures are used to monitor and control the cost of performing the service?

The following guideline questions should help the entrepreneur identify the type of information needed to develop an operations plan for a merchandising firm.

- To what merchandising category (specialty store, department store, off-price retailer, discount store, direct seller, wholesaler, etc.) does the business belong?
- What product or product line is sold?
- How does this product or product line provide a unique or competitive advantage?
- What are the major activities and procedures that make up the firm's merchandising process?
- What aspect, if any, of the merchandising process is unique?
- What is the key to success for the merchandising operation?
- How is product selection and purchasing conducted?
- How many staff members are required to handle sales, inventory control, purchasing, and management, and what are the costs associated with employee salaries?
- What is the firm's sales and pricing strategy (low profit margin/ high volume, quality, service, etc.), and why is it successful?
- What are the firm's sales figures per square foot of selling area, per labor dollar, and per sales employee?
- What percentages of the firm's total cost do variable and fixed costs represent?
- What is the contribution margin of major products or product lines?
- What is the firm's breakeven sales volume?
- What is the gross profit margin for the firm?
- What measures are used to monitor and control operating costs?

5. **Describing operating facilities and layout.** A successful operation requires sufficient space and an efficient combination of

physical and human resources. Physical resources include such assets as buildings, machinery, equipment, fixtures, and vehicles. Human resources are the labor and administrative skills needed to create value and manage the business. Whether operating activities take place in a store, office, or plant, or on-line there must be sufficient, correctly designed space to accommodate the flow of work and the movement of workers, materials, or customers. The primary objective in deciding the size of the work area needed to accommodate operations is the planned volume of output, the efficient placement of physical assets, and movement of people.

There are a number of ways to plan the layout of operations. Most, however, use some form of scaled model. For example, a diagram of the floor and wall space can be prepared and then templates or scaled models can be used to represent the amount of space that each requires. The templates or models can then be correctly located to determine whether a smooth flow of activity results. Computerized versions of this approach are readily available in the form of computer assisted drawing or design (CAD) programs.

There are three basic types of operating layouts: product, process, and some combination of the two. With a *product layout,* the arrangement of physical and human resources follows the sequence of operations to be performed. Products, people or work-flow move forward from one stage of operations to the next with little or no backtracking. One well-known production process using the product layout is an automobile assembly line. The food line and customer flow in a typical cafeteria are also arranged as product layouts. In general, the advantages of the product layout include faster movement, specialization of workers and machines, lower space requirements, and lower inventory requirements.

The *process layout* is based on the principle of grouping related functions. For instance, machines performing the same type of work, workers with similar skills or performing similar tasks, or merchandise serving the same function are grouped together. Common examples of process layouts include secretarial pools in offices, merchandise arrangements in department stores, or the grouping of special-purpose machinery and equipment in a machine shop. The primary advantages of the process layout are more efficient use of machines, labor, and time; the flexibility to handle variety and change; and the potential for higher productivity or lower cost through grouping similar functions.

Few layouts are all product or all process. Well-designed layouts attempt to capture the benefits of each. For example, the process layout typically reduces idle or down time compared to the product layout but often results in higher inventory cost. Combining the features of each may allow a balance that maximizes the benefits of both.

The following guideline questions should help identify the information needed to develop a plan for a firm's operating facilities and layout.

- What type of facility is required to produce the planned volume of output or to maximize sales?
- Are the facilities leased or owned? If leased, identify the lessor and describe the significant terms of the lease. If owned, identify outstanding liens against the asset, the lien holder, and the amount of the outstanding balance(s).
- How much space is required to effectively conduct operations?
- Has adequate space been allowed for people or product movement under normal and extreme conditions?
- What physical assets (building, machinery and equipment, vehicles, etc.) are required to conduct operations?
- How much space is required for the placement of physical assets?
- What is the most effective layout of physical assets, people, and work-flow?
- What aspects of the required facility or layout are unique or provide a competitive advantage?
- Why are facilities and layout cost-effective?
- How do facilities and layout contribute to the overall success of the business?
- What percentage of the firm's total assets do fixed (plant) assets represent?
- Are equipment, vehicles, and machinery leased or owned? If leased, identify the lessor and describe the significant terms of the lease. If owned, identify any outstanding liens against the assets, the lien holder, and the outstanding balance(s).
- What are the ages, expected useful lives, and operating condition of major fixed assets?
- Are the building and equipment adequately covered by insurance?
- How will the facility accommodate future growth? Is there room for expansion?
- Do the facilities, layout, and work-flow adequately meet safety and environmental standards and regulations?
- Do the facilities, layout, and work-flow meet reasonable standards for cleanliness and aesthetics?
- What procedures have been established to monitor and control efficiency of work-flow?

6. **Describe purchasing procedures.** To produce and/or sell a product or service, the typical business firm requires some form of incoming materials or finished goods. The process used to acquire these items is referred to as the *purchasing function.* In some businesses, purchasing may involve nothing more complicated than placing orders with sales representatives. In other firms, purchasing is complicated by the nature, assortment, volume, and price of the goods purchased. For example, some firms use basic raw materials and others use finished components; some use standardized products, while some use specially designed items; some materials must be stored, but others are not.

The following questions should help identify the type of information needed to develop a plan for a firm's purchasing procedures.

- Which purchases are critical to the firm's operation and why?
- What event indicates a purchase should be made, and which person makes this determination?
- How many staff members are required to fulfill the firm's purchasing needs, and what are their functions?
- How are purchase quantities determined?
- Are key items available from a limited number of suppliers or are they widely available?
- How long are the lead times of purchases, particularly specialty items, and what process will the firm utilize to ensure adequate inventory?
- What vendors are used by the firm, and what criteria influence this choice?
- How reliable are these suppliers in terms of product availability, meeting lead times, service, and quality control?
- What alternative sources of supply are available?
- If only a limited number of suppliers exist, what contingency plans have been made to avoid a disruption of operations?
- What procedures are in place to check incoming shipments for accuracy, quality, etc.
- What percentage of the firm's total operating cost does the purchasing function represent?
- What measures are employed to monitor and control purchasing costs?
- What record-keeping system is used to track purchase orders from the time an order is placed to the time the goods are received and stocked?
- What aspect, if any, of the purchasing function is unique or provides a competitive advantage?
- Does the firm purchase through an outside buying group?

- What unique or competitive advantage does purchasing through the outside buying group provide?
- What methods are used to ensure that suppliers are paid promptly and cash discounts are taken when available?

7. **Explain inventory management procedures.** Inventory requirements vary by type of firm and by how operations are conducted. The typical manufacturing firm has three levels of inventory: unprocessed raw materials inventory; partially processed work-in-process inventory; and finished goods inventory. Merchandising firms, such as retailers and wholesalers, carry only finished goods inventory. Service firms fall somewhere in between the two. Some service firms use raw materials or finished goods in rendering their service, while others have no inventory.

For those firms using inventory, purchases are typically made in advance of the time they are used in the operating process. This creates inventory levels which, for many firms, represent a sizable investment and a major cost item. For these reasons, it is important that inventory is carefully managed and controlled.

Sound inventory management is a prerequisite for maintaining satisfactory profit margins, minimizing invested dollars, minimizing operating costs, and avoiding cash-flow crises. Effective inventory management is also necessary to balance the important trade-off between the cost of carrying too much inventory and the cost of carrying too little. Too much means cash, credit, or borrowed funds are needlessly tied up in excessive inventory, while too little means stock-outs that result in lost sales or disruptions to production schedules.

The four major requirements for effective inventory management are:

- Effective sales forecasting, based on communication with sales staff and management and information derived from historical sales data and projections.
- Sound policies controlling which inventory items are carried, what inventory levels are maintained, the point at which inventory is ordered, the amount that is ordered, and the safety stock that is carried.
- An information system that provides reliable and timely inventory information from the point of purchase through the point of transformation and/or sale.
- Careful monitoring of the information produced by the inventory management system.

When inventory represents a sizable investment of funds, it is essential that the operating plan clearly detail the procedures used to manage this valuable asset. The intended reader of the business plan will search for this information because it signals the entrepreneur's understanding of the importance of inventory control and makes a statement about his or her managerial ability.

The following questions should help identify the type of information needed to develop inventory management procedures.

- What techniques are used to forecast sales and project inventory needs?
- How are inventory projections related to the sales forecast?
- What inventory items are critical to the operation of the business?
- What is the average daily usage or sales rate of key inventory items?
- What is the minimum level of inventory needed to conduct operations efficiently and to avoid disrupting production or losing sales?
- What measures have been established to identify when the minimum level has been reached and when the necessary purchase order should be placed?
- What controls have been established to ensure that a purchase order is placed when the minimum stock level is reached?
- What techniques are used to control the costs of ordering and carrying inventory?
- How is information on inventory status (purchase dates, balances on hand, inventory age, usage or turnover rates, etc.) generated and used in the inventory control process?
- What automated techniques are used in inventory control? For example, is the process computerized, is a just-in-time inventory system used, is a point-of-sale device such as an optical scanner or an automated cash register used as part of the inventory control system?
- What are the inventory costs and how are they monitored?
- How often is inventory control information reviewed by the person(s) responsible for inventory management?
- When, how often, and by whom are gross profit margins (sales minus cost of sales) or contribution margins (sales minus variable cost) reviewed?
- What methods are used to prevent inventory theft by employees?
- Why is the firm's inventory management and control system effective?
- What unique or competitive advantage does this inventory management system provide?

8. **Establish quality control and customer service procedures.** By necessity, the first goal of operations is the effective and efficient creation of value. Planning an effective operating process does not, however, end here. An important part of operations is maintaining an acceptable level of product quality and customer service. These ingredients are often as important to the success of the business as having the product or service available. When consumers can choose from a large number of substitutes, or when the firm operates in highly competitive markets, meeting the quality and service expectations of customers may be the firm's only key to success.

As is true of operations, quality control is often thought of only in the context of manufacturing. Again, this perspective is too narrow. In general, *quality* refers to conformity with perceived standards. *Quality control* can be defined as the process of measuring and comparing the firm's product or service against standards set by management and the customer.

Quality control was once thought of as a means of correcting problems after they had been discovered. Goods were checked for defects only after production, or customer complaints were not investigated until a large number were received. Productivity, quality control, and customer satisfaction were considered separate and mutually exclusive goals. This thinking has changed, with much of the credit for this change attributed to Dr. W. Edwards Deming.

Dr. Deming pioneered the idea that quality, productivity, and customer satisfaction are closely linked. In his view, quality cannot be "inspected into" a product after the fact. To be effective, quality control must be considered a *preventive* process. For example, in a manufacturing firm, the quality of a product begins with the goals set by management, the product's design, the design of the operations that produce it, and the attitude about quality of the operating personnel involved. In a merchandising or service firm, the quality of output begins with an organizational commitment to customer satisfaction and the recognition that it is the customer that must ultimately set the standards that define quality. The entrepreneur must take the steps necessary to identify customer expectations and to select and train personnel to be concerned with meeting these expectations.

As is true of other facets of the firm's operations, maintaining quality and customer satisfaction involves a cost/benefit trade-off. The costs associated with controlling quality or achieving customer satisfaction must be weighed against the benefits derived from meeting customer expectations. Again, the intended reader will search for evidence of this understanding.

The following guideline questions should help identify the type of information needed to develop the firm's quality control and customer service procedures.

- What policies have been established to ensure an acceptable level of quality and customer satisfaction?
- What methods are used to transmit the intent of these policies to managers and employees?
- How are customer attitudes about product quality and service determined?
- How are customer service needs determined?
- What quality standards have been established?
- How is output measured against these quality standards?
- At what point(s) in the operating process is output inspected and compared to quality standards?
- What methods are used to implement quality control and customer satisfaction standards?
- How is information on the effectiveness of quality control and customer satisfaction generated and used?
- What precautions have been taken to ensure that customer orders are handled properly from the point of sale to the point of delivery?
- What techniques or measures are taken to minimize the response time from order point to shipment date?
- What follow-up procedures are used to determine customer satisfaction subsequent to the sale?
- What percentage of orders are returned or require further attention because of customer dissatisfaction?
- How are quality control and customer service costs identified and measured?
- Why is the firm's quality control and customer service program effective?
- What unique or competitive advantage does the firm's quality control program provide?

TIPS FOR PREPARING THE OPERATING PLAN

▬ **An effective operation means effective management.** The operating plan not only provides the intended reader with an understanding of how the business operates, but also serves as an indicator of the entrepreneur's managerial ability. The most effective method for conveying this message is to identify the cost/benefit trade-offs that are associated with operations and how the entrepreneur intends to balance them.

━ **Explain how costs are controlled.** The intended reader of the operating plan will also be keenly interested in how the cost of operations will be controlled. The method used may consist of nothing more complicated than a systematic review of operating-cost data, or it may consist of a sophisticated computerized cost control system. Of most concern is evidence that the entrepreneur understands the need for cost control and has established effective control procedures.

━ **Explain how inventory is controlled.** For firms that carry inventory; control of this asset is as critical to successful operations as controlling costs. Excessive or obsolete inventory increases the cost of operations and is a major drain on cash flow and profits. Again, the particular inventory control method used is not as important as evidence that the entrepreneur understands the need for it and has established effective control procedures.

━ **Use graphic aids.** If operating activities are highly technical, visual aids such as layout sketches, schematic drawings, or flow charts are valuable tools for conveying complex information. Even when a manufacturing process is not unusually complicated, a simple flow chart showing steps in the process can aid understanding. Care must be taken, however, that graphics do not become an unintended substitute for substance.

FIGURE 8-1 *The Operating Plan of Industrial Metal Finishing*

Operating Plan Summary

This operating plan describes the business concept and operating strategy that have been the primary reasons for the success of Industrial Metal Finishing. The high level of productivity enjoyed at each stage of operations, the quality of the end product, and the high level of customer satisfaction have been achieved through rigid adherence to established standards and an ongoing process of evaluation and improvement. These operating procedures will be standardized as part of an operating policy manual, which will serve as the blueprint for operations.

Situational Review

Industrial Metal Finishing (IMF) is currently located in an industrial center that offers advantages of low rent and flexible space. In addition, a dock-height shipping and receiving facil-

FIGURE 8-1 *(continued)*

ity is in place and access to natural gas and 440 VAC3 phase electric service is available. The firm is located in a prime central region with ample access to shipping and transportation. In terms of disadvantages, however, work place is not custom suited to application and accommodations must be made for other businesses that occupy the same building. There is a three-year tenancy limit and Industrial Metal Finishing could easily outgrow its available space.

Operations

IMF provides power coatings on conductive metallic surfaces, chiefly not-rolled steel, cold-rolled steel, cast iron, stainless steel, rolled or extruded aluminum, and cast aluminum. The pieces accepted will vary in size from a few square inches of surface area to 70" × 54" × 63", which is the maximum size capacity of the current oven.

Technological advancements have allowed the expansion of power coating to nonmetal surfaces, such as ceramics, wood, plastic, and glass. These applications generally require specialized equipment that IMF will not have initially. If market demand for these types of services is great enough to justify the expense of additional equipment, IMF will consider expanding service to include them.

IMF will offer its customers their choice of most types of thick-film, functional end use, and thin-film decorative end use thermosetting powders that are currently available. These coatings are epoxy, polyester, new polyester, acrylic, silicone/epoxy, silicone acrylics, and silicone. Each material or blend of materials offers unique properties of hardness, color acceptance, flexibility, durability, temperature resistance, ultraviolet light resistance, and salt-spray resistance. The material to be used in any given application will be determined by consultation with the power supplier and the customer, using a "needs" checklist.

The three major steps in the powder coating process are surface preparation, powder application, and thermosetting (baking). Of the three steps, surface preparation is the most critical. Unlike wet painting with solvent-based paints, which are somewhat forgiving of scale and grime, the surface to be powder coated must be free of contaminants and have a good phosphatized or conversion coat. IMF uses a variety of clean-

FIGURE 8-1 *(continued)*

ing methods including a high-temperature, high-pressure phosphate wash. Additionally, IMF has identified a new metal finishing process that is an environmental alternative to clean chromate coating on aluminum.

Powder is applied in a spray booth designed specifically for powder coating. Because there are virtually no VOCs in the powder, the spray booth air can be drawn through a two-stage filter and recirculated directly back to the shop. As with all spray type applications there is a certain amount of overspray. Unlike most wet spray processes however, the powder overspray can be recovered and reused.

Facility Requirements

Climate control. Coating powders have a shelf life of about one year depending on storage conditions. Ideal storage would be in an area protected from rapid temperature and humidity changes.

Chemical storage. While the chemicals associated with IMF's operations are generally not highly reactive, the concentrations involved would dictate safe and prudent holding facilities. These facilities will comply with or exceed code requirements.

Receiving Equipment. This will be dictated by IMF's marketplace. As the customer base develops, appropriate equipment will be acquired. Initially, only clean, designated areas will be necessary.

Shipping Area. A minimum amount of fixtures have been necessary to date, although the shipping area has the potential to become the largest square foot area in the shop. The plan is to offer potential customers the option of light assembly of their product and packaging and shipping to their customer as an efficiency that would greatly reduce extra handling problems and increase customer satisfaction. Also, having an adequate shipping area will give IMF the ability to serve customers worldwide.

Waste Management. The two most challenging items requiring waste management are disposal of incoming packaging materials and discharge of spent cleaning solutions. Incoming packaging materials will consist mainly of corrugated kraft paper and polypropylene sheets. Wherever possible these materials will be reused or, if reuse is not feasible, they will be recycled. Liquid discharges will be minimal (less than 100 gallons per day of highly diluted waste water). Discharges are coordinated with city public works department personnel and monitored and adjusted by equipment purchased from chemical suppliers.

Product Handling Fixtures. Three mobile racks are sized to fit in the oven, strong enough to carry 250 pounds of product each. The dolly wheels, as well as other parts of the racks are designed to operate in and withstand temperatures of up to 500 degrees Fahrenheit.

Powder Application. The shop is equipped with a walk-in spray booth designed to minimize powder migration within shop confines. The applicator module is an industry standard model that provides the versatility necessary for job shop usage. Accessories and specialized parts will be purchased as the need arises.

Thermosetting. A previously owned, electrically heated convection oven has been purchased that should be sufficient initially and sufficiently modifiable to provide for some future needs. Conversion of the oven to a more efficient gas-fired unit will be considered when volume dictates. The size of the current oven is 6 feet deep 5 feet wide and 5 feet high. The small size of this oven is limiting productivity. An oven 12 feet deep with doors on both ends would more than double the hourly production capacity. The larger oven would also allow IMF to accommodate projects involving larger parts (i.e.: automotive and airplane frames, boat trailers and docks) that are currently turned away.

Facilities and Layout

With current equipment IMF's production capacity is capable of generating approximately $28,000 per month in sales. With the addition of a larger oven, priced at approximately $35,000, four additional employees and 1,200 square feet of manufacturing space, IMF could increase revenue generating capacity to approximately $40,000 per month.

CHAPTER PERSPECTIVE

Operations can be defined as the system or set of processes and procedures used to convert resource inputs into a valuable product/service output. The operating plan details where the firm will locate, the procedures that will be used to conduct operations, the facilities and layout that will be required to conduct operations, how inventory will be purchased and managed, how quality control and customer service will be conducted, as well as create accountability. The most effective method for addressing the issue of feasibility is to identify the cost/benefit trade-offs associated with operations and explain how they are balanced. If you can demonstrate to the funding source that your team can execute the concept in your plan and accomplish the goals of your firm, the likelihood of success will be much greater.

The Organization Plan

WHAT IS AN ORGANIZATION PLAN?

The management process of arranging human, physical, financial, and informational resources is *organizing.* The resulting blueprint is the *organization plan.* An effective plan for organizing the various resources used by the firm is important to the success of every business. To the growing firm, however, it is crucial. Unless there are clearly defined links between authority, job responsibilities, and the flow of information and communication, it becomes virtually impossible to effectively coordinate efforts and to achieve organization goals as the firm grows.

The organization plan also serves as the entrepreneur's vehicle to convince others that his or her decisions on form of ownership, organization structure, and organization staffing will lead to the success of the business. A well-written organization plan is evidence that the entrepreneur understands the factors that affect organizational effectiveness and has carefully planned for the design.

After studying the material in this chapter, you will:

■ Understand the role of the organization plan.

■ Know what information is needed to prepare the organization plan.

■ Know the steps to preparing an organization plan.

■ Understand the basic differences between the three major legal forms of business ownership.

■ Understand the basic principles that guide the organizing function.

INFORMATION NEEDED TO PREPARE THE ORGANIZATION PLAN

Information to prepare an organization plan falls into three major categories: the firm's legal form of ownership; the design of the firm's internal organization structure; and the identification of the human skills needed to fill the positions within that structure. There are three basic legal forms of ownership: the sole proprietorship, the partnership, and the corporation. To make the proper choice, the entrepreneur must understand the legal, financial, and personal considerations surrounding each ownership form. Given the complexity of the decision, a qualified consultant may need to study the ramifications of each choice.

A fundamental task of business managers is to design an organization structure that provides the most efficient mechanism for meeting the firm's goals; an effective match between people, skills, job requirements, and authority/responsibility relationships; and the physical and informational resources job-holders need to meet assigned duties and responsibilities. Making sound decisions on organization structure requires information such as:

- The key jobs that must be filled.
- How the duties and responsibilities of each job are divided.
- How job authority and responsibilities are grouped.
- How formal authority flows through the organization.
- The most effective organizational design given the firm's *primary task*. The primary task is the activity or set of activities that form the firm's reason for existence.

Most business experts say having productive employees is as important to the success of the firm as the product or service it provides. The reason is simple: An organization is only as effective as its people, and its people are only as effective as the managers who lead them. The management process that is concerned with personnel issues is referred to as *human resource management*. To perform this function effectively requires information such as:

- Requirements of each job in the organization.
- Job qualifications.
- Appropriate compensation for each job.
- Appropriate fringe benefits for each job.
- Recruitment and retention plans for capable employees.
- Standards by which job performance is measured and evaluated.

WHEN TO INCLUDE AN ORGANIZATION PLAN WITH THE BUSINESS PLAN

An organization plan will typically be included as a separate component of the business plan when one or more of the following conditions exist.

- Firm is large enough to require multiple management and staff positions.
- Firm's expected growth indicates that multiple management and staff positions will be needed.
- Firm's primary task is sufficiently technical or complex to require multiple staff and key operating positions.
- A major change in the organization structure is intended.

■ The organization plan is unique or complicated, or needs to be clarified for the reader.

If these conditions are not present, the extent to which organizational considerations are discussed is a matter of judgment. For example, an abridged version of the organization plan may be included as part of the operating plan. Regardless of what is decided, resumes of the entrepreneur, the management team, and other key personnel in the firm should be included in the appendix to the business plan. The intended reader of the business plan will be concerned about the qualifications of key personnel. He or she knows that all businesses, whether new ventures or going concerns, will periodically encounter varying degrees of adversity. The difference between the firms that survive setbacks and those that do not is capable, productive, people.

STEPS TO PREPARING AN ORGANIZATIONAL PLAN

The eight steps identified and discussed below offer a logical approach to gathering information and preparing the organization plan. As an aid, guideline questions are included where appropriate. Also, an organization plan for the hypothetical firm, Masterful Meals, appears at the end of this chapter as Figure 9-1.

1. **Consider an organization plan summary.** This optional section *may* be used when the organization plan is prepared for outside presentation. The summary is a convenience for the reader and should be no longer than what is needed to gain an understanding of the plan's major thrust. This usually can be accomplished in one paragraph.

2. **Prepare a situational review.** Normally, this section serves either of two purposes. It may be used to describe a major change that has occurred, or is intended to occur, in the organization of an existing firm; or, in the case of a new venture, the review may be used to describe the various stages of organization development that have been completed to date.

3. **Identify the legal form of ownership.** An important part of the organizing function is a decision on the appropriate legal form of business ownership. Since a number of legal, financial, and tax issues flow from this decision, it is important that the choice be carefully planned. The legal form of ownership should be matched to the basic mission of the firm, the firm's overall goals, and the entrepreneur's personal needs.

You must consider the following issues when determining which business form is best for your entity:

- **Risk.** How many others will be sharing control of the business with you? Is it wise to limit the number of people who control the business?
- **Taxes.** Which business form will allow you to absorb losses, usually present in your first year of operation?
- **Image.** Will a more formal business organization attract investors?
- **Control.** Will you have the desired amount of control if you share responsibilities? Are you willing to dilute your ownership control?
- **Transferability and Marketability.** Are there constraints in certain business forms that limit your ability to market and liquidate?

Various legal forms of ownership are available to the firm. Because some are appropriate only to specialized applications, only the characteristics, advantages, and disadvantages of three basic forms are discussed here. When considering these points, it is important to remember that most of the features identified are *not* absolute. What is an advantage or disadvantage of an organization form is relative to the current and expected circumstances for that firm and that entrepreneur.

For example, while the federal corporate income tax rate is higher than the rate for an individual taxpayer, absolute size of the tax rate is not the only tax issue that must be considered when choosing between the sole proprietorship and corporation. The total tax bill under the various forms of organization will differ depending on such factors as expected profits and losses over the planning horizon; expected growth of the firm and the need for future financing; wage, salary, and Federal Insurance Contributions Act (FICA) tax considerations (i.e., for Social Security and Medicare) for the entrepreneur or his or her family members; and the entrepreneur's estate plan.

A *sole proprietorship* is a business firm established and owned by one person. Legally, and in the eyes of the taxing authorities, a business organized as a sole proprietorship is indistinct from its owner. The firm's assets, liabilities, profits and losses, tax obligations, and legal responsibilities are also those of the owner. What's more, the life of the business is tied directly to the life of the owner. Technically, if the owner dies, the business dies as well.

Advantages generally associated with sole proprietorship are:
- It is the easiest and least costly ownership form to organize and dissolve.
- It is often the most appropriate form of ownership for a new business.

- The proprietor has total control and can make and implement decisions without interference, can sell the business to whomever he or she wishes, or can easily pass the business down to heirs if desired.
- All profits belong to the proprietor.
- Relative to the regular corporate form, there may be a potential tax advantage when losses occur, because the losses flow through to the owner's personal tax return.
- Relative to the regular corporate form, owner's withdrawals of funds from the business are taxed only once, at the proprietor's individual tax rate.
- Unlike the regular corporate form, which, by law, is required to disclose financial information, a sole proprietor can maintain complete confidentiality.

Disadvantages generally associated with sole proprietorship are:

- Assets of the business and the personal assets of its owner are subject to the claims of the firm's creditors. This characteristic is known as *unlimited liability*.
- Without prior provision for the allocation of business assets, the life of the business is limited to that of the owner.
- Financing available to the business is limited to what the proprietor can personally invest or borrow, as investors usually will not invest in proprietorships.
- Because of the firm's limited growth potential and the limited opportunity for employees to gain a share of the firm's ownership, it is often difficult for sole proprietors to attract and keep good employees and management talent.
- Since profits from the business flow through to the owner, there is no opportunity to protect cash flow retained in the business from income tax.
- Relative to the regular corporate form, there may be income tax disadvantages associated with income tax on the owner's or his or her family members' salary and FICA and Medicare tax payments.

The *general partnership form of ownership* shares many of the characteristics of the sole proprietorship. A general partnership is an association of two or more persons conducting business as co-owners. As is true of the proprietorship, the general partnership is legally and for tax purposes inseparable from the owners (partners) themselves. Each general partner shares in the firm's profits and losses, has management equality, is liable for the business-related actions and decisions of other partners, and has unlimited liability for the debts of the business. Also, the life of the partnership is, technically, tied to that of each partner.

There are variations of the general partnership status. Most common are the limited partner, silent partner, and secret partner. The liability of a *limited partner* is limited to the investment in the business, and he or she typically has no voice in managing the business. A *silent partner,* like a general partner, has unlimited liability but does not have an active voice in managing the business. A silent partner is known to the public to be a partner in the business. A *secret partner* is active in the firm's management and has unlimited liability, but is unknown to the public as a partner.

Advantages generally associated with the general partnership are:
- Partnerships, like sole proprietorships but to a somewhat lesser degree, have the advantage of ease and low cost of both organization and dissolution of the business.
- Because partners pool financial resources, partnerships often have access to greater amounts of capital than do sole proprietorships. For the same reason, partnerships often have better credit standing than sole proprietorships have. Also, because the losses of the firm are shared by the partners, the relative share of the risk to each partner is less relative to a proprietorship.
- The partnership has greater potential than the sole proprietorship for attracting and keeping management talent and good employees.
- In comparison to the regular corporate form, there may be a tax advantage, because losses from the business flow through to the personal tax returns of the partners.
- Relative to the regular corporate form, a partner's withdrawals are taxed only once, at the partner's personal tax rate. The partnership itself is not responsible for paying taxes on the income generated by the business.
- Unlike the regular corporate form, which, by law is required to disclose financial information, the partnership can maintain complete confidentiality.

Disadvantages generally associated with the general partnership are:
- Each partner has unlimited liability for business obligations.
- Each partner is responsible for the business actions of other partners and upon the death of a partner, the business dissolves.
- Potential for partnership disagreement and internal strife is great.
- Without prior provision for the disposition of the business in the event of a partner's death, the life of the business is limited to that of any partner.

- Financing available to the business is limited to what the partners can personally raise.
- Since profits from the business flow through to the partners, there is no opportunity to retain, free from income taxes, the cash flow from operations generated by the business.
- Relative to the regular corporate form, there may be income tax disadvantages associated with a partner's or his or her family members' salary, FICA, and Medicare tax payments. However, like a proprietorship, a partnership can deduct premiums for medical insurance coverage.

Several words of warning about forming a partnership:

- The potential for partnership conflicts is great. Business experts agree that long-term partnerships are the rare exception rather than the rule. Consequently, it will take much stronger justification to convince the intended reader that a partnership can be more successful than other ownership forms.
- A partnership is essentially a legal relationship between the partners. It is crucial, therefore, that the partners enter into an *articles of partnership* agreement. The Uniform Partnership Act or the Revised Uniform Partnership Act has been adopted in some form in every state but Louisiana.

As indicated below, this agreement should define in detail the role, involvement, duties, and responsibilities of each partner. The most common provisions contained in the articles of partnership are:

- Date and duration of the agreement (e.g., continue until terminated).
- Name and location of the firm and the nature of its business.
- Names of partners, their respective investments, and the agreed-upon distribution of profits and losses.
- Duties of each partner, the expected hours of personal service that are to be devoted to the business, and access of the partners to the books of the business.
- Salary of each partner.
- Each partner's percentage distribution of profits and responsibility for losses.
- Limitations on withdrawals of funds from the business.
- Procedures to be followed in the event of a partner's withdrawal from the firm.
- Procedure for admitting new partners
- Procedures to be followed in the event of a partner's death or incapacity.

The next form of ownership is the *corporation* that is chartered by the laws of the state in which it is incorporated. As such, a corporation is a legal and taxable entity that has a life, existence, and duties and responsibilities separate and distinct from its owners. Technically, a corporation is governed by its board of directors. This group makes major policy decisions and appoints the firm's officers and top-level management. The owners of the corporation are its common stockholders. Stockholders elect the board of directors and are entitled to all profits remaining after other claims on income (such as wages, payments to vendors, interest payments, and taxes) have been satisfied.

Advantages associated with the corporate form of ownership are:

- The corporation is a legal entity that can sue and be sued, enter into contract, own assets, and borrow in its own name.
- The corporation has an unlimited legal life that is separate from that of its owners (stockholders), whereas a sole proprietorship ceases existence with the death of the proprietor. As to the partnership, see above.
- A stockholder's liability is limited to the amount of his or her investment and the stockholder is not personally liable for the business debts, obligations, and liabilities of the corporation.
- Professional managers with no share of ownership can be hired and fired by the board of directors.
- Relative to the sole proprietorship and partnership, earnings can be retained in the business without being taxed as income to stockholders.
- Shares of ownership (common stock) can be sold, making it easier to raise capital and expand the business.
- Shares of ownership can be sold or transferred, making it easier to extend ownership interest to valuable employees, and easier for the entrepreneur to do estate planning.

Disadvantages generally associated with the corporate form, as compared to the sole proprietorship or partnership, are:

- It is more difficult and costly to organize a corporation.
- Unless the corporation is small and has elected the S corporation taxing option, it is a C corporation and subject to multiple taxation. Federal and state income taxes are levied on the corporation itself and again on the dividends and salaries paid its stockholders. In addition to this *double taxation* of income, corporations also may pay franchise taxes as well as taxes or fees to other states in which it does business.
- Corporations must keep records and prepare reports for state and federal agencies. Also, if the corporation's stock is publicly traded, it must keep audited accounting records and prepare reports for the Securities and Exchange Commission (SEC) and the exchange, if any, on which its stock is listed.

The next form of ownership is the Subchapter S corporation. The Internal Revenue Service (IRS) allows a small, closely held corporation (100 or fewer stockholders) to be taxed as a sole proprietorship or partnership while, at the same time, keeping its legal status as a corporation. Known as S corporation status, this tax status eliminates the double taxation of income associated with the regular corporate form. All owners, however, must be United States citizens or permanent residents, and there can be only one class of stock (no preferred stock). The S corporation does not pay income tax. Instead, corporate profits (and losses) flow directly to the personal tax returns of shareholders and are taxed at the stockholder's personal tax rate. To obtain S corporation status, the board of directors must elect this option by making a specific request to the IRS.

A special category of business is the limited liability company. It combines the pass-through tax benefit of a sole proprietorship or partnership. That is, one reports and pays tax on the firm's profits on his or her individual income tax return, with the limited liability afforded by a corporation, so that firm creditors cannot reach the personal assets of the owners. Thus, the owners report the firm's income, losses, deductions, and credits on their own tax returns. (That said, the limited liability company can elect corporate tax treatment should that prove more beneficial).

Most states do not restrict ownership—allowing for even single-member ownership—with no maximum number of members either. Certain businesses, such as banks and insurers, cannot qualify. Owners may apportion profits and losses based on relative ownership (e.g., 50–50), but need not do so. Such companies are managed by their members or by a single manager or group of managers consisting of one or more members. Note that a member will continue to be liable in tort for his own negligence, but not that of the other members. Further, as in other forms of business, if an owner agrees to personally guarantee a firm's debt or obligation, there will be no limited liability protection afforded to such personally guaranteed loans. Similarly, if a limited liability company, like a corporation, fails to pay the required federal or state taxes, the tax due may be sought from any of the so-called responsible persons.

For questions regarding how a firm's corporate veil may be pierced (e.g., where an owner treats business assets as his own), a consultation with legal counsel is recommended. Also, in some states, one may not practice certain professions (e.g., law) as either a corporation or a limited liability company—in such cases, one may limit one's liability somewhat by creating a limited liability partnership in which a partner will still be personally liable for his own negligence and that of employees whom he supervises, but not that of others in the firm. Thus, a limited liability partnership is itself a general partnership, whereas a limited partnership includes at least one general partner and one limited partner. With a limited liability partnership, incidentally, the partnership will not be taxed, with the partners paying taxes on their shares of the profits.

The entrepreneur should consider the following *guideline questions regarding legal form of ownership:*

- What is the total cost of organizing the firm as a corporation compared with organizing as a sole proprietorship or partnership?
- How will the entrepreneur's personal assets be protected from the firm's creditors if the corporate form is *not* used?
- How much total control does the entrepreneur want to have over the business?
- Given the firm's growth prospects over the next one to five years, what is the estimated amount of income tax that would be paid under the various forms of ownership?
- Given the expectations for business profits, dividends (owner's withdrawals), salaries and wages, and FICA withholdings for the entrepreneur and working family members, what amount of tax would be paid under the various forms of ownership?
- If the entrepreneur dies how will ownership interests in the business be taxed and transferred to heirs under the various forms of ownership?
- If the corporate form of ownership is chosen, what relative tax advantages and disadvantages are associated with the Subchapter S corporation?
- If a C corporation wishes to switch to an S corporation, will all shareholders consent as required by law?
- If the sole proprietorship form of ownership is chosen, can management talent and other key personnel be hired and retained?
- If the corporate form is selected, who will serve on the board of directors, and what can each director contribute to the success of the firm?

4. **Management philosophy.** An important consideration in organizational structure is the culture that evolves to determine the values, beliefs, and patterns of behavior that are accepted and practiced by the organization's members. The culture that eventually evolves is, either consciously or unconsciously, the result of the entrepreneur's management philosophy: how the role of manager is perceived by the entrepreneur and the pattern of behavior exhibited

when he or she makes decisions and exercises authority. While management philosophy is possibly more subtle than other determinants of the firm's success, it is no less important. How well the entrepreneur and other managers relate to those inside and outside of the business, determines how well they can motivate and lead employees, win the loyalty of customers, creditors, and the surrounding community, and create a positive image of the firm.

Management experts suggest that the most important factor influencing the culture and management style is the entrepreneur's actions. What the entrepreneur says or writes is not as convincing as what he or she does. The following actions have the most important influence.

- What the leader pays attention to, measures, and controls. For example, if the entrepreneur's actions enforce a customer-comes-first policy, employees will do so as well. By contrast, those things the entrepreneur ignores are perceived as unimportant by employees.
- How the leader reacts to critical situations. For example, assume that because of declining profits pay cuts are necessary for survival. If everyone from the CEO down takes pay cuts, the action emphasizes the belief that management and employees are, for better and for worse, on the same team. On the other hand, if only operating employees are made to sacrifice, the opposite message is sent.
- The leader serves as teacher and coach. By directly relating to and becoming involved with members of the organization, the leader establishes himself or herself as a role model.
- How the leader recognizes and rewards achievement. Leaders can quickly communicate their priorities by consistently linking pay increases and promotions, or the absence of pay increases and promotions, to particular behaviors.
- How much trust the leaders bestow on their employees through delegating key responsibilities can give employees pride and ownership of their work, resulting in loyalty to the firm. Conversely, if tasks are micromanaged, employees will feel devalued.

Consider these questions regarding management philosophy:

- How would the entrepreneur like employees to feel about the firm, himself or herself, and other managers or supervisors in the firm?
- What steps will be taken to ensure that employees will have positive feelings about the firm, the entrepreneur, and other managers?

- How will employees be motivated?
- How will employee achievements be recognized and rewarded?
- How will employees be disciplined?
- How will employee morale be gauged?
- To what extent should decision-making be centralized in one or a few top managers?
- To what extent should employees have a voice in planning, problem-solving, and decision-making?
- What philosophy should govern the firm's relationship with customers, suppliers, creditors, and the community?

5. **Organization structure.** An organization is a structured group of human, physical, informational, and financial resources combined to accomplish specific goals. The organizational design that results from this effort defines the relationships and formal lines of authority and communication that exist between people and positions.

The primary purpose of designing a formal organization structure is to effectively coordinate the efforts of each part of the firm. There are five basic principles or building blocks through which this is accomplished: division and specialization of labor, departmentalization, line and staff status, the hierarchy of authority, and span of control.

Division of labor is the process of partitioning jobs into smaller, manageable tasks and assigning these responsibilities to specific workers. *Specialization of labor* refers to dividing jobs into a set of tasks that can be repeated easily and efficiently.

Departmentalization groups jobs into major work units and places them under the authority and control of an identified manager. Decisions about how to departmentalize affect how authority is delegated, responsibilities are assigned, resources are distributed, performance is evaluated, and information and communication flow.

One of the most basic principles of organization involves the distinction between line and staff authority. *Line authority* is the formal right to make decisions and issue orders. This authority flows from the top of the organization down. For example, the firm's CEO delegates defined limits of authority to the vice president of production who, in turn, redefines and delegates areas of authority to production supervisors. Conversely, the term *staff* refers to the right to advise and assist line managers or other staff personnel in the staff member's area of expertise. The degree to which the assistance or advice must be followed by line personnel depends on the amount of authority that has been delegated to the staff position.

Closely related to the concepts of line and staff authority are the principles of managerial hierarchy, chain of command, and unity of command. *Managerial hierarchy* refers to the levels of management within the organization, and the organization's *chain of command* defines the authority relationships between these levels. Typically, the chain of command flows from the top of the organization down. The principle of *unity of command* establishes that each worker reports to and gets instructions from only one boss.

Span of control deals with the number of employees reporting to one manager. Once the work has been divided into major work units, the number of managers and workers must be decided. While a good rule of thumb for determining a manageable span of control is five to nine employees, the number should be determined by the capabilities of the manager and the nature of the work. This number is affected by:

- **Nature of the task:** The more complex the task, the narrower the span of control should be.
- **Level of employee skill and motivation:** The higher the skill level and motivation of employees, the wider the span of control can be.
- **Location of employees:** The more work locations at which workers are stationed, the narrower the span of control should be.
- **The degree to which authority is delegated:** The greater the ability and willingness of management to delegate authority, the wider the span of control can be.
- **The degree of interaction required:** The more interaction and feedback needed between manager and employees, the narrower the span of control should be.

The ultimate design of the firm's organization structure should depend on its primary task. In general, there are five basic ways a business can be organized or structured around its primary task. Consider these examples:

- **By product:** A chemical manufacturer may organize activities into industrial and agricultural chemical product divisions.
- **By function:** Many firms are organized around their production, marketing, information, and finance functions.
- **By process:** A hospital may be organized into process units based on the type of medical service provided (emergency care, cardiology, surgery, etc.).
- **By customer:** An electronics firm may set up divisions to serve its military, industrial, and consumer target markets.
- **By territory:** An international firm may establish strategic business units to serve the U.S., South American, and European markets.

If the firm's size requires multiple management and staff positions, the authority/responsibility relationships between them should be depicted in an organization chart. A partial chart for a firm organized by function is shown on Table 9-1.

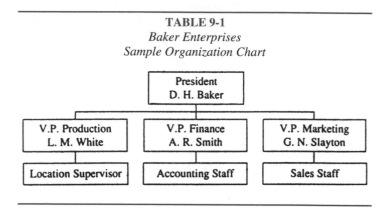

TABLE 9-1
Baker Enterprises
Sample Organization Chart

The boxes shown on the organization chart represent positions in the organization and the functional areas of responsibility (Production, Finance, etc.) associated with each. The vertical lines depict the flow of authority through various levels of the organization.

The entrepreneur should consider these questions when making decisions regarding organization structure:

- What is the firm's primary task?
- Are the activities surrounding the primary task most logically related to function (production, marketing, etc.), product, process, type of customer, or geography?
- What are the top-level management positions?
- What are the staff and middle-level management positions?
- What are the specific duties and responsibilities associated with each management and staff position?
- What decisions must be made to fulfill the duties and responsibilities associated with each management position?
- What number of immediate, lower-level employees can effectively be supervised by each management and staff position?
- What level of authority is assigned to each management staff position?
- What are the authority relationships between each management position?
- Who holds each management position?

- How effectively does each management and staff position-holder delegate authority to immediate, lower-level subordinates?
- What are the major work units or departments into which the firm's primary task can be best divided and re-grouped?
- How many supervisors are required for each major work unit or department?
- What duties, responsibilities, and level of authority are associated with each supervisory position?

6. **Key-personnel assessment.** This section of the organization plan should contain a brief summary of the job-related attributes of each key position-holder. The summaries should be prepared from complete resumes for each person. The resumes should be included in an appendix to the business plan and their location appropriately referenced in this section.

Job-related attributes refer to the background, skills, and accomplishments that enable the individual to effectively perform his or her assigned job. To correctly identify these attributes, the entrepreneur must first understand which skills and knowledge level are required for that position. This information is gathered through the process of *job analysis,* and the results are written into a formal document known as a *job description.* A sample job description for a hypothetical assistant store manager position is illustrated in Table 9-2.

TABLE 9-2
Sample Job Description

Job Title: Assistant Store Manager

Reports To: Store Manager

General Description of the Job:
Manages the daily functions of a specialty department in the retail operations. Assistant store manager is responsible for customer service, supervision of sales clerks, new employee training, merchandising, advising and coordinating purchases with purchasing manager, and inventory maintenance.

Principal Duties and Responsibilities:
1. Assists customers in merchandise selections, sales returns, and lay-aways as needed.
2. Clarifies any questions or problems that a sales clerk encounters.
3. Trains, coordinates, directs, and supervises department sales clerks daily.

TABLE 9-2 *(continued)*

4. Maintains inventory records.
5. Prepares the department for opening.
6. Ensures that the department remains professionally organized and orderly.

General Qualification Requirements:

1. Education:
   Minimum four-year college degree in marketing or related discipline from an accredited university.
2. Experience:
   Minimum of six months to one year in a retail environment. Preferred one to three years as sales clerk at [*Name of firm*].
3. Knowledge, Skills, Abilities:
   Basic math competency
   Effective interpersonal skills
   Good judgment and independent thinker
   Highly motivated self-starter
   High integrity
4. Physical Requirements:
   Standing and walking for more than 90% of the work time
   Ability to lift and carry boxes weighing about 15 pounds or less.

In general, the job-related attributes for each key position should include:

- **Education:** As used here, *education* means training that is directly related to the job or duties performed. This may include such training as job-related military training, formal education, or the successful completion of executive development programs.
- **Qualifications:** These are the tangible job skills and intangible attributes needed to effectively perform a particular job. For example, a sales manager should have marketing skills, leadership ability, and managerial talent commensurate with the requirements of that position in a given organization. On the other hand, training and job experience as an electrical engineer, while admirable attributes, do not qualify one for a sales management position.
- **Experience:** This term refers to the individual's exposure to the duties and responsibilities that are directly or indirectly

related to a particular job. The key to what is appropriate experience is job-related exposure. For example, experience as an aircraft mechanic's apprentice would qualify one for a mechanic's position. It does not, however, qualify one to fly a plane.

- **Successes:** This term refers to career or job-related accomplishments that indicate an individual's ability to succeed. Included are such considerations as superior work performance that has been recognized, promotions and awards received, and pay increases.
- **Strengths and weaknesses:** Strengths refer to the personal qualities that make him or her well-suited to a particular job. For example, if a particular management position were being filled, the candidate's ability to plan, motivate employees, and set and reach goals would be important strengths. Weaknesses refer to personal deficiencies that must be corrected to effectively perform the job. If individual weaknesses are identified, then a plan for correcting them should be included in this section as well.

Because the key-personnel assessment step and the next two steps are closely related, the guideline questions for all three are combined and appear at the end of Step 8.

7. **Planning human resource needs.** This section should describe the key positions that must be filled in the future and the reasons these positions will contribute to the success of the organization. The description should identify:

- Each position by job title.
- The duties, responsibilities, and degree of authority of each position.
- How the authority and responsibilities of each position fit into the organization structure.
- The job-related attributes needed to successfully carry out the duties and responsibilities of the position.
- How qualified people will be recruited to fill each position.

The discussion of why a particular position must be created and filled should focus on how and why it will add to the organization's existing strengths or correct its weaknesses. For example, the reason for creating a top-level marketing position may be stated as follows: "By hiring an experienced marketer, the firm would gain the expertise needed to establish realistic marketing goals and strategies, and to control its overall marketing activities."

For the guideline questions on human resources needs, see the end of Step 8.

8. **Compensation and incentives.** Readers of the business plan will be interested in the financial stake that management and other key personnel have or will have in the business. Consequently, information such as the following should be included for each key individual in the firm:

- The amount of personal financial investment in the business.
- The percentage of the total ownership interest in the firm that the individual's investment represents. If the firm is incorporated, this information should include shares of stock held, price at which they were acquired, percentage of the total shares outstanding that the shares represent, and a description of the terms of stock options held.
- The base salary received.
- A description of any bonus or commission opportunities afforded the individual.
- A description of any profit-sharing opportunities for the individual.

If the firm has employment agreements or management contracts that legally bind the individual to the job, these should be identified, explained, and justified. Such agreements often are viewed suspiciously by financiers, especially venture capitalists, because they may be used as instruments for perpetuating managerial incompetence. If the firm has existing or planned management contracts or employment agreements, justification should focus on how they contribute to the success of the firm. For example, a management contract may be the only way a highly qualified individual can be lured to the firm.

Also, if the firm is incorporated and has outside directors on the board, prepare a separate section that describes the qualifications of these individuals and the contribution that each makes to the success of the firm. Again, readers will become suspicious if it appears that director positions (especially paid positions) are being used as havens for relatives and friends.

The description of each director should include information such as:

- The director's identity.
- Background and experience the director brings to the firm.
- Position-related qualifications the director brings to the firm.
- The policy-setting role the director plays.
- Any gap in management skills the director fills.

In preparing the sections for Steps 6, 7, and 8, key-personnel assessment, human resources needs, and compensation and incentives, the entrepreneur should consider the following guideline questions:

- What job title will be assigned each key position?
- What is the purpose of each position and what outputs should it produce?
- What duties and specific tasks must be performed by each position-holder?
- What responsibilities are associated with each key position?
- What authority is associated with each position?
- What level of education, knowledge, skill, and experience is needed to perform the duties and responsibilities of each key position effectively?
- What personality or behavioral characteristics are required to perform the duties and responsibilities of each position effectively?
- How much job education or training will be required to perform duties effectively after the person is hired?
- How will any additional education or training be provided?
- What materials and equipment must nonmanagement jobholders use?
- How much time is required to complete the important tasks associated with nonmanagement jobs?
- In what environment and under what working conditions will nonmanagement jobs be performed?
- What environmental hazards are associated with these jobs?
- How are workers protected against environmental hazards?
- Will these protections satisfy federal and state safety requirements?
- What salary or wage compensation, including fringe benefits, is assigned to the management and nonmanagement jobs?
- How is the compensation level for management and nonmanagement jobs established, and is this amount sufficiently competitive to attract qualified individuals?
- What monetary and other incentives will be used to motivate job-holders?
- How will qualified personnel be recruited?
- What strategy will be used to replace key management that leave the firm and manage responsibilities in the interim?
- How will job recruits be evaluated and screened?
- How will job performance be evaluated?

Good managers can set levels of expectations on which to judge performance of employees. For example, your employee responds to customer e-mail inquiries. You help her set a realistic and attainable goal of answering the inquiries within four hours. But to further enhance your ability to judge her performance, you can add levels to that goal. Perhaps she would meet the minimum standard by answering all requests within four hours, but would exceed your expectations by answering 50 percent of the requests within two hours. With more detailed goals, you're not only enhancing customer service, but you're giving yourself and your employee a better tool on which to assess performance.

- What promotion opportunities exist for each job-holder?
- Based on the firm's overall goals and objectives, what key personnel will be needed in the future, and when?

TIPS FOR PREPARING THE ORGANIZATION PLAN

■ **Stress feasibility.** The entrepreneur should not underestimate either the contribution a strong organization makes to the success of the firm or the significance the intended reader will attach to this factor. In all likelihood, the reader will understand the importance of capable people to the success of the firm. For this reason, he or she will pay particular attention to the qualifications of key personnel and to organizational needs that must be filled in the future. If the organization plan does not contain this information, it is impossible to make a convincing case for *why* the organization structure is feasible and *why* the business will succeed.

■ **Evidence a strong commitment.** The intended reader of the business plan also will know that the entrepreneur must make a strong personal commitment to the business for success. An entrepreneur who is in a position to suffer a large personal loss if the firm fails will work hard to achieve success and is less likely to walk away from the business when adversity strikes. The entrepreneur's commitment to the business can be indicated in a number of ways, including the size of his or her personal financial investment, the personal assets the entrepreneur has or is willing to pledge as collateral for financing, the time devoted to the business, and how the entrepreneur deals with work and personal priorities, or balances business commitments with family responsibilities.

■ **Management experience is expected.** Usually, it is not enough that an entrepreneur has specific technical skills in his or her business area. The intended reader also will expect the entrepreneur to have management experience. He or she will carefully search the business plan and question the entrepreneur to verify that this experience exists or, if it does not, that the entrepreneur recognizes the deficiency and has a plan for correcting it.

■ **Do not exaggerate strengths.** The qualifications of the key position-holders in the firm are an important ingredient of a convincing organization plan. These qualifications should be presented as favorably as possible. In doing so, however, it is important to resist the temptation to exaggerate or misrepresent the facts. Anyone seriously considering a professional or financial interest in the business will verify what is written. Exaggerations or misrepresentations will be discovered, which will destroy the entrepreneur's credibility.

▬ **Do not whitewash weaknesses.** It is as self-defeating to hide or omit organizational weaknesses as it is to exaggerate strengths. If the entrepreneur or other key personnel have job-related deficiencies, they should be identified *along with* plans for correcting the problem. For example, an entrepreneur lacking certain managerial qualifications may compensate by using an outside consultant for major decisions, or by hiring an experienced person to fill the position. Hiding or failing to recognize weaknesses indicates a person who either cannot be trusted or, equally disastrous, one who does not recognize problems.

▬ **Be prudent about employing friends and relatives.** Placing unqualified friends or relatives in key positions or creating unnecessary positions for them has been the death knell for all too many firms. A business represents a large investment of the entrepreneur's time and money. There is too much at stake not to select people who have the background and skills needed to contribute to the firm's success. The intended reader of the business plan will immediately be suspicious if there is a hint that the firm is being used as an employment sanctuary for unqualified people.

FIGURE 9-1 *The Organization Plan of Zupermail Inc.* *

Organization Plan Summary

This plan describes the organization structure and key personnel that will be required to support Zupermail, Inc.'s operations.

Situational Review

Zupermail, Inc. is a C corporation formed under the laws of the state of Delaware in June of 2007. The company is an Arizona-based developer of "opt-in" (permission-based) e-mail direct marketing and database services. As the founder of Zupermail, Inc., Mr. _____ is assembling a corporate management team and a staff of accredited employees with the experience, skill, and vision to launch and position the company as a leader in the opt-in e-mail direct marketing industry, targeting specific demographic segments. A long-time and successful business-

FIGURE 9-1 *(continued)*

man, Mr. _____ has been involved in specialty retail leasing and retail industry publishing for over 20 years.

Zupermail, Inc. has created its web site and developed all back-end infrastructures needed to utilize its database. Having launched the site in October of 2007, the company has seen membership rise from a base of a few hundred individuals to over 14,000 as of February 2008. Zupermail, Inc. is currently in the beta-testing phase of the company focusing on increasing membership and verifying all data of members. The company is also currently creating an advisory board of respected industry and business leaders.

Key Personnel

As a service organization, Zupermail, Inc. will dedicate concerted effort towards operational staffing and human resource concerns. Actively pursuing people in each of the following areas, the company is in talks with several individuals to fill positions as growth dictates.

Administrative
Accounting Staff
Office Manager
Administrative Staff

Web Site
Webmaster
Programmer
Content Developer
Site Administrator
Affiliate Director
Research Director

Marketing and Advertising
Display/Traditional
Promotion/PR/Partnerships
Broker Sales
Sales People/List Sales

Management Team
CEO/President of Sales: Mr. _____
During his tenure as president and founder of *Sales Dynamics, Inc.,* Mr. _____ led the company to become a premier spe-

FIGURE 9-1 *(continued)*

cialty retail leasing company in the US. Operating in over 150 malls in 40 states with a staff of more than 100, sales generated exceeded $16 million annually. Among his other accomplishments, he founded two retail industry publications, one of which was sold to a billion-dollar corporation.

President of Marketing: Ms. _____

Ms. _____ served as Vice President of Operations at *Sales Dynamics, Inc.,* leading a team of eight regional directors and 90 employees. She also served as Senior Vice President of Sales for *National Mall Monitor* magazine, and personally sold $2 million dollars of advertising while supervising a national sales staff.

CFO
In talks with prospective individuals.
Reporting to the CEO, this position will be responsible for executing all internal accounting and financial duties of the company, including internal financial statements, budgeting and forecasting, investments, and allocation of funds.

Honorary Advisory Board
Management has identified the need for an Advisory Board that will assist the company in its direction, both from a technology and marketing standpoint. The board will consist of six (6) members that are specialists in the areas of e-mail marketing and technology.
Budgeted fees: stock options negotiated for each board member

Other Consultants
The company believes that research and development will continue well into the second year of operations, both domestically and internationally. To this end, there may be a need to employ further researchers and/or training staff to insure quality of all research. No budgets have been determined at this stage, although R&D budgets have been increased from year two to cover additional staffing and research needs.

---

* Sample provided by Jamie Hait, Partner, NextLevelPlan.com, a strategic business planning firm that specializes in creating comprehensive business plans for small to mid-sized ventures.

CHAPTER PERSPECTIVE

An organization plan details how the firm's resources will be organized and structured to coordinate activities and meet established goals. The organization structure should give consideration to the most effective method for carrying out the firm's primary task, the duties and responsibilities of each key position in the firm, how authority should flow through the firm, and the most effective matching of job requirements and job qualifications. The typical organization plan contains a summary, a situational review, a statement of management philosophy, a description of the chosen legal form of ownership and organization structure, an assessment of key personnel and planned human resource needs, and a description of the compensation and incentives received by key personnel.

The Financial Plan

WHAT IS A FINANCIAL PLAN?

The various operating plans prepared by the entrepreneur indicate where the firm is expected to go and how it will get there. The financial plan estimates and plans for the financing needed to implement these intentions. It, along with the market analysis and marketing plan, is the most critical component of the business plan. A convincing financial plan answers these key questions:

▬ What amount of financing is needed to make plans feasible?

▬ When and in what amounts will financing be needed?

▬ In what form will financing be needed?

▬ Who will provide financing?

▬ What short- and long-term financial projections does the firm estimate, particularly as they relate to paying back loans and other types of financial backing?

Generating convincing responses to these questions requires business knowledge, the factors that determine the success or failure of its operation, a basic understanding of the financial side of the business, and the ability to translate this information into a sound financial game plan.

Although some entrepreneurs might think of the financial plan as being strictly "about the numbers," it is much more than that by providing a basis for making many decisions about the business. Decisions such as how many employees to hire, what suppliers will be used, and what equipment will be purchased will be largely made while completing the financial plan. As is true with marketing and operations, one plan has to be streamlined with the other. The financial plan needs to reflect the marketing activities and the level of production that were outlined previously in the plan.

Likewise, as is true with the other parts of the business plan, the reader's interests need to be kept in mind. If the plan is to be used internally, more emphasis will be placed on items such as cash flow to help the entrepreneur manage fixed and operating costs. Conversely, if the plan will be primarily used to secure a bank loan, the significant emphasis will need to be placed on the firm's ability to service its debt obligations.

After studying the material in this chapter, you will:

- Understand the role of the financial plan.
- Know what information is required to prepare the financial plan.
- Know the steps to preparing the financial plan.
- Know how to prepare a cash budget and use this tool to estimate the firm's short-term financing needs.
- Know how to prepare pro forma financial statements and use them to estimate the firm's long-term financing needs.
- Understand the basic features of the major forms of financing.
- Understand the basics of financial ratio analysis.

INFORMATION NEEDED TO PREPARE A FINANCIAL PLAN

Information for the financial plan comes from other sections of the business plan and, possibly, from published secondary sources. Included among these are:

- The firm's operating plans and budgets, and the sales forecast that drives them. For example, the sales forecast is the starting point for the cash budget and pro forma (projected) financial statements; the marketing budget provides estimates of product revenues and marketing expenditures; and the operating budget provides data on asset requirements and production schedules.

- Historical financial statements and the cash budgets and pro forma financial statements prepared for previous planning periods. For the existing firm, these sources provide many of the key financial relationships needed to prepare planning documents.

- Published financial data such as *Annual Statement Studies,* published by Robert Morris and Associates, and *The Almanac of Business and Industrial Financial Ratios,* published by Prentice Hall. These references provide key financial statement data for large samples of firms in different size categories from a wide variety of industries. This data can be used as general benchmarks in deciding on financial estimates.

- The firm's operating policies. For example, personnel policies determine the cost of fringe benefits such as holiday and vacation pay; inventory policy establishes appropriate inventory order quantities and purchasing procedures; and credit policy determines the average length of time accounts receivable (credit sales) are outstanding.

FORMS OF FINANCING

Before beginning the financial planning effort, the entrepreneur should be familiar with the major forms of financing used by businesses. In general, there are two major categories of financing: debt and equity; two basic sources of financing: internal and external; and four primary types of financing: seed money, start-up capital, working capital, and long-term financing.

Debt and Equity Capital

Debt financing represents funds borrowed from a creditor under a legally binding, contractual agreement. The contract obligates the borrower (debtor) to repay the obligation plus stipulated interest at some designated future date(s) and to honor all other specified provisions of the contract. While the debt agreement gives the creditor a legally enforceable claim on the firm's cash flow and assets, it also limits the creditor's relationship with the firm. Normally, a creditor has no voice in management; does not share in the firm's earnings beyond contractual payments; and has no ties to the firm beyond the duration of the debt agreement.

Debt financing used by business firms is generally thought of as having either a short-term or long-term maturity. *Short-term debt financing* usually takes the form of trade credit, which is credit extended by suppliers for purchased goods, and short-term loans from financial institutions. Obligations such as these appear on the firm's balance sheet in the current liabilities section.

Long-term debt financing may have maturities as long as 30 or more years and consists of such obligations as a term (installment) loan, mortgage loans for the purchase of real property, and bonds. These obligations appear on the firm's balance sheet in the long-term liability section.

Equity capital represents the ownership interest(s) in the business. It consists of funds invested by or stock purchases of the owner(s) and, if the firm is a going concern, the cash flow that has been retained in the business rather than paid out as dividends to the owner(s). In contrast to creditor's claims, the owner's claim is residual and, unless otherwise specifically agreed, is assumed to continue for the life of the firm. As residual claimant, the owner is entitled to all cash flows and asset values remaining after other claims on the firm have been satisfied.

Internal and External Financing

Internal financing refers to the funds generated by normal operations that remain after creditors and taxes are paid, or to the additional investment (purchase of stock) of existing owners. These funds belong to the owners and are available for reinvestment in the business or for payment to the owners as dividends (withdrawals).

External financing represents debt or equity capital raised outside the firm. External debt financing takes the form of negotiated loans from creditors such as banks or commercial finance companies or debt obligations such as bonds that are sold in the open market. External equity capital is ownership financing raised through the sale of some portion of the ownership interest in the business to an outside investor.

Types of Financing

Seed money is the financing needed to develop and refine the business concept. The development stage of a business firm may be as involved as designing and producing a prototype product or as simple as having enough capital to reach the start-up stage. The amount of seed money depends on the complexity of the development stage and can range from nominal sums to millions of dollars. Unfortunately, seed money must usually be furnished by the entrepreneur. Finding outside investors willing to take the large-scale risk that exists when the firm is nothing more than an embryo is difficult at best.

Start-up capital is the money to get the business going. It usually consists of the short-term working capital to finance initial operations and the long-term capital to obtain physical and human resources. While it may be somewhat easier to find start-up capital than seed money, sparking the interest of an outside investor at this stage is difficult as well. Normally, banks and other lending institutions will not make start-up loans. The degree of risk involved is too high for limited-return loans. Some private investors and possibly a few venture capitalists may furnish start-up capital if:

- There is solid evidence of market acceptance of the concept.
- There is the likelihood of exceptional commercial success.
- There is the promise of large-scale returns on the money invested.
- The entrepreneur and other management are deemed to be capable administrators.

Working capital is short-term financing to support recurring build-ups in current assets (inventory, accounts receivable, and cash). These assets play a large role in the firm's normal operating cycle and are expected to turn themselves into free cash flow at the end of that period. The major suppliers of working capital are typically commercial banks and trade creditors. The latter entities do not supply money per se but extend credit in the form of delayed payment under specified credit terms. Commercial banks and other lending institutions make working-capital loans to qualified businesses. In general, this type of financing is the easiest for a viable firm to obtain.

Long-term financing and/or *growth capital* finances the firm's fixed (plant) asset base. These are the firm's more permanent or long-lived assets, such as buildings and equipment. The financing for fixed assets usually consists of some combination of long-term debt and owner's equity capital. The ability to borrow on a long-term basis requires an adequate base of owner's equity capital, an acceptable credit standing, adequate collateral, and a profitable track record.

Self-financing. Fast-growth companies with healthy profit margins can self-finance the bulk of their planned investments. Whenever higher interest rates make borrowing less attractive, it drives new loans and credit development lower. When gross margins are robust, some companies can self-fund many initiatives through cash flow.

However, exercise caution when making equity contributions of personal assets to your business. Your rights to that funding may take a back seat to the rights of business creditors if your business fails.

GUIDELINE QUESTIONS

The preceding discussions provide potential sources for the information to prepare the firm's financial plan and an overview of forms of financing. By answering the following questions, the entrepreneur will have guidelines for identifying what information is needed and when enough information has been gathered to complete the effort.

■ Given the current stage of the firm's development, what category and amount of financing should be used?

■ In what form, debt or equity capital, will this financing be raised?

■ Given the degree of risk to which the business is exposed, what is the maximum percentage of debt financing that should be used?

■ If debt financing is contemplated, would the proportion of debt existing after the financing violate the maximum?

■ Who can realistically be approached to provide financing?

■ If the firm is an existing business, what has been its financial performance for the past three years as measured by the trend in key ratio values, such as return on investments or sales growth?

■ If the firm is an existing business, what is its current financial position as measured by key indicators, such as cash flow from operations, profit margins, and the debt ratio?

■ If the financial plan is prepared for a new venture, what key balance sheet and income statement relationships exist for the representative business in the firm's industry?

■ What attainable financial goals have been established for the upcoming planning period?

■ What control mechanism will monitor the firm's progress toward meeting established financial goals?

■ What monthly sales are forecast for the next 12 months, and what annual sales are forecast for the next three years?

■ What is the expected percentage breakdown of monthly sales between cash and credit?

■ What is the expected accounts receivable collection pattern?

■ Given the sales forecast, what is the average level of inventory purchases each period?

■ How many days will elapse between the time inventory is purchased and the time payment is made to the supplier?

■ What cash expenses, including taxes and loan repayments, will be incurred and paid each month?

■ What is the minimum cash balance the firm should keep as a precaution against unforeseen emergencies?

■ As shown by the "Cumulative Financing" figure on the cash budget, what amount of seasonal working-capital financing is needed during this planning period?

■ Which financing sources can realistically provide this financing?

■ What are the historical percent-of-sales relationships between those asset and liability accounts that are directly related to sales?

■ What adjustments, if any, to the historical percent-of-sales relationships should be made to reflect expected changes during the planning period?

■ What dividend payouts (owner's withdrawals) are anticipated during the planning period?

■ As shown by the pro forma balance sheet, how much external financing must be raised to support anticipated growth during the planning period?

■ In what form should the required external financing be raised?

■ Which financing sources can realistically provide this financing?

WHEN TO INCLUDE A FINANCIAL PLAN WITH THE BUSINESS PLAN

As is true of the marketing plan, information from the financial plan is a critical component of any convincing business plan. This is true whether a complete business plan is prepared for outside presentation, whether the presentation package is limited to selected business plan information, or whether the financial plan is used internally. A well-prepared financial game plan is important to effective management and it also affirms the entrepreneur's understanding of finances.

SEVEN STEPS TO PREPARING A FINANCIAL PLAN

The seven steps discussed below offer a logical sequence for gathering information and preparing the financial plan.

1. **Financial plan summary.** This optional section *may* be used when the financial plan is prepared for outside presentation. The summary is convenient for the reader and should be no longer than what is needed for him or her to gain an understanding of the plan's major thrust. This can usually be accomplished in a paragraph that identifies the amount(s) and type(s) of financing required.

2. **The situational review.** If the firm is a going concern, this section should contain a review of the firm's financial performance for the past three to five years, or since inception if less than three years. The review should be sufficiently detailed to provide the reader with an understanding of where the firm has been, the progress it has made, and the current financial position from which the business plan departs.

To support the narrative for this section, key financial indicators should be presented in supporting tables or graphs. The historical financial statements (balance sheets, income statements, and cash-flow statements) from which this data is taken should be included in an appendix. Their existence and location can be appropriately referenced in the review. The historical financial statements for A&D Sales and Service, the hypothetical firm used in the sample financial plan (Figure 10-1), are shown as Tables 10-3, 10-4, and 10-5. A list of key financial indicators calculated from these statements is shown as Table 10-2 in the plan. Also, a short tutorial on the basics of ratio analysis and calculating a breakeven point are contained in the Appendix to this chapter.

If the financial plan is prepared for a new venture, the entrepreneur may wish to use this section to present the financial profile of the representative firm in the industry. As used in this context, a *financial profile* is a common-size balance sheet and income statement. These statements show the dollar amounts as percentages of sales or of a specific category total. As noted earlier, this information is readily available from published sources such as the *Annual Statement Studies* and *The Almanac of Business and Industrial Financial Ratios.*

The presentation of a representative financial profile in this section serves three important purposes:

- Gives the entrepreneur guidelines for making estimates for the venture's pro forma statements.
- Provides the reader with a benchmark for evaluating the new venture.

- Offers additional evidence of the quality and depth of the research effort for the financial plan.

3. **Financial goals.** Financial goals are the benchmarks to guide and measure the firm's progress. If a business does not enjoy financial success, it cannot remain viable. This means generating cash flow sufficient to:

- Meet out-of-pocket expenses.
- Service debt obligations.
- Replace assets as they wear out or become technologically obsolete.
- Implement and carry out planned activities.
- Earn a compensatory rate of return for the owner(s).

The financial goals set by the entrepreneur must reflect these fundamental needs. They should be clearly stated, realistic, measurable, and expressed in terms such as these examples:

- **Financial ratio values:** "It is our goal to achieve a return on investment (ROI) of 20% and to increase inventory turnover to five times per year."
- **Percentage growth rates:** "An annual growth in sales, assets, cash flow, and profits of 10% is expected over the three-year planning horizon."
- **Percent profit margins:** "Management intends to increase gross profit margin on the major product line to 48%."
- **Cost and expense relationships:** "The investment in new equipment is expected to reduce labor cost by 25%, or the cost-control program that has been implemented is expected to reduce operating cost by 10%."

4. **Cash-flow planning—the cash budget.** Cash-flow planning is the process of estimating financial resources (money and credit) needed to carry out planned operations and to keep the firm financially viable. Planning horizons usually are divided into short- and long-term time frames. *Long-term cash planning* covers three to five years, and pro forma (projected) statements are used to make estimates. *Short-term cash plans* typically are prepared for one year, and these detailed projections are made through a cash budget.

A *cash budget* is a period-by-period estimate of the amount and timing of the cash inflows (receipts) and outflows (disbursements) associated with planned operations. The budget is usually prepared for one year, which is divided into either monthly or weekly budget intervals. Estimated cash inflows consist of:

- Cash receipts produced by normal operations. This includes the receipts from cash sales plus the collection of accounts receivable (credit sales).

- Cash receipts arising from nonoperating sources, such as the sale of a fixed asset or a tax refund.

Cash outflows consist of:

- Cash disbursements associated with normal operations, including the payments for purchases (accounts payable), payments for cash operating expenses such as wages and salaries, and tax payments.
- Cash disbursements associated with fixed asset purchases, repayment of debt obligations, and the payment of dividends (owner's withdrawals).

A typical format for the cash budget is shown as Table 10-6 in the Appendix to the sample financial plan at the end of this chapter. We now turn our focus to preparation of the cash budget.

While the cash budgeting process begins with a sales forecast, forecast sales are not a part of the actual budget. Rather, forecast sales values serve as reference numbers in the estimation of the cash inflows that sales produce. For most businesses, some portion of sales are cash sales. These estimates are included in the budget as cash inflows. However, most business sales are made on credit, and a credit sale does not become a cash inflow until the outstanding account is actually collected. Projecting the cash inflows from this source requires an estimate of the percentage of outstanding accounts that are collected in a given period. These percentages are referred to as the *receivables collection pattern.*

If the firm is a going concern, the cash sales and the receivables-collection-pattern percentages can be estimated using the firm's past sales and collection experience, adjusted, if necessary, for changes the entrepreneur expects to occur. The estimated cash-sales percentage for a going concern can be established using the following approach:

- First, select a representative sample of historical sales figures for periods that correspond to the periods in the cash budget. For example, if the budget is prepared in monthly intervals, compile monthly historical sales figures.
- Next, identify the dollar amount of sales in each period that were made for cash. Convert these amounts to percentages by dividing the dollar amount of cash sales for each period by total sales for that period. Use this formula:

  Cash Sales Percentage = Cash Sales/Total Sales
- Then, apply the cash-sales percentage for each month to forecast sales for that month to obtain the estimate of cash inflow from cash sales.

The estimated cash inflow from the collection of receivables is determined by applying collection-pattern percentages to the forecast sales values for each period. These percentages represent the proportion of credit sales from a given budget period that is expected to be collected in the current or subsequent budget periods.

For the going concern, collection-pattern percentages can be established using information from the firm's historical sales and receivables records, and a technique known as the *payments pattern approach.* The payments pattern approach uses customer payments data to determine the percentage of a given month's credit sales that have been collected in that month and subsequent months. The following steps outline the approach used to establish collection-pattern percentages. Check business finance textbooks for more details.

- First, select a representative sample of historical credit-sales figures for periods that correspond to those used in the cash budget. For example, the percentages used to estimate collections for June, the first quarter, or the fall holiday season should be derived from their historical counterparts.
- Next, the sample of historical credit sales for each period should be separated into sales by individual customer or by groups of customers of the same size. Sales must be isolated by customer to determine when that customer pays the outstanding account.
- Then trace a given customer's receivable payment in a given month back to the time the sale was made. These payments would then be converted to percentages by dividing the receivable payment in a given month by the amount of the sales in the month the sale was made.
- Next, average the collection percentages in a given month and identify them in terms of the lag time between the month of sale and the month of collection. For example, the collection-pattern percentages may indicate that 50% of the credit sales made in January are collected one month later (in February), 40% are collected two months later (in March), and 10% are collected three months later (in April).
- Finally, apply the historical collection-pattern percentages to forecast sales to obtain the monthly estimates of cash inflow from receivables collections used in the cash budget.

Assume that the management of the XYZ Company, after examining historical credit sales and customer payments on accounts receivable, has decided that June is a representative month. The historical data for the most recent June indicate the following breakdown of credit sales by major customer. The Alex Shop, Avanti, Sunbloc, and Dosta Sports are XYZ's major customers, and credit sales to its remaining small customers are lumped together.

Credit Sales for Major Customers During June

Customer	June Sales
Alex Shop	$15
Avanti	10
Sunbloc	10
Dosta Sports	8
All Other Credit Sales	7
Total Credit Sales for October	$50

Analysis of the accounts receivable ledger below indicated that these customers paid their accounts according to the pattern shown. Since the goal is to associate payments received in a given month with the month in which the associated sale was made, these dollar amounts represent collections on sales originating in June. The collection pattern for June sales is indicated by the percentages in the last row of the table. The 40% figure under the July column ($20/$50) represents the proportion of June credit sales collected one month after the month of sale. Likewise, the 60% figure for August ($30/$50) represents the percentage of credit sales in June collected two months after the month of sale.

Receivables Collection Pattern for June Sales

Customer	July	August
Alex Shop	$ –	$15
Sunblock	10	–
Avanti	10	–
Dosta Sports		8
All Other Credit Sales	___	7
Total Payments	$20	$30
Total Credit Sales During June	$50	
Percentage of June Sales Collected In:	40%	60%

To ensure that June was a representative month, XYZ's management performed the same analysis for several other sample periods. The collection pattern for these samples was about the same as that for June, so the 40% and 60% estimates were used in the cash budget.

If the financial plan is prepared for a new venture, initial cash sales and collection estimates must be derived from the firm's intended sales and credit policies and the information garnered from the entrepreneur's research. For example, the research done on the firm's industry, market, and competitors should produce sufficient information to estimate sales and credit norms for the firm's industry or its competitors. Also, if credit is to be extended to customers, then the adopted credit terms provide some indication of the receivables-collection pattern.

A convenient device for making the calculations associated with cash inflow estimates is the *cash budget worksheet.* A worksheet covering the first four months of the cash budget period for A&D Sales and Service is shown as Table 10-1. Note from the table that while the budget period starts with January 20X4, historical sales for the previous November and December are shown. These months are included because of the lag between the time when a credit sale is made and the time the outstanding receivable is collected.

A&D's cash sales and collection pattern appears in the section of Table 10-1 labeled Collections. The Cash Sales figure indicates that 10% of forecast sales in a given month are expected to be cash sales. For example, the forecast sales figure for January is $54,000 and cash sales for that month are estimated to be $5,400 (.10 × $54,000).

TABLE 10-1
The Cash Budget Worksheet
A&D Sales and Service
for the Pro Forma Period January to April, 20X4

Nov	Dec			Jan	Feb	Mar	Apr
$57,000	$55,000	Projected Sales		$54,000	$56,200	$93,400	$116,700
		Collections:					
		Cash Sales	10%	$ 5,400	$ 5,620	$ 9,340	$ 11,670
		1-Month Lag	60%	33,000	32,400	33,720	56,040
		2-Month Lag	30%	17,100	16,500	16,200	16,860
		Total Cash Inflows		$55,500	$54,520	$59,260	$ 84,570

The 1-Month Lag figure indicates that 60% of the sales in a given month are expected to be collected in the next month. Thus, the $33,000 figure for January represents 60% of credit sales from the previous December ($55,000). Likewise, the 2-Month Lag figure indicates that 30% of the sales in a given month are expected to be collected two months after the month of sales. For example, the

March amount of \$16,200 represents 30% of the forecast sales figure for January of \$54,000.

The total of operating and nonoperating cash inflows for each period are transferred from the worksheet to the cash budget. By transferring only Total Cash Inflows, the cash budget is free of any possible confusion caused by numerical clutter.

Estimating cash outflows is the easier part of the cash budgeting process. Given the short-term nature of the cash budget, most cash outflows are the result of predetermined events and the firm's planned operations. For example, cash outflows for salaries and lease payments are fixed over the short run. Likewise, other cash outflows, such as labor costs or advertising expenditures, are predetermined by management through plans and budgets. The remaining outflows usually can be estimated from historical patterns, established operating policies, or by working backward, estimating expenses that are contingent on other fixed costs. For example, energy costs can be estimated through looking at amount of production being completed, which is determined by forecasted sales.

Similarly, payments for inventory purchases are a function of the firm's purchases or production policy and the credit terms extended by suppliers. Purchasing and production policies, which are normally based on estimated sales in a subsequent month, determine the cost incurred. The credit terms, if any, extended by suppliers determine when the payment should be made for purchases. Other cost items such as telephone and utility expenses, vehicle expenses, and office supplies can be extrapolated from historical trends if the firm is a going concern, or estimated using research information gathered by the entrepreneur if the firm is a new venture. Estimated cash inflows and outflows for A&D Sales and Service are shown on the firm's 20X4 cash budget (see Table 10-6 at the end of this chapter).

The final cash budget issue to be resolved is the size of the *cash contingency balance* (i.e., the minimum cash balance that should be maintained to protect against unforeseen developments and forecasting error). The cash budget primarily identifies the funds needed to support anticipated business activity. The entrepreneur must decide how much additional cash to maintain over and above this amount.

In general, the size of this contingency balance should be sufficient to allow the entrepreneur to sleep worry-free, but yet not so large that the firm is needlessly foregoing earnings on idle funds that could be put to work. While there is no precise answer to the question of what amount is appropriate, the size of the contingency balance should be determined by the stability of the business and its cash-flow pattern. If operations and cash flows are relatively stable and reasonably predictable, only minimal contingency balances are required. If operations and cash flows fluctuate dramatically from period to period, larger balances must be maintained.

Regardless of how proficient the entrepreneur's forecasting skills, cash projections are rarely precise. The firm operates in an uncertain world and forecasts are subject to error. The entrepreneur can, however, deal with uncertainty by allowing for it in the planning and budgeting process. One widely used method is scenario analysis.

As applied to cash budgeting, *scenario analysis* means preparing multiple cash budgets for a given planning period. Each budget reflects a different set of assumptions. Usually, three sets of assumptions are used: best-case scenario, worst-case scenario, and most likely scenario. For example, the worst-case scenario might reflect the entrepreneur's estimate of the least amount of sales, the slowest receivables-collection pattern, and the highest cash outflows that could reasonably be expected to occur. On the other hand, the most likely and best-case scenarios would reflect more optimistic assumptions for key forecast variables.

Consider this example of a cash flow gap: Ted makes custom furniture with two employees. He pays himself and the workers biweekly. He requires 10 percent down with every order; the customer pays the remainder when the furniture is delivered. A recent order is $10,000, with material to complete the job priced at $2,500. Considering salary payouts, Ted will be in a negative cash-flow situation by day 13 of the job, reaching a negative $4,450 just before collecting the balance from the customer. Proper management will help narrow the gap. Any business owner will be on his way to improved cash-flow management if he or she can answer the following questions:

■ How much cash does my business have?

■ How much cash does my business need to operate and when is it needed?

■ Where does my business get its cash and spend its cash?

■ What credit terms will my customer expect and my suppliers extend?

■ How do my income and expenses affect the amount of cash I need to expand my business?

■ What circumstances can possibly occur that could affect cash flow, and how much cash reserves would I be comfortable with to overcome that time period?

Another concept to consider for effective cash-flow management: cash flow and profit are very different concepts. For example, if a retail business is able to buy an item for $1,000 and sell it for

$2,000, it makes a profit of $1,000. But what if the buyer is slow to pay the bill, and five months pass before the bill is paid? Using accrual accounting, the retail business still shows a profit, but what about the bills it has to pay during the five months? It will not have the cash to pay them, despite the profit earned on the sale.

The *what if* focus of scenario analysis provides an estimate of the range of possible outcomes for key decision variables, such as net cash flow and required financing. This information allows the entrepreneur to prepare one set of plans based on the most likely conditions and an alternate set of contingency plans reflecting the extreme cases.

5. **Cash-flow planning—pro forma financial statements.** *Pro forma* in the context of cash planning means projected or "as if" forecast conditions and planned activity had actually occurred. For example, the pro forma income statement or balance sheet is prepared in the same format as its historical counterpart, but the numbers reflect the assumption that planned events had actually occurred. Annual pro forma statements are typically used as part of the firm's long-term cash planning process and often cover a planning horizon of three to five years.

The *pro forma income statement* depicts the effect of planned operations on sales, expenses, and profits. The key variables are forecast sales values for each year in the planning horizon as well as an estimate of the expenses associated with these sales. The *percent-of-sales method* is the most common technique for estimating starting values for expense items. This technique is based on the idea that expenses vary with sales and the relationship between the two can be expressed as a percentage of that key variable.

For example, the Cost of Sales account that appears on the pro forma income statements for A&D Sales and Service was assumed to be 51% of sales (see Table 10-7). Since forecast sales for 20X4 are $1,203,600, the dollar amount for Cost of Sales is estimated to be $613,836 ($1,203,600 × .51). The remaining expense items shown on the pro forma income statements for A&D's three planning periods were calculated in the same manner. For instance, the Wages & Salaries expense figure of $81,250 is 11.2% of the 20X1 Sales figure of $725,000 ($81,250/$725,000) and the Utilities expense figure of $12,805 is 1.77% of Sales ($12,805/$725,000). These percentages were applied to the pro forma 20X4 sales estimate of $1,203,600 to obtain the Wage & Salaries expense estimate of $134,886 ($1,203,600 × .112) and $21,258 ($1,203,600 × .0177) respectively.

To obtain the three profit levels, Gross Profit, Net Operating Income, and Net Income, the appropriate expense amounts are subtracted from Sales or the preceding profit level. A&D's pro forma income statements appear as Table 10-7 in the Appendix to the sample financial plan.

The next task is to determine *percent-of-sales values.* If the financial plan is prepared for an existing business, the percent-of-sales values used to make the initial expense estimates are usually determined from historical financial statement relationships. These percentages can be calculated from the most current income statement, from a statement for a year considered typical, or as averages of statement values for several years. If the initial percentages are not appropriate indicators of expected future conditions, they should be adjusted to reflect the entrepreneur's expectations.

To illustrate percent-of-sales calculations, assume the management of A&D Sales and Service anticipates a 20% annual growth in sales for the planning period 20X4 through 20X6. This translates to projected sales levels of $1,203,600 ($1,003,000 × 1.2), $1,444,320 ($1,203,600 × 1.2), and $1,733,184 ($1,444,320 × 1.2) respectively. Because the cost-control problems that caused profit margins to deteriorate during 20X2 and 20X3 have been corrected, A&D's management thinks that the percent-of-sales figures from those statement years do not accurately indicate the future. As shown by the historical income statements on Table 10-3, the Gross Profit of $355,000 in 20X1 is 49% of sales ($355,000/$275,000). The Gross Profit figures for 20X2 and 20X3 are 43% ($363,750/$850,000) and 41% ($411,230/$1,003,000), respectively.

An investigation shows that the percentage relationships from the 20X1 income statement are representative of what could be accomplished over the planning horizon. These percentages are calculated by dividing each expense category on the 20X1 income statement by the sales figure for that year. The resulting percentages are applied to forecast sales to obtain the expense estimates for A&D's pro forma income statements (see Table 10-7).

If the financial plan is prepared for a new venture, percent-of-sales values for the typical firm in the same industry may be used as starting values or indicators for the venture's pro forma statements. These percentages would be adjusted, where appropriate, to fit the entrepreneur's expectations. Common-size income statements and balance sheets are available from a number of published sources. The most popular are *Annual Statement Studies, The Almanac of Business and Industrial Financial Ratios,* and various industry and trade association publications.

The next financial statement prepared is the *pro forma balance sheet*. A pro forma balance sheet translates the effects of planned operations into projected levels of assets, liabilities, and owner's equity. It provides a rough estimate of the financing that will be required to support long-term plans. The logic behind this key estimate is straightforward. If sales are to grow, then the firm's asset base must grow to accommodate the increase in sales, and these assets must be financed.

For example, sales growth normally requires the purchase of additional inventory, gives rise to more accounts receivable, and often requires additional fixed assets such as buildings, machinery, or equipment. The investment in additional assets requires financing. Some of this financing comes from the cash flow generated by the firm's operations, some from the normal time lag in routine payments such as wages and taxes (accrued liabilities) and, if the firm has established credit with suppliers, some from the credit extended by the firm's suppliers (accounts payable). If these *spontaneous sources,* as they are referred to in finance, are insufficient to finance the growth in sales and assets, then additional debt and/or equity financing beyond spontaneous sources also will be required. This *external financing required (plug figure)* is the focal point of the pro forma balance sheet.

As is true of the pro forma income statement, a pro forma balance sheet can be prepared using assumed relationships between balance sheet items and projected sales. Over long-term planning horizons, most asset, liability, and equity items vary with sales, and the percent-of-sales method provides reasonable approximations for these amounts. Where necessary, historical percent-of-sales relationships can be adjusted to reflect anticipated conditions.

The percent-of-sales method was used to prepare the pro forma balance sheets for A&D's three-year planning horizon. These statements appear as Table 10-8 in the Appendix to the sample financial plan. The historical percentages were calculated by dividing applicable balance sheet values for 20X1 by the 20X1 sales figure. These values, as well as the dollar amounts that are carried forward from the 20X3 balance sheet, are shown below. The values for the asset accounts Vehicles and Equipment shown or the pro forma balance sheets are supplied by management. These amounts reflect management's estimates of the firm's long-range needs. A step-by-step illustration of the preparation of A&D's 20X4 pro forma balance sheet is included on pages 194–197.

Statement Item	Percent-of-Sales or Specified Dollar Amount
Cash	4.5%
Accounts Receivable	8.9%
Inventory	8.3%
Prepaid Expense	0.0%
Accounts Payable	4.2%
Accruals Payable	.8%

Actual 19X3 Account Values

Land	$ 75,000
Buildings	$375,000
Notes Payable	$112,100
Term Loan Payable	$ 60,000
Mortgage Payable	$260,921
Capital Stock	$ 75,000

Specific dollar amounts are transferred from the most recent balance sheet to the pro forma statements because:

- A&D's management thinks that no additional land will be needed to accommodate the anticipated growth. Consequently, the $75,000 in this account is carried forward to all three pro forma balance sheets.
- The combination of the Notes Payable (typically short-term loans from a bank or commercial finance company), Term Loan Payable (installment debt from a financial institution), Mortgage Payable, and Capital Stock accounts represents external financing that was used to finance the firm's 20X3 asset base. Since these assets are essentially carried forward into 20X4, so is the financing that funded them.

The question resolved by the pro forma balance sheet, therefore, is how much additional external financing will be needed to support the additional assets that growth creates. If sales growth creates a need for financing beyond what spontaneous sources are able to provide, the shortfall should be raised through some combination of additional notes payable, long-term debt, or owner's equity capital. The external financing required figure or plug figure shown on the pro forma balance sheet indicates this amount.

A balance sheet contains an important owner's equity account labeled *retained earnings*. In accounting parlance, this account represents that portion of net income earned in a fiscal period that has been retained and reinvested in the business rather than paid out as dividends (owner's withdrawals). The retained earnings value is calculated as (a) the retained earnings from the previous year, plus (b) net income earned in the current year, minus (c) dividends paid (owner's withdrawals).

For example, the Retained Earnings value shown on A&D's 20X5 pro forma balance sheet of $601,937 (see Table 10-8), is calculated as the 20X4 Retained Earnings of $455,840 plus pro forma net income for 20X5 of $146,097 (see Table 10-7). In this case, the full amount of net income was added to the previous retained earnings figure because dividend payments are not anticipated during the planning period.

The *external financing required* figure shown on the pro forma balance sheet is an adjustment value that balances any difference between total assets and the sum of total liabilities and owner's equity. Accounting systems are based on the principle of *double entry bookkeeping*. This means the balance sheet must balance. In other words, total sources of funds (total liabilities and owner's equity) must equal total uses (total assets). Note, for example that the value of Total Assets equals the value of Total Liabilities & Owner's Equity on A&D's historical balance sheets.

On a pro forma balance, however, the growth in sales can result in an increase in total assets that exceeds total liabilities and owner's equity. This occurs when the growth rate is higher than what can be financed by:

- Spontaneous sources: cash flow generated by normal operations as indicated by the increase in the retained earnings account, and the increases in accounts payable and accrued liabilities.
- The value of negotiated, external financing represented by notes payable, long-term debt, and owner's equity that has been carried forward from the last actual balance sheet.

When projected total assets exceed these sources of financing, the plug figure not only brings the balance sheet into balance, but it also represents the estimated additional financing for that period.

The *pro forma balance sheet plug figure* should be interpreted as:

- A negative value (minus figure) indicates that total assets exceed total liabilities and owner's equity. In this case, required financing should come from some combination of external sources (additional notes payable, long-term debt, or owner's equity).
- A zero value indicates that total assets and total liabilities and owner's equity are equal. In this case, spontaneous financing is just sufficient to accommodate the planned increase in sales and assets, and no additional financing is needed.

- A positive value indicates that total liabilities & owner's equity are greater than total assets. In this case, surplus funds exist, because spontaneous financing is more than sufficient to meet planned growth.

Understanding the rationale behind the plug figure is the key to understanding how the pro forma balance sheet is used for long-term cash planning. A&D's pro forma balance sheets illustrate this point. In 20X4, the anticipated 20% growth in sales causes Total Assets to increase to $1,114,842. Total Liabilities & Owner's Equity, however, increase to only $1,024,041 creating a shortfall or Plug Figure of ($90,801). Presumably, this amount would be financed with either additional notes payable, long-term debt, owner's equity, or some combination of these sources. As shown on the 20X5 balance sheet, an additional $11,175 must be raised in the form of external financing. By 20X6, however, the firm's ability to generate spontaneous financing is more than sufficient to meet the expected increases in assets. As shown by the positive Plug Figure, A&D should anticipate a $86,401 funds surplus in that year.

Preparing The Pro Forma Balance Sheet: An Illustration

The steps involved in preparing a pro forma balance sheet can be illustrated using the 20X4 data for A&D Sales and Service.

- **First, gather the appropriate data.** The required data includes percent-of-sales values and, if the statement is prepared for an existing business, those account values that are carried forward. This data for A&D are shown on pages 186–187. As indicated, the percent-of-sales values were calculated using 20X1 data. For example, the Cash percentage, 4.5%, was calculated as Cash from the 20X1 balance sheet of $32,500 divided by Sales from the 20X1 income statement of $725,000. The remaining percent-of-sales values were calculated in the same manner. The account values to be carried forward were, as suggested on pages 186–187, a combination of management judgment and percent-of-sales procedure.
- **Next, calculate and enter asset values.** These amounts represent the addition to the firm's asset base; that is, the assets required to accommodate forecast sales and the financing required to obtain any of these assets. For A&D, the asset values consist of both percent-of-sales calculations and management estimates. The percent-of-sales calculations involve applying the appropriate percentages to the forecast sales fig-

ure. For example, Cash as shown on A&D's 20X4 pro forma balance sheet of $53,594 was calculated as $1,203,600 (forecast sales) × .045. Next, enter management's estimated values. In this case, these include the Land, Buildings, Vehicles, Equipment, and Accumulated Depreciation figures. After the asset values have been entered, the 20X4 pro forma balance sheet would appear as follows:

Assets

Current Assets:	
Cash	$ 54,162
Accounts Receivable	107,120
Inventory	99,899
Prepaid Expenses	0
Total Current Assets	$ 261,181
Fixed (Plant) Assets:	
Land	$ 75,000
Buildings	650,000
Vehicles	132,811
Equipment	83,007
Accumulated Depreciation	(87,157)
Total Fixed Assets	$ 853,660
Total Assets	$1,114,842

- **Then, calculate current liabilities.** For A&D, current liabilities consist of notes payable (which figure is carried forward from the most recent historical balance sheet), the percent-of-sales or spontaneous liability items, accounts payable, and accrued liabilities. The 20X4 Accounts Payable and Accrued Liabilities values, $50,551 and $9,629, are calculated by multiplying the Forecast Sales figure, $1,203,600, by .042 and .008, respectively.
- **Next, enter the remaining carry-forward values.** These items include the Term Loan, Mortgage Payable, and Capital Stock accounts. After entering these values and those for the current liabilities as calculated above, the pro forma balance sheet would appear as shown below.

<u>Assets</u>

Current Assets:	
Cash	$ 54,162
Accounts Receivable	107,120
Inventory	99,899
Prepaid Expenses	0
Total Current Assets	$ 261,181

Fixed (Plant) Assets:	
Land	$ 75,000
Buildings	650,000
Vehicles	132,811
Equipment	83,007
Accumulated Depreciation	(87,157)
Total Fixed Assets	$ 853,660

Total Assets	$1,114,842

<u>Liabilities & Owner's Equity</u>

Current Liabilities:	
Notes Payable	$ 112,100
Accounts Payable	50,551
Accrued Liabilities	9,629
Total Current Liabilities	$ 172,280

Long-Term Liabilities:	
Term Loan Payable	$ 60,000
Mortgage Payable	260,921
Total Long-Term Liabilities	$ 320,921

Total Liabilities	$ 493,201

Owner's Equity:	
Capital Stock	$ 75,000

- **Finally, calculate retained earnings and plug figure.** The retained earnings value for the current year is the Retained Earnings value for the previous year, plus the net income for the current year, minus dividend payments. Thus, the retained earnings figure for the 20X4 pro forma balance sheet, $455,840, is calculated as 20X3 Retained Earnings of $334,692 plus 20X4 Projected Net Income of $121,148. After this value is entered on the pro forma balance sheet, Total Owner's Equity equals $530,840 and Total Liabilities and Owner's Equity equals $1,024,041. Note, however, the Total

Asset value is $1,114,842. That is, Total Assets are $90,801 ($1,114,842 − $1,024,041) larger than Total Liabilities and Owner's Equity, and the balance sheet does not balance. The Plug Figure of ($90,801) as shown on Table 10-8 serves as the balancing amount and, as such, is the amount of external financing that is required.

6. **Capital structure planning.** The term *capital structure* refers to the firm's financing mix—the proportions of debt and owner's equity capital that are used to finance assets. The larger the proportion of debt financing used relative to equity capital, the greater the degree of financial risk to which the firm is exposed. Conversely, the larger the equity capital base, the lower the degree of financial risk and the more secure are the firm's creditors and owners. The base of equity capital is a cushion for the firm's creditors, and it also serves as the foundation from which the firm develops and grows. An adequate equity base also is a necessary precondition for raising debt capital.

As previously discussed, debt financing represents borrowed funds and a legal obligation for the timely repayment of interest and principal. Failure to meet these payments gives the creditor the right to exercise his or her claim on the firm's assets. What's more, if the borrower has personally signed for or endorsed the promissory note evidencing the obligation, the lender also has a claim on the borrower's personal assets. In short, default on a loan could mean losing the business and, possibly, a good deal more. The message for the entrepreneur then, is clear: Debt financing means assuming a serious obligation and it must be used judiciously. This means striking an appropriate balance between the firm's debt- and equity-capital mix.

The appropriate goal for the firm's capital structure mix is to maximize the benefits that debt financing provides while, at the same time, reducing the risk and cost involved. To do so, the entrepreneur must understand and carefully consider the factors that determine how much debt financing the firm can use. These factors are the *ability to borrow, the ability to repay, the business risk, and the quality of assets.* Each is discussed below.

Regardless of the entrepreneur's willingness to assume the obligations and risk of debt financing, their *ability to borrow* is determined by the creditor's willingness to lend. It is important, therefore, that the entrepreneur understand what a given lending institution can and cannot do before approaching it with a financing request. For example, banks and commercial finance institutions are not venture capitalists. The returns from the loans they make are limited to the rate of interest charged. Consequently, these institutions must limit the risk they can assume when making a loan. In general, lenders expect these qualifications to be present before a loan is made:

- **An adequate base of equity capital.** In general, creditors will not make loans when they are supplying more capital to the business, and implicitly assuming more financial risk, than the owner(s). While rules of thumb are usually not reliable gauges for making decisions, banks and other lending institutions often use the 50% debt and 50% equity capital structure rule as a rough guideline for the maximum proportion of debt financing they will supply.

- **A favorable earnings record and good prospects for continued success.** The firm's ability to meet loan obligations depends on the continuing ability to generate positive cash flows.

- **Evidence of good management.** Experienced lenders know that all businesses experience difficult periods, and it is usually good management that separates the survivors from the failures.

- **Adequate collateral where needed.** When the firm's future is uncertain or its earnings record questionable or unproven, the lender will demand adequate collateral to reduce the loss in the event of default. In general, good collateral for a loan is characterized as assets that are legally and physically controllable, are easily liquidated, and can be sold in a market that has relatively stable prices. Examples are financial securities such as bonds, stocks, and savings certificates; land and buildings; and selected equipment, accounts receivable, and inventory.

The primary consideration for both the prospective lender and the entrepreneur is the firm's *ability to repay* its debt obligations. Normally, this is not a problem when the economy is booming and businesses are doing well. The major concern is the firm's ability to generate free cash flow during business downturns. The amount of cash flow that is expected to be available for servicing debt during business downturns should determine the maximum amount of debt the firm can safely carry.

Business risk refers to the uncertainty surrounding the firm's ability to generate net operating income and positive cash flows. Some businesses are, by their very nature, more risky than others. In general, business risk is high when:

- **Sales and earnings are subject to wide fluctuation.** For example, industries characterized by widely fluctuating product demand due to rapid technological change, consumer whims and fads, or changes in general economic conditions have high business risk.

- **The firm's cost structure has a high proportion of fixed costs.** Fixed costs cannot be reduced when the firm experiences a sales downturn.
- **The firm has little or no control over the selling price of its product/service or the cost of the resources it uses.** In these cases, the firm's profit margins are heavily influenced by external factors rather than management control.

If business risk is high, lenders are more cautious about making loans. They expect the firm to have a higher proportion of equity capital in the financing mix and also demand more collateral to support the loan.

The last factor to be examined is *quality of assets*. If all else fails, the creditor first looks to the firm's asset base to satisfy unpaid obligations. In general, the easier it is to liquidate an asset and the greater its liquidation value, the greater its collateral value, and the more likely the lender is to make the loan. All things being equal, firms with tangible assets such as real property or financial securities are able to borrow more than those whose assets consist primarily of intangibles such as copyrights, patents, or growth prospects. Likewise, firms with assets that are highly marketable and free from existing creditor claims are able to borrow more than those having assets that are not.

With regard to collateral, it is important to note that rarely, if ever, will a lender consider good collateral as a substitute for good credit standing and the ability to repay. To the lender, collateral serves as a safety net. It reduces the risk of loss in the event that plans and expectations for future cash flow do not materialize and the borrower defaults. A lender will not, however, make a loan when the likelihood is high that the asset will eventually have to be seized and liquidated. The limited return on a loan does not compensate for the risk, cost, and headaches involved with such a loan.

7. **Financial controls.** Financial controls are an essential component of the entrepreneur's arsenal of management control tools. The budgets that evolve from the firm's operating plans are expressed in numerical terms, and these numbers serve as standards for evaluating actual operations. *Budgeted financial goals* may be expressed as:

- Percentage growth measures, such as a goal of 20% growth in sales, cash flows, and profits.
- Financial ratios, such as a goal to increase the inventory turnover rate to five times per year, or to increase the firm's ROI to 15%.

- Cost measures, such as a goal to reduce operating costs by 10%.
- Cash flows or profits, such as a goal of generating a given dollar amount of free cash flow each year.

Since monitoring actual operations is the basis of managerial control, it is important that the firm's financial information system provides the data needed to do so. It is not enough to have an accounting system that produces basic financial statements. The firm must have a system that has the flexibility to output data in the form needed for control. It is up to the entrepreneur to define what data are needed and in what form they should be produced.

TIPS FOR PREPARING A FINANCIAL PLAN

▬ Cash planning is necessary. The cash plan is an important part of both the business plan and of the entrepreneur's day-to-day management of operations. First, cash planning puts the entrepreneur in touch with the realities of a financing request. This understanding will help clearly identify the amount of financing needed, the purpose for the funds, the length of time the funds are needed, and how the financing will be repaid. These issues are of key concern to the prospective financier. Second, a sound cash plan increases the entrepreneur's credibility. Financiers are acutely aware of the small-firm manager stereotype: overburdened and administratively deficient. This image is substantiated when a financing request is poorly prepared or undocumented. On the other hand, the financier's confidence is bolstered when a sound, well-documented cash plan accompanies the proposal.

▬ Practice by doing. Quality of financial planning and the effectiveness of the cash budget and pro forma statements increase as the entrepreneur gains experience. Financial planning on a regular basis should be a top priority, and the financial plan should clearly indicate the entrepreneur's intention of making it that.

▬ Document underlying assumptions. Improving the art of financial planning requires an after-the-fact understanding of which underlying assumptions were valid and which were not. With this understanding, the entrepreneur knows what to repeat and what to correct. To make after-the-fact comparisons between actual and assumed, underlying assumptions should be carefully documented at the time plans are prepared. It also is important to note that a financial plan lacking documentation will be considered a pipe dream by the intended reader.

▬ Expert assistance may be necessary. Given the importance of this component of the business plan, it *may* be in the entrepreneur's best interest to seek expert assistance, if needed, with either preparing the financial plan or checking the validity of a completed plan. Such assistance can be obtained on a fee basis from a financial consultant or a professional accountant, or possibly at no cost through a consultant from the U.S. Small Business Administration or the local small business development center.

■ **Be a financial manager.** The firm's financial performance and financial condition do not manage themselves. The entrepreneur must understand the financial side of the business, and this understanding must be conveyed to the intended reader of the business plan. A financier is not going to provide financing if there is doubt about the entrepreneur's ability to effectively manage it.

■ **Use debt financing judiciously.** While financiers are naturally cautious about extending too much debt, the entrepreneur should be even more cautious about overuse. He or she has much more to lose. It is important that the financial plan convey this understanding. The most effective method for doing so is a well-documented cash-flow analysis indicating the firm's ability to service its debt.

■ **Save for a rainy day.** Cash flows retained in the business increase owner's equity and provide a margin of safety against periods of adversity. Therefore, it is important that the entrepreneur resist the temptation to take extravagant bonuses and dividends when times are good. A reasonable, clearly stated retention policy improves the firm's liquidity position, provides the financial strength necessary to weather the inevitable business downturn, and sends a strong message to the reader about the entrepeneur's financial judgment.

■ **Closely monitor accounts receivables and inventory.** The entrepreneur's control efforts should focus on the critical areas of the business. For most firms, the level of accounts receivable and inventory are two of the most critical. Experienced businesspeople and financiers are aware of the serious problems that are created by the liberal extension of credit and sloppy or nonexistent inventory control. If credit is to be extended, sound credit standards and the procedure for monitoring receivables should be established and clearly stated in the financial plan. The same holds true if the business will have raw materials and/or finished goods inventory.

A SAMPLE FINANCIAL PLAN

A&D Sales and Service sells and services medium-sized equipment, such as forklifts and backhoes. The firm is incorporated, but 100% of its shares are held by the owner, Alex Duke, and other family members. A&D has been in business for three and one-half years. The company has had an exclusive distributorship for its main product line for a well-known equipment manufacturer for the past two years. The financial statements for the firm's first three years of operation are shown as Tables 10-3, 10-4, and 10-5.

A&D has experienced rapid growth over the past two years, and Mr. Duke is even more optimistic about the next three years. He estimates that sales will increase by 20% per year over this planning horizon. However, as noted in the Situation Review section of the Plan, growth has been a mixed blessing. The benefits from increases in sales and earnings have been offset by the consequences of poor financial management practices.

Alex Duke has recognized these problems and has developed a financial strategy for dealing with them. This strategy is detailed in the firm's business plan [*not shown*], which will be presented to a bank as part of a financing proposal. The major points from A&D's Financial Plan are highlighted below.

FIGURE 10-1 *The Financial Plan for A&D Sales and Service*

Financial Plan Summary

This Financial Plan outlines the financial strategy to effectively manage the firm's anticipated 20% annual growth in sales, cash flows, and earnings over the next three years. As discussed in the Cash Planning sections of this Plan, total financing of $173,850 will be needed. Of this amount, $72,000 (rounded) is needed in the form of a line of credit to support seasonal working-capital needs. The cash budget indicates that the line of credit, if granted, should be repaid in full by July. The remainder of A&D's financing needs, $103,000 (rounded), are long-term. The management of A&D thinks that if the firm's existing term loan is restructured to provide the needed financing, both the existing balance on the term loan and the additional debt will be repaid by 20XX.

Situational Review

The annual financial statements for the first three years of the company's operation are shown as Tables 10-3, 10-4, and 10-5. The key financial indicator values for this three-year period appear below in Table 10-2. (More information on how to effectively utilize financial ratio analysis is provided in the appendix to this chapter.)

FIGURE 10-1 *(continued)*

TABLE 10-2

Key Financial Ratios for the A&D Sales and Service
20X1 Through 20X3

	20X1	20X2	20X3
Sales Growth	—	17%	18%
Net Profit Growth	—	3.7%	0.6%
Net Cash Flow	—	($67,225)	($20,125)
Average Collection Period (in days)	32	59	59
Inventory Turnover (times per year)	6.1	3.4	3.6
Cash Cycle in Days	61.8	136.3	130.5
Total Asset Turnover	1.25	1.02	1.11
Times Interest Earned	18.3	16.4	13.3
Total Debt to Total Assets	53.0%	57.0%	55.0%
Gross Profit Margin	49.0%	42.8%	41.0%
Operating Profit Margin	17.7%	15.9%	13.8%
Net Profit Margin	10.0%	8.9%	7.6%
Return on Investment	18.7%	15.7%	15.3%
Return on Owner's Equity	22.6%	21.0%	18.5%

The data from Table 10-2 shows the rapid growth A&D has enjoyed since gaining exclusive distributorship rights for its primary equipment line in 20X2. Sales increased by 17% in 20X2 and 18% in 20X3 and, as indicated by the historical balance sheets, Table 10-4, total assets grew by 21.9% and 8.3% respectively. These gains have not, however, been free of problems. The absence of effective controls has, as indicated by the Average Collection Period, Inventory Turnover, and Profit Margin ratios, resulted in an unwarranted buildup in accounts receivable and inventory and a deterioration in profit margins. These problems also caused the large cash drain indicated by the 20X2 and 20X3 Net Cash Flow figures. These figures appear on the Statement Of Changes In Cash Position (Table 10-5) for those years.

Management recognizes these problems and has implemented strong corrective measures. As indicated by the firm's financial goals and shown on the pro forma statements for 20X4 through 20X6, the corrective measures should return profit margins, cash flow, inventory, and accounts receivable to a level of efficiency equivalent to that experienced in 20X1.

FIGURE 10-1 *(continued)*

Financial Goals

The management of A&D has instituted control measures designed to accommodate the anticipated 20% growth in sales and assets and, at the same time, produce a sound liquidity position and acceptable profit margins. Specifically, management expects to meet the following financial goals over the next three years.

- Enjoy a 20% growth rate in sales, assets, profits, and cash flows.
- Retire short-term working-capital loans by midyear of the year in which the line of credit is granted.
- Retire the existing balance on the outstanding term loan and the additional funds extended on this loan by the end of 20X6.
- Reduce the average collection period on accounts receivable to 40 days or less.
- Increase inventory turnover to six times per year.
- Restore the gross profit margin and net profit margin to 51% and 10% respectively.
- Reduce the total debt ratio to 40% or less by 20X6.

Cash Flow Planning—The Cash Budget

A&D's 20X4 short-term cash plan was prepared using the cash budget contained in the Appendix to this Plan. The cash-flow data clearly indicate the highly seasonal nature of A&D's business. Operations are at a peak during spring and summer months and slow down dramatically during fall and winter months. As indicated by the largest Cumulative Financing figure on the cash budget, peak activity months create the firm needs of temporary working-capital financing of $71,733.

The effects of A&D's inventory and receivables control measures are best reflected in the pattern of Net Cash Flow figures on the cash budget. As shown by these values, A&D should be in position to repay the full amount of temporary working capital financing by July 20X4. Management proposes, therefore, that the Bank grant A&D a Line Of Credit of $75,000.

Cash Flow Planning—Pro Forma Financial Statements

A&D's long-term financing needs for the planning period 20X4 through 20X6 were estimated using pro forma financial statements. These statements, which are shown as Tables 10-7 and 10-8 in the Appendix to this Plan, were prepared using the percent-of-sales method. The data from these statements reflect these key assumptions:

- Annual sales growth rate of 20%.
- Cost-to-sales and profit-to-sales relationships equivalent to those experienced in 20X1.
- Asset-to-sales and spontaneous-liabilities-to-sales relationships equivalent to those experienced in 20X1.

The decision to use 20X1 financial relationships reflects management's belief that the cost and current asset control measures implemented to correct the cash-flow and profit-margin problems of 20X2 and 20X3 will return operations to 20X1 efficiency. The benefits of this program are reflected on the pro forma statements for 20X4 through 20X6. The income statements reflect the substantial increases in gross profit, operating income, and net profit that should occur as a result of expected sales growth and tighter cost control; and the balance sheets reflect the effects of the reduced average collection period and improved inventory turnover relationships.

To increase the equity capital proportion of the firm's anticipated financing needs, A&D's owners have elected to forgo dividend payments during this period. This decision allows 100% of earnings to be retained in the business and ensures that growth will be financed with a prudent mix of internally generated owner's capital and debt.

As indicated by the plug figures for 20X4 and 20X5, the anticipated growth will create the need for $103,000 ($91,305 + $10,811) of external financing. Management proposes that this amount be borrowed through a restructuring of the existing term loan. This restructuring would require the bank to add the new financing to the existing principal and extend the maturity of the loan for two more years. As indicated by the 20X6 plug figure, the bank can anticipate that A&D will generate surplus funds in an amount sufficient to retire the full amount of the term loan by the end of that year.

Capital Structure Planning

A&D is currently using more debt in its capital structure than the 40% target debt ratio deemed appropriate by management. While the debt ratio will temporarily rise to 52.4% in 20X4 [($493,201 + $90,801)/$1,114,842], if the proposed loan restructuring is done, this condition will be corrected by the end of 20X6. At that time, the combination of a retired term loan, anticipated growth in profits over the planning period, and dividend omissions will produce an equity capital base that will comfortably accommodate the firm's expected growth beyond 20X6.

Financial Controls

Operating costs and inventory and accounts receivable levels will be monitored monthly to ensure that control measures remain effective. The data necessary to do so is produced monthly by the firm's accountant, including:

- Common-size income statements.
- Summary reports on order quantities and item costs.
- Inventory turnover ratio results, and data from a physical inventory taken each quarter.
- Average collection period ratio results and accounts receivable aging reports.

TABLE 10-3
A&D Sales and Service
Annual Income Statements
for the Periods 20X1 Through 20X3

	20X1	20X2	20X3
Net Sales	$725,000	$850,000	$1,003,000
Cost of Sales	370,000	486,250	591,770
Gross Profit	$355,000	$363,750	$ 411,230
Operating Expenses:			
Wages & Salaries	$ 81,250	$ 82,600	$ 98,707
Payroll Taxes	11,250	17,400	20,793
Rent & Lease Expense	13,500	9,000	10,755
Utilities	12,805	13,045	15,589
Insurance	31,750	31,750	37,941
Advertising	15,000	13,750	16,431
Vehicle Expense	50,945	49,790	59,499
Accounting & Legal	6,000	6,000	7,170
Depreciation Expense	4,500	5,000	5,975
Total Operating Expenses	$227,000	$228,335	$ 272,860
Net Operating Income	$128,000	$135,415	$ 138,370
Less: Interest Expense	7,000	8,250	10,400
Net Income Before Taxes	$121,000	$127,165	$ 127,970
Less: Income Taxes	48,373	51,833	52,160
Net Income	$ 72,628	$ 75,333	$ 75,809

TABLE 10-4
A&D Sales and Service
Annual Balance Sheets
for the Periods 20X1 Through 20X3

Assets	20X1	20X2	20X3
Current Assets:			
Cash	$ 32,500	$ 7,500	$ 8,850
Accounts Receivable	64,445	136,500	161,070
Inventory	60,418	140,313	165,569
Prepaid Expenses	0	12,500	14,750
Total Current Assets	$157,363	$296,813	$350,239
Fixed (Plant) Assets:			
Land	$ 75,000	$ 75,000	$ 75,000
Buildings	375,000	375,000	375,000
Vehicles	80,000	96,500	125,100
Equipment	50,000	48,500	46,000
Accumulated Depreciation	(52,500)	(57,500)	(67,850)
Total Fixed Assets	$527,500	$537,500	$553,250
Total Assets	$684,863	$834,313	$903,489
Liabilities & Owner's Equity			
Current Liabilities:			
Notes Payable	$ 52,775	$ 95,000	$112,100
Accounts Payable	30,500	42,280	49,890
Accrued Liabilities	5,700	9,225	10,886
Total Current Liabilities	$ 88,975	$146,505	$172,876
Long-Term Liabilities:			
Term Loan Payable	$ 0	$ 64,170	$ 60,000
Mortgage Payable	275,000	265,000	260,921
Total Long-Term Liabilities	$275,000	$329,170	$320,921
Total Liabilities	$363,975	$475,675	$493,797
Owner's Equity:			
Capital Stock	$ 75,000	$ 75,000	$ 75,000
Retained Earnings	245,888	283,638	334,692
Total Owner's Equity	$320,888	$358,638	$409,692
Total Liabilities & Owner's Equity	$684,863	$834,313	$903,489

TABLE 10-5
A&D Sales and Service
Statement of Changes in Cash Position
for the Periods 20X2 and 20X3

	20X2	20X3
Cash Flow From Operating Activities:		
Net Income	$75,333	$75,809
Plus: Depreciation Expense	5,000	5,975
Less: Increase in Receivables	(72,055)	(24,570)
Less: Increase in Inventory	(79,895)	(25,256)
Less: Increase in Prepaids	(12,500)	(2,250)
Plus: Increase in Payables	11,780	7,610
Plus: Increase in Accruals	3,525	1,661
Total Cash Flow From Operating Activities	($68,813)	$38,979
Cash Flow From Investing Activities:		
Less: Increase in Fixed Assets	($15,000)	($26,100)
Cash Flow From Financing Activities:		
Plus: Increase in Term Loan Payable	$64,170	($ 4,170)
Less: Decrease in Mortgage Payable	(10,000)	(4,079)
Less: Dividends Paid	(37,583)	(24,754)
Total Cash Flows From Financing Activities	$16,588	($33,003)
Net Cash Flow	($67,225)	($20,125)

TABLE 10-6
A&D Sales and Service
The Cash Budget
for Pro Forma 20X4

	Jan	Feb	Mar	Apr	May
Total Cash Inflows	$ 55,500	$54,520	$59,260	$ 84,570	$110,570
Cash Outflows:					
Payment for Purchases	$ 49,890	$30,525	$29,986	$ 32,593	$ 46,514
Wages & Salaries	11,239	11,239	11,239	11,239	11,239
Payroll Taxes	1,556	1,556	1,556	1,556	1,556
Rent & Leases	1,868	1,868	1,868	1,868	1,868
Utilities	1,772	1,772	1,772	1,772	1,772
Insurance	13,177	0	0	13,177	0
Advertising	6,226	0	0	6,226	0
Vehicle Expense	7,048	7,048	7,048	7,048	7,048
Accounting & Legal	830	830	830	830	830
Income Taxes	20,191	0	0	20,191	0
Total Cash Outflows	$113,797	$54,838	$54,299	$ 96,500	$ 70,826
Net Cash Flow	$(58,297)	$ (318)	$ 4,961	$(11,930)	$ 39,744
Plus: Beg. Cash Balance	8,850	15,000	15,000	15,000	15,000
Total Cash This Month	(49,447)	14,682	19,961	3,071	54,744
Less: Minimum Balance	15,000	15,000	15,000	15,000	15,000
Financing Needed					
(Repaid)	64,447	318	(4,961)	11,929	(39,744)
Cumulative Financing	64,447	64,765	59,804	71,733	31,989
Excess Cash	0	0	0	0	0
Ending Cash Balance	$ 15,000	$15,000	$15,000	$15,000	$ 15,000

June	July	Aug	Sept	Oct	Nov	Dec
$125,490	$145,390	$155,400	$141,100	$120,200	$84,900	$63,100
$ 60,814	$ 69,020	$ 79,965	$ 85,470	$ 77,605	$66,110	$46,695
11,239	11,239	11,239	11,239	11,239	11,239	11,239
1,556	1,556	1,556	1,556	1,556	1,556	1,556
1,868	1,868	1,868	1,868	1,868	1,868	1,868
1,772	1,772	1,772	1,772	1,772	1,772	1,772
0	13,177	0	0	13,177	0	0
0	6,226	0	0	6,226	0	0
7,048	7,048	7,048	7,048	7,048	7,048	7,048
830	830	830	830	830	830	830
0	20,191	0	0	20,191	0	0
$ 85,126	$132,926	$104,277	$109,783	$141,512	$90,423	$71,008

TABLE 10-6 *(continued)*

$ 40,364	$ 12,464	$ 51,123	$ 31,318	$(21,312)	$(5,523)	$(7,908)
15,000	23,375	35,989	87,112	118,430	97,119	91,597
55,364	35,839	87,112	118,430	97,119	91,597	83,690
15,000	15,000	15,000	15,000	15,000	15,000	15,000
(31,989)	0	0	0	0	0	0
0	0	0	0	0	0	0
8,375	20,839	72,112	103,430	82,119	76,597	68,690
$ 23,375	$ 35,989	$ 87,112	$118,430	$ 97,119	$91,597	$83,690

TABLE 10-7
A&D Sales and Service
Pro Forma Income Statements
for the Planning Periods 20X4 Through 20X6

	20X4	20X5	20X6
Net Sales	$1,203,600	$1,444,320	$1,733,184
Cost of Sales	613,836	736,603	883,924
Gross Profit	$ 589,764	$ 707,717	$ 849,260
Operating Expenses:			
Wages & Salaries	$ 134,886	$ 161,863	$ 194,236
Payroll Taxes	18,677	22,412	26,894
Rent & Lease Expense	22,412	26,894	32,273
Utilities	21,258	25,510	30,612
Insurance	52,709	63,251	75,902
Advertising	24,902	29,882	35,859
Vehicle Expense	84,576	101,491	121,789
Accounting & Legal	9,961	11,953	14,344
Depreciation Expense	7,471	8,965	10,758
Total Operating Expenses	$ 376,851	$ 452,222	$ 542,666
Net Operating Income	$ 212,913	$ 255,495	$ 306,594
Less: Interest Expense	11,000	12,000	13,000
Net Income Before Taxes	$ 201,913	$ 243,495	$ 293,594
Less: Income Taxes	80,765	97,398	117,438
Net Income	$ 121,148	$ 146,097	$ 176,157

TABLE 10-8
A&D Sales and Service
Pro Forma Balance Sheets
for the Planning Periods 20X4 Through 20X6

Assets	20X4	20X5	20X6
Current Assets:			
Cash	$ 54,162	$ 64,994	$ 77,993
Accounts Receivable	107,120	128,544	154,253
Inventory	99,899	119,879	143,854
Prepaid Expenses	0	0	0
Total Current Assets	$ 261,181	$ 313,417	$ 376,101
Fixed (Plant) Assets:			
Land	$ 75,000	$ 75,000	$75,000
Buildings	650,000	650,000	650,000
Vehicles	132,811	159,373	191,248
Equipment	83,007	99,608	119,530
Accumulated Depreciation	(87,157)	(104,589)	(125,506)
Total Fixed Assets	$ 853,660	$ 879,392	$ 910,272
Total Assets	$1,114,842	$1,192,809	$1,286,373
Liabilities & Owner's Equity			
Current Liabilities:			
Notes Payable	$ 112,100	$ 112,100	$ 112,100
Accounts Payable	50,551	60,661	72,794
Accrued Liabilities	9,629	11,555	13,626
Total Current Liabilities	$ 172,280	$ 184,316	$ 198,759
Long-Term Liabilities:			
Term Loan Payable	$ 60,000	$ 60,000	$ 60,000
Mortgage Payable	260,921	260,921	260,921
Total Long-Term Liabilities	$ 320,921	$ 320,921	$ 320,921
Total Liabilities	$ 493,201	$ 505,237	$ 519,680
Owner's Equity:			
Capital Stock	$ 75,000	$ 75,000	$ 75,000
Retained Earnings	455,840	601,937	778,094
Total Owner's Equity	$ 530,840	$ 676,937	$ 853,094
Total Liabilities & Owner's Equity	$1,024,041	$1,181,634	$1,372,774
External Financing Required (Plug Figure)	$ (90,801)	$ (11,175)	$ 86,401

An Internet resource listed at the back of this book offers worksheets and other tools for managing financial statements.

CHAPTER PERSPECTIVE

The financial plan contains estimates of the types and amounts of financing that are needed to carry out the firm's strategic and operating plans. Components include the summary and situational review, financial goals, cash-flow planning, capital structure planning, and financial controls. The primary tools of financial planning are the cash budget and pro forma financial statements. Financial ratios are tools used to analyze the firm's financial statements to evaluate its financial position and performance.

Small-business owners can also turn to the web as a day-to-day resource for financial management. For example, you don't always have to pay an accountant for information. That accountant's firm may be posting valuable tips on the web. Seek it out. Here's what you can find on many financial sites:

▬ Affordable software. Many accounting web sites offer basic accounting system software. This strategy may be particularly good for a small, but rapidly growing firm. Rent the software during growth until you know which software will be best to suit your needs.

▬ Remote-access records. Some accounting firms offer their clients access to current and past financial data and reports via a web-based site with login access. You get access to what you need, when you need it.

In addition, consultants through the SBDC, Small Business Development Centers, run by the Small Business Administration, can often review and assess financial statements for free or for a nominal fee. Find a center near you through *www.sba.gov*.

Appendix to Chapter 10
What Is Financial Ratio Analysis?

INTRODUCTION

Balance sheets and income statements can offer insight into a firm's financial condition and financial performance. The trick is knowing how to extract the appropriate information. Financial ratio analysis is, when properly used, the tool that provides this information. This Appendix offers a brief tutorial on ratio analysis.

A *financial ratio* is simply a fraction that compares a balance sheet or income statement numerator value to a balance sheet or income statement denominator value. The result is an index number or percentage that, when compared to some meaningful standard, can provide insights into some aspect of the firm's financial performance. The keys to effective ratio analysis are:

▬ Choosing financial relationships that provide useful information about the important facets of a firm's financial operations.

▬ Focusing on trends of ratio values rather than single-period measures.

The following discussion uses data from the A&D Sales and Service financial statements for 20X1, 20X2, and 20X3 to illustrate how several of the more common ratios are calculated and interpreted. The ratio results are shown on Table 10-2. (See page 203.)

WIDELY USED FINANCIAL RATIOS
Average Collection Period (ACP)

This ratio, also known as the *average days credit sales outstanding,* is calculated as (accounts receivable × 365)/net sales. It measures the average number of days that credit sales are uncollected. In general, the shorter the time period (the lower the number of days) that credit sales remain outstanding, the shorter the time period that the firm's scarce cash is tied up. A rising trend of ACP values signals a red flag. Failure to control credit and investment in accounts receivable has caused the demise of many firms, both small and large. Note from Table 10-2 (see page 203) that the ACPs for A&D are sending ominous danger signals. This ratio almost doubled from 32 days [($64,445 × 365)/$725,000] in 20X1 to 59 days in 20X3.

Inventory Turnover

This ratio is calculated as (cost of sales/inventory) and represents the average number of times per year that inventory is purchased (or produced) and converted to sales. All other things being equal, the higher the turnover figure the more liquid and more profitable the firm. Table 10-2 indicates that A&D's inventory turnover rate slowed dramatically from 6.1 ($370,000/$60,418) in 20X1, to 3.6 ($194,500/$165,569) in 20X3. This is a signal that inventory is building to excessive levels and severely straining the firm's liquidity.

Total Asset Turnover

This ratio measures the productivity of the firm's asset base. *Productivity* in this case means the dollars of sales that the firm is able to generate for each dollar invested in assets. All other things being equal, the greater the number of sales dollars generated per dollar of assets, the more productive the asset base, and the greater the firm's earning power. The ratio is calculated as (sales/total assets). Table 10-2 indicates a slight decline in A&D's asset turnover from 1.25 in 20X1 ($725,000/$684,863) to 1.11 in 20X3.

Times Interest Earned

This ratio is most often calculated as (net operating income/interest expense). The calculation represents the dollars of operating income that are generated to meet interest obligations. The more dollars of earnings a firm generates relative to its interest charges, the bigger the financial cushion and the lower the financial risk. A declining trend is a sign of increasing financial risk and a clear danger signal. The decline in A&D's ratio to 13.3 in 20X3 ($138,370/$10,400), while a matter of concern, is not as yet so low as to be alarming.

Debt Ratio

This ratio is calculated as total debt/total liabilities and owner's equity (or total assets). It measures the percentage of the firm's total financing (assets) that has been provided by creditors relative to the percentage invested by the owners. When the firm's asset base is financed with increasing amounts of debt (higher debt-ratio values), mandatory payment obligations are increased and the degree of financial risk to which the firm is exposed increases. The slight increase in A&D's debt ratio to 55% in 20X3 ($493,797/$903,489) is not as yet alarming.

Gross Profit Margin

This ratio is calculated as (gross profit/net sales). The resulting percentage indicates the proportion of each sales dollar remaining after cost of sales has been deducted. For example, A&D's gross profit margin of 41.0% in 20X3 ($411,230/$1,003,000) means that $.41 out of each dollar of sales remained after $.59 was deducted as cost of sales. This was an alarming decline from the 49% figure for 20X1.

Net Operating Profit Margin

This ratio is calculated as net operating income divided by net sales and reflects the amount of each sales dollar remaining after all normal costs of operations have been deducted. A&D experienced a decline in the operating profit margin from 17.7% in 20X1 ($128,000/$725,000) to 13.8% in 20X3. As suggested by the gross profit margin results, the decline in net operating income margin is attributed to increasing cost of sales.

Net Profit Margin

This ratio is calculated as net income divided by sales. It measures the percentage of each sales dollar remaining after all costs of operations, including taxes, have been deducted from sales. On a continuing basis, the net profit margin on sales represents the long-run capacity of the firm to generate dividends for the owner (owner's withdrawals) and produce satisfactory returns on the owner's investment. For A&D, the decline in net profit margin to 7.6% ($75,809/$1,003,000) in 20X3 is further evidence of the alarming increase in the overall cost of operations.

Return On Investment (ROI)

This ratio is most often calculated as net operating income divided by total assets. The resulting percentage reflects the dollars of income earned per dollar invested in assets. The larger the ROI, the more efficiently operations and assets (as well as the capital used to finance them) have been utilized, and the more profitable the firm. The decline in A&D's ratio to 15.3% in 20X3 ($138,370/$903,489) reflects the deterioration of profit margins and the excessive buildup of accounts receivable and inventory.

Return on Owner's Equity (ROE)

This ratio is calculated as net income divided by owner's equity. It measures the dollars of net income earned per dollar of owner's investment. The result of this calculation reflects the efficiency with which the owner's invested capital has been employed. Generating a satisfactory return is the reason an entrepreneur risks time, effort, and capital. If the firm does not generate a fair rate of return for the owners, then there is no economic justification for its existence. The decline in A&D's ROE to 18.5% in 20X3 ($75,809/$409,692) is additional evidence of the deterioration in profitability.

A Note on Ratios, the Cash Cycle, and Working Capital

Working capital refers to the investment (dollars tied up) in cash, accounts receivable, and inventory that is required to conduct normal operations, as well as the financing that is used to support operations. Many businesses experience seasonal increases in operations (production or purchasing and sales) and, as a result, a temporary buildup in cash, accounts receivable, and inventory. This buildup creates the need for temporary financing.

The length of time required for the asset buildup to be converted into cash is referred to as the firm's *working-capital cycle* or *cash cycle*. It is determined by the average number of days required to turn over its inventory, plus the average number of days required to collect its receivables (ACP) (see page 213), minus the average number of days the firm is able to defer payment for its purchases and operating expenses (average payment period, or APP). Assuming A&D's suppliers offer 30-day credit terms, the number of days in its cash cycle in 20X3 is determined as follows:

$$
\begin{aligned}
\text{Cash Cycle} &= \text{(Inventory Turnover in Days + ACP)} - \text{APP} \\
&= (365/3.6 + 59) - 30 \\
&= 130 \text{ days}
\end{aligned}
$$

The number of days in the cash cycle, along with an estimate of the firm's average expenditures per day, can be used to make a rough estimate of the amount of financing needed to support seasonal working capital. To obtain this estimate, first calculate the firm's average cash expenditures per day by dividing cash operating expenses (operating expenses – depreciation expense) by 365. For A&D, average cash expenditures per day in 20X3 is determined as follows:

$$
\begin{aligned}
\text{Average Expenditures per Day} &= \text{Cash Operating Expenses}/365 \\
&= \$266,885/365 \\
&= \$731
\end{aligned}
$$

Second, calculate the amount of working-capital financing required as the number of days in the cash cycle times the average cash expenditure per day. For A&D, this is:

$$\text{Required Financing} = \text{Cash Cycle} \quad \text{Average Expenditure per Day}$$
$$= 130 \times \$731$$
$$= \$95,030$$

BREAKEVEN ANALYSIS

As used in business, the term *breakeven* most often refers to the level of operations at which sales revenue and total cost are equal. That is, the level of operations that produces net operating income of zero. The breakeven point can be calculated in terms of either units or sales revenue, and it can be calculated for a single product, a product line, or for overall operations.

To make the breakeven calculation, the firm's cost structure as shown on its income statement must be reclassified into variable and fixed costs. *Variable costs* are those that vary directly and proportionately with changes in sales. For example, XYZ Company manufactures bicycles, and one of the parts it uses has a variable cost of $10. If one bicycle is produced and sold, one part is used and total variable cost is $10. If sales double (increase by 100%), the cost of the component also doubles, to $20. If 100 units are produced and sold, total variable cost is $1,000.

Fixed costs are those that remain the same when sales vary. For example, the rent on the building is fixed regardless of the number of units produced and sold. Given the firm's variable and fixed costs, the breakeven point is calculated as follows:

$$\text{Breakeven (Units)} = \frac{\text{Fixed Cost}}{\text{Selling Price per Unit} - \text{Variable Cost per Unit}}$$

$$\text{Breakeven (Sales)} = \frac{\text{Fixed Cost}}{(\text{Sales} - \text{Variable Cost})/\text{Sales}}$$

These simple calculations can be illustrated using the abbreviated, hypothetical income statement for the XYZ Company shown below. Assume the firm's financial officer has analyzed the cost data and indicated variable and fixed cost with a (V) or (F).

Sales (30,000 units @ $300/unit)	$3,000,000
Cost of Sales (V)	1,500,000
Gross Profit	$1,500,000
Operating Expenses:	
Wages & Payroll Taxes (V)	$ 380,000
Salaries & Payroll Taxes (F)	190,000
Rent (F)	100,000

Utilities (V)	40,000
Maintenance & Repairs (V)	50,000
Advertising (V)	30,000
Depreciation (F)	20,000
Total Operating Expenses	$ 810,000
Net Operating Income	$ 690,000

These expenses can be reclassified using an alternative format known as the *contribution format income statement*. This format is useful for a wide range of decisions, including the breakeven calculations. As shown below, sales minus variable cost, the denominator of the breakeven calculation, is referred to as *contribution margin*. It is the amount remaining from sales after deducting those costs that vary directly with sales.

	Total	Per Unit
Sales (10,000 units @ $300/unit)	$3,000,000	$300
Less: Variable Costs		
Cost of Sales	$1,500,000	
Wages & Payroll Taxes	380,000	
Utilities (V)	40,000	
Maintenance & Repairs (V)	50,000	
Advertising (V)	30,000	
Total Variable Cost	$2,000,000	$200
Contribution Margin	$1,000,000	$100
Less: Fixed Costs		
Salaries & Payroll Taxes (F)	190,000	
Rent (F)	100,000	
Depreciation (F)	20,000	
Total Fixed Cost	$ 310,000	
Net Operating Income	$ 690,000	

Given these data and calculating the contribution margin ratio of 33.333% (contribution margin of $1,000,000/sales of $3,000,000), the unit and sales breakeven points can be calculated as follows:

$$\text{Breakeven (Units)} = \frac{\text{Fixed Costs}}{\text{Selling Price per Unit} - \text{Variable Cost per Unit}}$$

$$= \frac{\$310}{\$300 - 200}$$

$$= 3{,}100 \text{ units}$$

$$\text{Breakeven (Sales)} = \frac{\$310{,}000}{.33333} = \$930{,}000$$

Financing Fundamentals and Financing Sources

INTRODUCTION

A continuous supply of internally generated funds and externally raised financing is the lifeblood of any business. All too often, however, the entrepreneur finds financiers apathetic to the needs of the firm. This even can occur when the firm is an acceptable candidate for a loan or investment. While it is virtually impossible to improve the financing opportunities for an unqualified business, the odds of doing so for the qualified and nearly qualified firm can be improved by approaching the appropriate financier with the proper information.

After studying the material in this chapter, you will:
- Understand the fundamentals of risk and return.
- Know what information is needed before approaching a financier.
- Understand the basic differences between the major types of financial institutions.
- Know which financier to approach for a particular type of financing.

INFORMATION NEEDS

Before approaching a prospective financier, the entrepreneur should have this knowledge:
- Clear understanding of the firm's financing needs and repayment capabilities.
- Clear understanding of the risk/return trade-off the financing request represents for the prospective financier.
- Basic understanding of the nature of the prospective financier's business.

As stressed in previous chapters, the quest for financing begins with a sound financial plan and financing proposal. The proposal should effectively summarize the important supporting information from the financial plan. It should identify:
- The specific amount, type, and maturity of the financing needed.
- How the financing will be used.

■ When and how it will be repaid.

■ What collateral is available, if needed, to secure a loan.

An effective financing proposal also must convince the financier of a successful transaction. This means a financing arrangement that is equally beneficial to the firm and the financier. Success to the firm means financing that will be profitably invested and will generate compensatory cash flows. To the financier, success means the funds will be in the hands of a competent, scrupulous entrepreneur, with an acceptable level of risk.

An effective financing proposal also must be presented to the appropriate financier. Financial institutions are not monolithic. They differ in such fundamentals as basic purpose, the types of loans or investments made, lending and investing policies, and attitude toward risk. Given these differences, it is important for the entrepreneur to approach the financier who provides the type of financing needed and who is in a position to accept the degree of risk exposure the financing represents. Selecting an appropriate financier sends an important message: The entrepreneur understands the financier's business and major concerns about the financing request.

THE FUNDAMENTALS OF RISK AND RETURN

Both creditors and equity investors have an important stake in any business they finance. They can avoid loss and earn a compensatory rate of return only if the firm is successful. This means financiers are exposed to the same risks as the firm and the entrepreneur. If the financing proposal is to convince the prospective financier that his or her risk exposure will be minimized, the entrepreneur must first understand the risk/return trade-off the firm represents.

What Is Risk?

Risk is the uncertainty about the occurrence of some future event or, alternatively, the possibility that a less than desirable outcome can occur. Risk is present whenever future events, such as the amount of sales or cash flow the firm will generate, are not completely predictable. The risks faced by the typical business firm fall into two basic categories: business risk and financial risk.

Business risk. Business risk is the underlying uncertainty to which any business firm is exposed regardless of how it is financed. It consists of the unpredictable fluctuations in sales and operating cash flows that result from changes in the general level of business and economic activity (such as a recession or rapidly escalating interest rates), from changing conditions within the firm's particular market (such as demographic changes or a competitor's development of a superior product), and from changes in the degree of competition faced by the firm. The more sensitive the firm's sales, costs, and prices are to these influences, the greater the degree of business risk to which it is exposed. As business risk increases, there is greater uncertainty over the firm's ability to generate a level of sales and cash flows that will fully compensate creditors and owners.

Financial risk. Debt financing means borrowing money that is to be repaid over a period of time, usually with interest. It can be short-term (payment in less than a year) or long-term (more than a year). Financial risk arises through debt financing. Borrowing creates a legal obligation to repay the creditor and to meet the terms and stipulations of the underlying debt contract. If the firm defaults on its debt obligations, creditors can bring suit and, if necessary, put the firm into bankruptcy. Bankruptcy generally means that all parties with a vested interest in the firm lose. The entrepreneur and other equity investors, however, will lose the most. In the typical bankruptcy proceeding, creditors end up with less than the amount of their claims and the owner(s) end up with nothing. What's more, if the entrepreneur or other owners have personally endorsed the note, their personal assets also are at risk.

While debt obligations are certain, there is no guarantee that the firm will generate sufficient cash flow to meet them. This uncertainty is known as financial risk. The greater the amount of debt financing used by the firm, the greater the financial risk and the greater the risk exposure of creditors, equity investors, and the entrepreneur.

For the entrepreneur seeking financing, three important points on risk should be kept in mind.

■ There is no financial risk associated with equity financing. As opposed to debt, equity financing does not involve mandatory payments and poses no threat of insolvency. It provides a financial cushion for creditors and reduces some of the impact of the firm's business risk.

■ Firms with a high degree of business risk should avoid using large amounts of debt financing. Heaping financial risk on business risk magnifies the firm's overall risk exposure and endangers the position of all parties with a vested interest in the firm. Substantial business risk means large fluctuations in sales and cash flow and an increased likelihood that fixed financial obligations cannot be paid.

■ The major concerns of any financier are loss of the amount loaned or invested and failure to earn a rate of return that is consistent with the risk assumed. The creditor wants assurances that cash flows will be sufficient to repay principal and make the required interest payments. The equity investor wants assurances that the firm will generate the earning power to pay dividends and provide capital appreciation. To make a convincing case for the firm's ability to do so, the entrepreneur must provide credible cash-flow projections. The financier must be convinced that the numbers from the cash budget and pro forma statements will materialize.

Rate of Return

A positive relationship between risk and return is a fundamental financial principle governing the dealings of all rational financial decision-makers. That is, the greater the degree of risk associated with a financial venture, the greater the rate of return the rational individual would require as compensation. Financiers rigidly adhere to this principle. Lending institutions, such as commercial banks, earn returns that are limited to the amount of interest charged on loans. The reality of limited returns forces banks to assume limited risk in their lending and investing activities. On the other hand, the venture capitalist making an equity investment in a firm knowingly assumes a large degree of calculated risk. This risk is accepted when the firm offers the promise of large-scale returns.

To send the correct message to the financier, the entrepreneur must do his or her homework and identify the appropriate financier to approach given the firm's particular needs and circumstances.

MAJOR SOURCES OF FINANCING
Credit Extended by Suppliers

Suppliers are usually eager to establish an ongoing, profitable credit relationship if:

- the firm is not overextended;
- obligations are met on time; and
- the firm is properly managed.

The credit extended on inventory purchases by a firm's suppliers is an important form of financing for virtually all businesses. Known as *trade credit,* this form of financing does not involve the direct loan of funds. Rather, trade credit involves delayed payment for goods or services received. The time period for which payment can be delayed depends on the credit terms offered by the supplier. Normally, this will be at least 30 days, and there may be the additional advantage of a discounted invoice price for early payment.

Trade credit also is an important form of financing because it is spontaneous or self-generating. Once the firm establishes a creditworthy relationship with its supplier, the amount of credit used automatically rises and falls with changes in the volume of operations. No negotiation or conscious decision on the part of management is necessary. Accounts payable swells automatically when purchases are made and shrinks when payment is made. During the interim credit period, the firm is receiving an interest-free loan of the goods or services purchased.

The most important determinants of the entrepreneur's ability to obtain trade credit are integrity and the practice of sound business and financial management. Given the importance of trade credit to most businesses, it is in the firm's best interest to jealously safeguard this source of financing.

Commercial Banks

The next most important source of financing is from commercial banks. Since the business practices of banks are typical of many lending institutions, the entrepreneur should understand the mechanics of banking.

Essentially, a bank is a privately owned dealer in debt. The primary reason for a bank's existence is accepting deposits and lending. The majority of the funds used to make loans comes from deposits to checking accounts and savings accounts. To a much lesser extent, banks also receive working capital through occasional borrowing from other lenders, borrowing through the sale of debt securities in public markets, or from the proceeds of the sale of common stock.

Commercial banks receive the right to operate as a regulated, depository institution through a charter granted by either the state or federal government. With the charter goes the responsibility to help service the financial needs of the community in which it operates. Equally important, the charter obligates the bank to submit to supervision of its lending and investing activities and to abide by banking regulations.

Factors influencing loans. A banker's choice of which loans and investments to make is influenced by three primary considerations:
- The type of deposits held by the bank.
- Expectations of bank examiners
- Risk/return perspective of its officers.

A bank, like other businesses, attempts to synchronize its cash inflows and outflows. It does this by confining the maturity of its loans and investments to a time period that is roughly equivalent to the deposits it holds. If the bulk of a bank's depositors hold checking accounts, it must guard against the instability and sudden cash drains that are characteristics of these short-term balances. It does so by concentrating on short-term loans and investments. On the other hand, savings deposits tend to be more stable, thereby allowing the bank to make longer-term loans and investments.

The types of loans and investments banks make also are influenced by the possible adverse reaction of examiners to its dealings. As a regulated institution, a bank's portfolio of loans and investments is subject to periodic scrutiny by examiners from the various bank regulatory agencies. If deviations from regulations or acceptable policy are found, the bank is subject to penalties that can range from reprimands to the loss of its charter. The intimidation caused by the jaundiced eye of a bank examiner goes a long way toward explaining the conservative attitude of bankers.

A banker's attitude toward risk also is tempered by a realistic view of the risk/return trade-off inherent in the choice between lending versus investing in low-risk securities. When the typical bank officer considers making a business loan, he or she naturally compares this use of funds to the return that could be earned on a low-risk investment such as U.S. Treasury bills, notes, or bonds. The comparison is made by estimating the degree of default risk inherent in the loan relative to that of the low-risk investment alternative. To compensate for the higher degree of risk associated with the loan, the banker charges an interest rate higher than what could be earned on the low-risk investment.

Theoretically, a bank could make loans with any degree of risk by simply charging a sufficiently high interest rate. In the real world, this is not possible. There are state usury laws that set upper limits on the rate of interest that can be charged. In the case of high-risk loans, a bank could not legally charge a compensatory interest rate. Since interest returns are limited, a bank is not in position to suffer the potential loss on high-risk loans. The bank carefully screens borrowers and requires loans to be fully collateralized by all but their most credit-worthy borrowers.

Types of bank loans. Although banks today make a greater variety of loans and are more aggressive lenders than in the past, their most important loans are still short-term working-capital loans and intermediate-term installment loans to businesses. To a lesser extent, most banks make mortgage loans and asset-backed loans, and larger banks often have industrial leasing departments.

■ **Working-capital loans:** Working-capital or self-liquidating loans are typically made for less than one year, may be either unsecured or secured depending on the borrower's credit capability, and are used to finance temporary increases in working capital (inventory, accounts receivable, and liquid cash balances). These loans take two basic forms: a secured or unsecured transaction loan or a secured or unsecured line of credit. The *transaction loan* is a single-payment financing arrangement that is evidenced by a promissory note. The single payment covers either the loan principal if the interest has been deducted from the original proceeds of the loan (a discounted loan), or principal and interest if it has not. Accounts receivable or inventory often are used as collateral to support working-capital loans.

The maturity on a transaction loan is usually between one and six months but can range up to slightly less than one year. While it is possible for a good customer of the bank to pay the interest at maturity and renegotiate (roll over) the loan for another maturity period, commercial banks generally require short-term business borrowers to "clean up" loans for a 30- to 60-day period each year. This simply means that the borrower must be free from short-term bank debt for that period. The purpose of this requirement is to ensure that the borrower is not attempting to meet long-term financing needs by manipulating lower-cost, short-term bank credit.

A *line of credit* is a commitment from a bank to provide a creditworthy business customer with a specified maximum amount (credit line) of short-term financing for a specified time period. This time period, which is intended to coincide with the firm's working-capital cycle, may extend 11 months. As is true of the transaction loan, the bank expects the credit line to be cleaned up once per year. The firm can draw down or borrow against its credit line as needed, and the borrowing can be paid back at any time during the credit period. Interest is paid only on the funds actually used and only for the time period they were used. Banks may require a fee for granting the credit line and will typically impose a compensating balance requirement on both transaction loans and lines of credit. A *compensating balance provision* requires the borrowing firm to maintain a minimum average monthly balance in its checking account that is equal to a specified percentage of the loan amount.

■ **Accounts receivable financing:** When receivables are used as collateral for a bank loan, the agreement has four important components: (a) the specific receivables that will be accepted as collateral, (b) percentage of the face value of accepted receivables that will be advanced, (c) the notification system that will be used, and (d) the interest rate that will be charged.

The collateral value of a receivable depends on its quality. The quality of a receivable is a function of the credit standing of the borrowing firm's customers, the borrowing firm's returns and allowances record, the credit standing of the borrowing firm, and the integrity of the borrowing firm's management. In general, the higher the overall quality of the receivables pledged, the lower the firm's sales-returns-

and-allowances experience. And the higher the firm's standing as a customer of the lending institution, the larger the percentage of the face value of the receivables that will be advanced.

If the borrowing firm is perceived as an acceptable credit risk, the loan against pledged receivables normally will be made on a non-notification basis. This means the borrowing firm's customers are not notified of the firm's financing arrangement, and payment of the outstanding receivable is made in the normal manner. Under the non-notification arrangement, the lender must either trust that the borrower will remit customer payments as they are received or conduct periodic audits of the borrower's books to ensure that loan payments are made. Under a notification arrangement, the customers whose accounts have been used as collateral are instructed to make payments directly to the lender.

The interest rate charged depends on the borrower's credit standing and the quality of the receivables pledged as collateral. In addition to the interest rate, the bank adds an administrative charge of from 1% to 3% of the face value of the loan.

■ **Inventory financing:** The process surrounding inventory financing is, in principle, the same as that of pledging receivables. The bank may use a general lien to secure all of the borrower's inventory holdings or a lien pinpointing the specific items of inventory that will be used as collateral. A common method for the bank to maintain physical and legal control over finished goods inventory is to have the items stored in a bonded warehouse. In this case, the bank retains the warehouse receipt and releases goods only when sales are made or the loan is repaid.

For inventory to qualify as collateral, it must have characteristics that allow the bank to easily maintain legal and physical control and to repossess and liquidate in the event of borrower default. For example, nonperishable raw materials sold in active markets at reasonably stable prices, such as grain, crude oil, or integrated electronic circuits, are desirable collateral. Finished goods that are easily identified, readily sold if the borrower defaults, and easily monitored or controlled by the lender, such as automobiles or major appliances, are also considered suitable collateral. On the other hand, work-in-process inventory does not make suitable collateral.

As is true of loans on accounts receivable, the interest rate charged on inventory loans depends on the borrower's credit standing and the value of the inventory. Also, if the inventory loan takes the form of warehouse receipt financing, there will be warehouse and administrative fees added to the interest rate. This latter cost can range from 1% to 3% of the amount of the loan.

■ **Term loans:** A term loan is the title given by lenders to traditional business installment debt. It is defined as amortized, intermediate-term financing covering a period from one to ten years. As its name implies, the typical term loan is repayable in equal installments over the life of the contract. Occasionally, one of three alternative repayment arrangements may be negotiated: a balloon payment, a recapture clause, or an equity sweetener.

A *balloon payment* is a large, lump-sum payment made at the end of the loan period. The payment compensates the bank for payments that are either smaller than normal or limited in number during the loan period. A *recapture clause* is an agreement that requires the borrower to repay the loan more quickly if the firm's sales and cash flows, or some other performance measure, exceed expectations. An *equity sweetener* is a stock option that grants the lender, in addition to the fixed interest charges on the loan, the right to purchase a specified number of shares of common stock in the borrower's firm at an attractive price. The sweetener is designed to compensate the lender for higher risk exposure by raising the potential return above that provided by the fixed interest charges. Equity sweeteners are not, however, normally used by commercial banks.

Term loans usually are secured with a lien on the asset(s) purchased with the loan proceeds, with other fixed assets of the firm, or with personal assets of the owner. The maturity of the term loan usually is tied to the expected service life of the purchased asset. The assets most commonly financed through term loans are equipment, real property, and the permanent component of working capital.

The interest charged on term loans depends on the borrowing firm's credit standing and the asset(s) pledged as collateral. Because a term loan has a longer maturity than a working-capital loan, the interest rate will be scaled up from the bank's prime rate. In addition to the interest cost, the borrower may also be required to maintain a compensating balance and to pay service charges to cover the costs of credit analysis, loan origination fees, or legal fees.

■ **Revolving credit loans:** An offshoot of the standard term loan is a revolving credit loan. This arrangement combines the features of a term loan with those of a line of credit. Under a revolving credit agreement, the lender makes a legally binding commitment to (a) loan the firm a specified amount of funds over an extended time period (usually up to five years), and (b) to continue lending up to the stated amount until the end of the agreement period. As is the case with a line of credit, a revolving credit loan provides the flexibility to use financing only when it is needed. In addition, as the original principal is reduced through repayment, the firm can re-borrow up to the stated maximum. For this privilege, the firm pays a commitment fee on the unused portion of the loan in addition to the established interest rate on the financing.

■ **Mortgage loans:** Mortgage lending is financing provided by a security interest in real property (land and buildings). Mortgage loans are virtually identical in character to term loans. They are amortized over the life of the agreement, but because of the nature of the asset involved, usually have longer maturities than term loans. Mortgage loans made to businesses are similar to those made for residential financing except for slightly shorter maturities and the use of quarterly rather than monthly installments.

The rate of interest charged on commercial mortgage financing depends on the characteristics of the secured property and the credit standing of the borrower. If the borrowing firm has acceptable credit and the property has multiple uses, is high in resale value, and is easily liquidated, interest rates will be competitive with the general level of mortgage rates. Conversely, the weaker the borrowing firm's credit standing and the more specialized the asset, the greater the risk to the bank and the higher the interest rate demanded.

■ **Asset-backed loans:** Equipment that is owned free of any liens and is in good operating order may serve as collateral for *extended-term financing*. The financing arrangement used normally is a term loan with a maturity tied to the remaining service life of the asset. As is true of all secured financing, the bank takes a security interest in the pledged asset and limits the amount of the loan to some percentage of its estimated liquidation value. The liquidation value is often established by a qualified appraiser who must be hired and paid by the borrowing firm. The term *asset-backed loan* also is used at times to refer to a receivables- or inventory-backed business loan.

Loan policies on asset-backed loans vary among lenders. While some commercial finance companies rely solely on the value of the pledged asset to judge the merits of the loan, commercial banks require the borrower to have an acceptable credit standing and the ability to generate adequate cash flow. The interest rate charged by banks on asset-backed loans is normally equivalent to that charged on term loans. In addition to the interest cost, the borrower may also be required to maintain a compensating balance and to pay service charges to cover the costs of credit analysis, loan origination fees, or legal fees.

■ **Leasing:** Leasing business assets is simply a specialized, alternative form of debt financing in which the lessee (the firm) enters into a binding contract to rent the services of the asset in question from the lessor (the financial institution). The usual procedure is for the lessor to buy the asset required by the lessee and lease its services according to the terms of the lease agreement. This arrangement allows virtually any business asset, including specialized plant or equipment items, to be leased. The lessor remains the legal owner of the asset and is entitled to depreciation and any other tax benefits that ownership provides. If the lease agreement meets IRS guidelines, the lease payments made by the lessee are tax deductible.

Business leases fall into two basic categories, operating leases and financial leases. An *operating lease* is a short-term transaction akin to property rental. In contrast, the *financial lease* has a longer maturity and is equivalent in principle to a secured term loan. The financial lease may not be canceled without full payment of all amortized costs to the lessor bank. The lease amortization process provides the bank with the return of principal and the expected interest yield (rate of return) on that principal.

▬ **Consider a simplified bank loan package.** Small businesses *may* have the opportunity to use a simplified, low-cost, loan application package when applying for bank financing. This loan package, known as the Business Credit Information Package (BCIP), was developed by an association of bank lending officers known as Robert Morris Associates (RMA) in conjunction with the American Institute of Certified Public Accountants (AICPA). It is designed to provide the lender with minimum accounting, financial, and business information through a questionnaire the borrower completes and an accountant's Compilation Report. The latter item summarizes and compares key financial statement data for the last two years. These data are used in place of the requirement that the borrower supply costly CPA-audited financial statements. To use the BCIP, two conditions must be met:

1. The bank must agree in writing through a Request Letter issued to the borrower to accept the financial data prepared in the BCIP format along with the accountant's Compilation Report in lieu of audited financial statements.
2. The borrower must agree in advance to complete the RMA Business Borrower Questionnaire.

▬ **Another option—a business credit card—can be a risky form of financing.** Entrepreneurs are accustomed to thinking of credit cards as last-resort financing for their businesses. However, depending on economic factors, cash from credit cards can seem inexpensive. Some introductory cards offer rates at 2.9 percent or lower. But should you bypass your banker? If you're vigilant about reading the fine print on the credit card offers and make payments diligently that are above the minimum, business credit cards can be a potential source of cheap capital. Although many individuals have difficulty controlling spending with credit cards, resulting in a downward spiral of financial debt, for those who use them wisely (and do not necessarily require a huge sum of money), they can be an efficient source of short-term capital. There is little paperwork to complete, and in some cases you can obtain instant approval. If a business owner simply needs some funds to bridge a slow cycle in the business, the actual interest paid will be relatively little, especially for a card with an introductory rate. In addition, points earned on most major credit cards can also be leveraged toward travel costs or other business expenses.

Commercial Finance Companies

Commercial finance companies are the business-world counterpart to consumer finance companies. They are lending institutions that make secured working-capital and plant and equipment loans to businesses. Like commercial banks, typical commercial finance companies also engage in industrial leasing. Unlike banks, finance companies are not permitted to hold checking account and savings account deposits. They are strictly lending institutions that raise loan funds through the sale of debt securities in the open market. Because commercial finance companies must cover the cost of the funds raised and because they lend to higher-risk borrowers, the interest rates charged on loans are generally higher than those charged by banks.

Factors

Factors are specialized financial institutions that provide receivables-backed financing to businesses through a process known as *factoring.* As opposed to pledging accounts receivable to secure a loan, factoring involves the outright sale of the firm's accounts to the factor. That is, the title to the receivables passes from the firm to the factor. The procedures, conditions, and charges associated with factoring are detailed in a factoring agreement contract.

A factor performs three important functions for the borrowing firm. These are financing, credit analysis and collection, and risk bearing.

■ **Financing:** The factor provides funds for the firm through either of two methods: maturity factoring or advance (discount) factoring. Under *maturity factoring,* the firm receives payment for receivables sold to the factor on the date the customer's payment is received or on the last day of the credit period, whichever comes first. When *advance factoring* is used, the factor advances funds to the firm when the customer is invoiced for the purchase.

■ **Credit analysis and collection:** As a normal part of the factoring arrangement, the factor evaluates the credit standing of each of the firm's customers. The receivables of customers not meeting the factor's credit standards are not accepted for purchase. In contrast, the factor takes full responsibility for collecting all amounts due and for any bad-debt loss on all accepted receivables. By performing the credit and collection functions, the factor relieves the firm of the cost and responsibility of each.

■ **Risk bearing:** Most factoring arrangements call for the purchase of receivables on a *nonrecourse* basis. This means that the factor must absorb the loss of a default on the accepted receivable. The nonrecourse arrangement passes title as well as default risk to the factor and also relieves the firm of bad-debt expense.

Equipment Manufacturers

Often manufacturers of business equipment make secured financing available to customers directly or through a financing subsidiary known as a captive financing company. The financing may take the form of a standard term loan or an operating or financial lease. Providing financing for its customers has important advantages for a manufacturer and for its buyers.

First, by offering financing, the manufacturer increases product sales. Second, since financing a sale produces both the profit margin on the sale and the interest return on the financing, the manufacturer can sell and extend credit to higher-risk customers. This may allow for marginally qualified firms to obtain financing that would otherwise not be available from a traditional financial institution. Also, dealing directly with a manufacturer makes it convenient for the buyer to combine the purchasing and financing functions in one transaction. Last, this type of financing usually requires a smaller down payment and the debt or lease contract will have less stringent covenants than a bank loan.

Savings and Loan Associations

A savings and loan (S&L) is a depository or thrift institution that raises funds by offering savings deposits and certificates to the public. Prior to the deregulation of commercial banks and S&Ls in the 1980s, S&L lending was limited to residential mortgages and to temporary financing for the initial stages of residential and commercial construction. While these loans still make up the bulk of the typical S&L's portfolio, most S&Ls have expanded their lending to include extended-term mortgage financing to businesses.

Life Insurance Companies

The typical life insurance company has sizable amounts of premium dollars that must be invested on a regular basis. For the most part, these dollars are in marketable, fixed-income securities (such as corporate bonds), industrial leases, and fixed-rate term and mortgage loans to businesses.

Term loans and commercial mortgage loans made by insurance companies differ in two important respects from those of commercial banks. First, insurance companies are willing to offer longer maturities than typically offered by banks. Second, the loan agreement for both loans either prohibit prepayments or the early retirement of principal, or impose a stiff penalty for the right to do so.

A recent trend in insurance company lending has been the addition of an *equity sweetener* or *equity kicker* on riskier business loans. This provision justifies assuming higher risk by allowing the lender to share in the earnings success of the firm as well as to enjoy the interest yield on the loan. The sweetener may take several different forms. Common among these are a share of the earnings from the commercial real estate that has been financed; warrants that allow the lender to buy stock in the borrowing firm at an attractive price; or, in the case of bond financing, a conversion privilege that allows the lender to exchange the bond for a specified number of shares of common stock in the borrowing firm.

Independent Leasing Companies
The largest volume of business lease financing is provided by specialized financial institutions known as independent or industrial leasing companies. These firms specialize in operating or financial leases. The former group of lessors concentrates on leases of standardized, short-lived business assets such as computers and commercial vehicles. The latter group writes financial leases for the specialized asset needs of the lessee.

Industrial Development Financing
Virtually all state and local governments have economic development agencies charged with the responsibility to promote business and economic growth in their jurisdictions. The incentives offered to qualifying businesses take a variety of forms, including financing assistance at attractive rates. Most often, this financing comes in the form of packaged loans in which the agency, local lenders such as commercial banks, and possibly the U.S. Small Business Administration participate.

The purpose of the financing is to create jobs by inducing businesses to locate in the area and to encourage local businesses to make job-creating investments in new plants and equipment. Some agencies also offer leases on land, buildings, or other plant assets on attractive terms. While the bulk of the financing made available has an intermediate-term or long-term maturity, some agencies also provide working-capital financing.

U.S. Small Business Administration

The U.S. Small Business Administration (SBA) is an independent government agency created by Congress in 1953 to provide assistance to small businesses. This assistance takes a variety of forms, including these activities:

■ Providing free business and technical counseling for small-firm entrepreneurs.

■ Providing educational services to small firm entrepreneurs through workshops, seminars, and topical literature on small business management.

■ Ensuring that small firms receive an equitable proportion of government purchases, contracts, and subcontracts.

■ Licensing, regulating, and lending to small business investment companies (SBICs).

■ Helping qualified small business entrepreneurs obtain financing. To be eligible for financing assistance, a business firm must first meet the criteria set by the SBA's definition of "small firm," which varies by industry.

SBA loan activity takes a variety of forms, including disaster loans, economic injury loans, surety bond guarantees, loans to economic development agencies, loans to SBICs, and direct and participating small business loans. Since its inception, the SBA has maintained a direct business loan program. The purpose of the program is to fulfill its intended role as "lender of last resort" for qualified firms unable to raise funds in the private sector. Financing for this program comes directly from Congress through budget appropriations. The amount of these appropriations has declined steadily since 1980, however, and the SBA has increasingly removed itself from direct lending.

In recent years, the SBA/bank loan participation program has been the primary focus of the agency's financing activity. Under this program, the small firm entrepreneur applies directly to and negotiates with a local commercial bank interested in making such loans. If the applicant is deemed an acceptable credit risk by both the bank and the SBA, the bank makes the loan and the SBA guarantees up to 90% of the outstanding principal for the lending bank. Participating loans made to finance permanent working capital and equipment are in the form of standard term loans with maturities of up to approximately seven years. Principal and interest on these loans are amortized through monthly or quarterly installments. Guaranteed loans for the purchase or construction of real property may have maturities of up to 20 years.

The outlook has improved for women who want to enter the business world. Since 1992 loans backed by the SBA to women business owners have almost tripled. To help women get started, the SBA offers a loan prequalification program that helps them through the application process.

However, women may not be aware of financing sources backed by the SBA. In 1999 the SBA's Small Business Investment Company Program invested $4.2 billion in small firms, but only $55 million or one percent went to women-owned businesses.

The SBA is also trying to increase federal contracting opportunities for women. In 1998, women-owned companies won $4 billion worth of federal contracts. The agency has signed contracts with ten federal agencies and 15 business and professional women's organizations to help promote SBA programs.

Venture Capitalists

Financing from a venture capitalist may be available for businesses offering attractive growth potential or the start-up firm with an innovation that has large-scale profit potential. Venture capitalists fall into two broad categories: (a) those licensed and regulated by the federal government through the U.S. Small Business Administration and (b) nonregulated firms. The former group consists of small business investment companies (SBICs) and the latter are venture-capital companies or simply venture capitalists.

Venture-capital companies have a wide variety of operating philosophies and investment interests. They do, however, share a common trait: The firms are made up of professional business investors who are attracted to higher-risk business opportunities offering potentially large-scale sales and profits. To obtain returns sufficient to compensate for both the inevitable losses associated with high-risk investment and the extended time period over which financing is committed, the venture capitalist must share in the earnings success of a highly promising firm through an equity interest. This financing usually will have the following characteristics:

▬ The first equity financing for the firm outside that of the original owners. While venture capital will cost the firm a substantial share of its common stock, the amount will usually be less than 50% of the ownership of the firm.

▬ Provided in the form of intermediate or gap financing that fills the firm's needs until the firm is taken public.

▬ Accompanied by the expectation of (a) providing management assistance to the target firm in those areas of identified administra-

tive weakness, and (b) taking an active voice in the firm's policy-
and decision-making process.

■ Provided with the expectation of earning large returns. Depending
on the financing stage at which funds are provided, the typical venture
capitalist limits investments to opportunities that provide expected
returns from 25% to better than 50% per annum on invested funds.

■ Expected to require a lengthy investment period. Successful venture-capital investments often take five to seven years to come to
fruition.

■ Accompanied by an agreement specifying a clearly defined
opportunity for the venture capitalist to exit the target firm. Normally
a venture capitalist expects to liquidate his or her investment through
an agreement to repurchase his or her shares at a specified date, to go
public with a common stock offering, or to seek a suitable merger
partner interested in buying the target firm.

Some venture capital firms specialize by industry, and have a preference regarding the stage of development to be financed and regarding
the size of the deal itself. For information on trends, see the National
Venture Capital Association (NVCA) web site at *www.nvca.org*.

SBICs fall into two broad categories: captive firms whose management and operating policies are dictated by a parent organization,
which is often a bank or insurance company; and privately owned and
operated noncaptive firms. As is true with venture capitalists in general, SBICs have divergent philosophies and operating policies. Some
specialize in equity financing, while others provide debt financing in
several different forms. This latter group of SBICs is the richest source
of debt financing for small businesses outside commercial banks.

In general, SBICs do not confine their financing to specific
industries or business types. Rather, an SBIC tends to focus on businesses whose opportunities are consistent with its particular investment policy. SBICs specializing in equity or equity-participation
financing lean toward small firms with extraordinary growth potential. Those specializing in debt financing favor stable firms with a
history of profitability. To qualify for SBIC consideration, the target
firm must meet the SBA's definition of a "small business." Beyond
meeting these standards, the individual SBIC has total discretion
over whether financing is extended, and over the specific terms and
features of the financing agreement.

The Internet is giving venture capitalists a new source of investment
possibilities. The dot.coms have proved intriguing, so intriguing that
venture capital firms have been launched by Sun Microsystems,

Oracle, Dell, and Nokia. These established technology firms are trying to deal with start-ups that could become serious competitors. The solution: befriend the startup with an early investment. For example, in about 15 percent of the companies it acquires, Cisco has contributed seed funding. Two hundred and thirty-five venture capital firms raised $34.7 billion in 2007 according to Thomson Financial and the National Venture Capital Association (NVCA).

Despite the outlay, web-based startups have been extremely risky, even for a venture capitalist. Consider this web start-up gone sour:

In the mid-1990s, an Internet-based gourmet meal server in California sold its idea to traditional lenders and to venture capitalist Oracle. But about three years later, it declared bankruptcy, filing more than $2 million in debts. The bankruptcy decision came after 15 Silicon Valley venture capital firms rejected the company's financing requests.

There's no doubt the Net has powered an economic surge, but many startups are slipping. In turn, venture capitalists are losing patience with dot.coms that don't produce profits. Some experts say Net companies went public too early. Others predict that most Internet companies will never make a profit.

Publicly held Internet companies need to be aware that a depressed stock price can cause employees to leave, investors to moan, and can severely limit a company's ability to raise more money in the market. These firms will find that raising capital will be nearly impossible because investors expect to see profits. The market capitalization of some Internet firms is so low that large institutional funds won't purchase their stocks. Many of the Internet companies may experience this cycle: raise money; spend money; issue an IPO; stock dips below opening price; employees defect; shift business emphasis; and finally, develop an exit plan.

Angels

Another source of financing is through private investors. Commonly called "angels," these people are seeking new business investments for a host of personal and economic reasons. Frequently angels are other business owners. Some angels will even serve on your board of directors or offer business and investment advice. How does an angel compare with a venture capitalist? In a five-year period, angels may want a return that's three to five times their original investment. A venture capital firm is seeking a return of five to ten times the original outlay. There are "angel networks" to help business owners find new sources of cash. Consider these sources:

■ Capital Network, Austin, Texas, (512) 305-0640.
■ Small Business Administration angel network: *www.sba.gov/services/financialassistance*

Crowdfunding is an innovation wherein funds are raised from a large number of potential backers. In the credit mode, prospective borrowers are matched with nonbank potential investors who are willing to accept the credit terms (e.g., *Prosper.com*). Kickstarter is a very popular site with limited rules, but one can still not fundraise for charity, offer prohibited items, or offer financial incentives, like equity or repayment. In the equity mode (e.g., Equitynet), investors will receive equity for their investments. Regardless, the funding portals are essentially designed to introduce the parties to each other. The Jumpstart Our Business Startups (JOBS) Act of 2012 specifically provides for the solicitation of funds from investors to raise funds from up to 2,000 shareholders before registration with the Securities and Exchange Commission (SEC) is triggered. The JOBS Act does not just apply to microcap companies, incidentally, but to firms raising capital more generally.

Initial Public Offering—First Sale of Stock to the Public

Some companies have seemingly become "overnight successes" by going public. These companies have decided to sell ownership shares of the business to the general public. In addition to the lure of additional working capital, an initial public offering can make a business more attractive to potential and existing employees if stock programs are available. Words of caution: Any sale of securities is complex and subject to state and federal regulation. Businesses who sell stock are required to disclose material information about the company to investors and must prohibit misrepresentation and fraud in the sale of stock.

Franchise

Another common form of financing is through franchising. It's been one of the fastest growing areas of new business development during the past 15 years. You can enter into a product and trade name franchise or a business format franchise. For the franchisee, it's a way to reduce the risks of a new business by getting involved with an established product or concept. For the franchisor, it's a method of expanding your business faster, by sharing costs, risks, and rewards with franchisees.

The following chart may give business owners or startups another view of the various sources of financing. The chart is organized according to the general age of the business and whether the financing is for long- or short-term needs.

STARTUP BUSINESS

Primary Sources

Long-term financing	Short-term financing
Personal financing	Personal financing
Insider (family, friends, associates)	Insider financing
Angels	Credit cards
Equity financing	Credit unions
Leasing	Trade credit
SBA loans	SBA loans
Credit unions	Banks

Secondary Sources

Long-term financing	Short-term financing
Business alliances	SBA loans
SBA loans	Consumer finance
Venture capital	Commercial finance companies
Small Business Investment Companies	State and local public financing
State and local public financing	
Franchising	

GROWING/MATURE BUSINESS

Primary Sources

Long-term financing	Short-term financing
Debt financing	Debt financing
Equity financing	Asset-based financing
Bank lending	Bank lending (lines of credit)
Leasing	Trade credit
Business alliances	Factoring
Venture capital	Commercial finance companies
Limited private offerings	
SBA loans	

Secondary Sources

Long-term financing	Short-term financing
Initial public offering	SBA loans
Franchising	State and local public financing
Angels	SBA loan guarantee program
SBA loans	
Insurance companies	
Commercial finance companies	
Employee Stock Ownership Plans	
SBA International Loan Program	

More information about each of these financing sources can be found on-line. The search engine www.lycos.com is an excellent source of business information.

TIPS FOR NEGOTIATING FINANCING

■ Be realistic. Seed money and start-up money is difficult if not impossible to find. Rarely will a traditional lending institution provide this type of financing. The risk is too great for the limited return received. Convincing a lender to make a loan for these purposes normally requires pledging virtually risk-free collateral, such as government bonds or bank savings certificates in an amount greater than the amount of the loan. Venture capitalists do make seed money or start-up financing available, but only when the opportunity promises large-scale returns.

■ Be cautious. The decision to enter into a debt agreement must not be taken lightly, or made in haste. Entering into a debt contract places the firm's assets at risk and, most likely, risks the personal assets of the entrepreneur. Also, the entrepreneur not only suffers the constant pressure of the possibility of loss from loan default, but he or she also must live with the terms and covenants of the loan contract. Before making the decision, the entrepreneur must objectively evaluate and justify every detail of the debt contract.

■ Be prepared for the negotiation process. To effectively and convincingly discuss the firm's financing needs with a financier, the entrepreneur must be certain of the needs. If he or she has not personally justified the risk/return trade-off associated with the financing, the financing request cannot be articulated and justified to the prospective financier.

■ Consider all relevant factors. While cost is an important consideration in any financing decision, nonfinancial factors also should be carefully evaluated. To remain viable, the firm must be sufficiently flexible to alter operations or change directions as needed. The entrepreneur must be certain, therefore, that restrictive provisions in a financial contract do not eliminate this advantage. Also, a strong relationship with a financial institution that serves the firm's financing needs may be more important in the long run than minor cost savings from another institution. Factors such as control and oversight must also be considered, as various sources of funding will differ in the amount of input demanded.

■ Shop carefully. Financial institutions vary in their operating philosophy and policies. It is in the entrepreneur's best interest to shop for financing. This is especially true if a financing request is rejected. A financing proposal that one financier finds unsuitable may be acceptable to another.

■ Learn from rejection. The rejection of a financing proposal can often be a valuable educational experience for the entrepreneur. As in athletics, the important lessons are learned from losing, not winning. A rejection should be carefully evaluated to identify the under-lying reasons and to determine whether the problem can be remedied. Often, the financier with whom the negotiation has been conducted is willing to discuss the reasons for the rejection. This knowledge may make the difference between success or failure on the next attempt and may provide valuable insight into operational weaknesses that require the entrepreneur's attention.

TIPS FROM THE LENDER'S PERSPECTIVE

Obtaining financing can be complex, frustrating, and intimidating since more than 50 percent of small-business loan applications are turned down.

Put yourself in the best possible light with lenders by following these tips:

■ **Be organized and prepared.** You must prepare to convince your lender that you are a good credit risk. Do your homework. Calculate the amount of money you will need, why it's needed, and how it will be repaid. The best way to do this is with a convincing business plan.

■ **Ensure that your credit history is accurate.** Make sure the credit-reporting agencies are presenting accurate details about your business. You should also gather letters of recommendation as an indicator of your credit status.

■ **Be sure to present adequate collateral.** As always, the lender will focus on your assets and those of other principals of your company.

■ **Invest in yourself to inspire confidence.** Show the lender that you are confident about your business or business idea. They want to know that your commitment is strong enough to invest your own money as well. You also need to understand that a lender will not finance all of your business.

■ **Prepare a strong business plan.** A convincing business plan is an important assessment tool for lenders. Not only will you provide details of how you'll repay your lender, your plan must present a comprehensive view of your business, your managers or partners, the market, costs, and why you believe you'll succeed.

■ **Present a strong track record.** Using a results-oriented format, present your past accomplishments, employment, previous businesses, and technical skills.

CHAPTER PERSPECTIVE

This chapter stressed the importance of approaching the right financier for financing. In addition to having a convincing business plan and financing proposal, the entrepreneur should understand the nature of the prospective financier's business, the type of financing normally provided, and his or her attitude toward risk. The major sources of financing available to businesses range from the highly conservative financiers—commercial banks (with their very specific lending criteria)—to the risk-seekers, such as venture capitalists and angel investors. If the funding source rejects the request, try to determine the reason in order to avoid a repetition when making future requests.

Glossary

Accounts receivable the money owed to a firm for goods or services sold on credit. Accounts receivable are shown on the firm's balance sheet as a current asset.

Advertising any paid form of nonpersonal persuasive message delivered through mass media.

Amortization when applied to debt financing, amortization means making a scheduled series of periodic payments over the life of the loan that cover interest for the period and provide for the gradual retirement of principal.

Angel an investor looking to invest anywhere from $5,000 to $50,000 of their own money. Typically, angels look for startups with large market potential and a competitive advantage.

Articles of partnership a legal agreement between partners that specifies the role, involvement, duties, and responsibilities of each partner.

Asset something that is owned by and is of value to the business.

Asset-backed (based) loan a loan made with business assets, such as machinery or equipment, used as collateral. Occasionally, the term is also used to refer to a loan made with accounts receivable or inventory used as collateral.

Bonded warehouse an insured, independent, public warehouse that will not release stored items without presentation of the issued warehouse receipt. This vehicle is popular with lenders who must maintain close physical or legal control over finished goods inventory that the borrower has pledged as collateral for the loan.

Breakeven point level of operations where sales revenue is equal to operating expenses; that is, the volume of sales that results in a net operating income of zero.

Budget a plan expressed in quantitative terms, such as units of a product in a production budget, revenues and expenses in a marketing budget, or cash inflows and outflows in a cash budget.

Business concept is a statement summarizing what the business is, how it will meet the needs of its customers, why it can do this better than its competitors, and what resources are required to do so. Usually expressed in a business plan.

Business description the component of the business plan that provides the reader with a summary of the plan's important points and conclusions.

Business plan a detailed study of what the business or business concept is, where and to whom the business will market its product or service, and how it will conduct its operations.

Business risk the uncertainty and fluctuation surrounding the firm's ability to generate sales, cash flows, and earnings.

Capital structure the mix or proportion of long-term debt and owner's equity capital to finance the firm's fixed assets.

Cash budget a financial-planning tool showing the period-by-period estimates of the amount and timing of expected cash inflows and outflows.

Cash discount a reduction from the invoice price of purchased goods for early payment. For example, the credit terms "2/10, in 30" mean the buyer can deduct 2% of the invoice price if payment is made within 10 days. Otherwise, the full invoice price is due in 30 days.

Channels of distribution the interconnected series of marketing middlemen used to get a product from the producer to the consumer.

Collateral assets that have been pledged to secure a loan. The creditor (lender) holds a lien on the assets and can claim them if the borrower defaults.

Commercial bank a state or federally chartered financial institution that accepts demand deposits (checking accounts) and makes loans to businesses.

Commercial finance company a non-depository financial institution that loans and leases to businesses.

Commercial success (feasibility) a volume of sales sufficient to provide a satisfactory level of cash flow and profits.

Commitment fee is charged by the bank for granting the loan and committing to the maximum amount that can be borrowed against the line of credit or rendering credit agreement. It also is the fee charged against the amount of the credit line not used by the borrower during the agreement period.

Compensating balance bank loan provision requiring the borrowing firm to maintain a minimum average balance in its checking account that is equal to a specified percentage of the loan amount.

Consumer goods four major product classes that identify the goods consumers buy, including convenience, shopping, specialty, and unsought products.

Contribution format income statement an alternative format income statement that classifies costs, variable and fixed, by their relationship to sales.

Control a basic management function that involves comparing actual events to planned expectations to determine whether remedial action is required.

Corporation legal and taxable entity that has a life, existence, duties, and responsibilities separate and distinct from its stockholders (owners).

Cover letter introductory letter accompanying a business plan that identifies the entrepreneur, the firm, and the reason for presenting the business plan.

Credit policy combination of the firm's credit standards used to gauge customer credit-worthiness, the credit terms offered its customers, and its collection policy.

Current assets assets of the firm consisting of cash and the assets expected to turn over or be converted into cash in less than one year. Typically, these latter assets are accounts receivable and inventory.

Customer profile distinguishing geographic, demographic, psychographic, and behavioral characteristics that define a specific group of consumers.

Cyclical business pattern recurring swings in general business activity that move production, sales, cash flows, profits, and employment through a recession phase to the peak of an upswing.

Debt capital funds borrowed under a legally binding contract that requires, among other possible enforceable provisions, the payment of interest and repayment of principal.

Dividends distributions of profits to stockholders.

Entrepreneur the term comes from French and literally translated means go-between or between-taker: one positioned between the financier of a venture and the ultimate consumer but who does not risk financial capital. In this book, we use the term entrepreneur to mean an individual who recognizes a market opportunity that promises a suitable return; is willing to accept the risk associated with acquiring and organizing resources (land, buildings, money, people, etc.) to take advantage of this opportunity; and has the initiative, drive, tenacity, and skills to start the venture and see it through to completion.

Equity capital ownership funds that represent a proportionate claim on the firm's cash flows and profits and a proportionate right to a voice in operating the business.

External environment a set of aggregate variables, such as the economic, industry, market, and competitive environment, that affect the firm's performance but are outside management's direct control.

Factoring sale of the firm's accounts receivable to a specialized financial institution known as a factor to raise funds.

Feasibility study detailed study of how and why a business or business concept is expected to succeed. Justifiable rationale and evidence for how and why a business will succeed is the central theme for each component of a business plan.

Financial lease a contract used in the leasing of business assets that has the characteristics of a debt contract.

Financial plan the plan that reflects the amount of financing needed to make operating plans feasible, when and in what form the financing is needed, and who will be approached for the needed funds.

Financial risk uncertainty surrounding the firm's ability to generate the cash flows needed to meet its contractual financial obligations.

Financial success (feasibility) a business firm able to generate a level of cash flow and profit sufficient to compensate its owner(s) for the time, effort, investment, and risk assumed is a financial success.

Financing proposal a supporting document to the business plan that details the nature and purpose of the financing request.

Fixed (plant) assets a firm's long-term assets such as land, buildings, and equipment.

Free cash flow the cash flow remaining after meeting operating needs, debt service, the replacement of assets, and dividend payments.

General partnership an association of two or more persons to conduct business as co-owners. Each general partner has management equality and unlimited personal liability for the debts of the partnership.

Gross domestic product (GDP) a measure of the value of all goods and services produced in an economy in a given time period. Formerly known as gross national product (GNP), GDP is the most widely quoted indicator of the health of an economy.

Growth capital the long-term financing needed to finance additions to the firm's fixed asset base.

Industry group of businesses supplying related products or services and the complementary businesses that support them.

Industry analysis a study of the set of characteristics that define and influence a group of primary and secondary businesses supplying a related product or service. The industry analysis is a major component of the business plan.

Industry classification the various segments (retailing, wholesaling, etc.) into which the primary businesses (merchandising, manufacturing, etc.) of the industry are divided.

Internal environment facets of the business, such as basic operations or its marketing and financial strategies, that are under management's direct control.

Inventory those current assets that will be converted into salable products or services, those that have been partially converted into salable products or services, or those finished products available for resale. Inventory is shown on the firm's balance sheet as raw materials, work-in-process, or finished goods.

Job analysis a study of the job-qualifications needed to effectively perform the duties and responsibilities of a job.

Job description a written description of the duties, responsibilities, and job qualifications associated with a given job.

Just-in-time inventory system an inventory management system designed to reduce inventory costs by pressuring suppliers to ship parts just as they are needed.

Lien a lender's legal claim on the borrower's assets that have been pledged as collateral for a loan.

Life-cycle concept *life cycle* refers to the various stages of existence for a product, firm, or industry. These periods are usually identified as the development stage, the growth stage, the maturity stage, and the decline stage.

Limited partner a co-owner of a partnership whose liability is limited to his or her investment in the firm and who typically has no voice in management.

Market geographical boundaries within which a product or service is offered for sale, the customers for that product or service, and firms competing for the customers' business.

Market analysis a study of the basic factors that define the market for the firm's product or service and how the firm must be positioned to reach this market.

Marketing budget the estimate of sales revenues and marketing expenses that are expected to result from planned marketing activities.

Marketing mix the combination of product/service, price, distribution, and promotion that has been determined as best suited to meet the needs and expectations of the firm's target market.

Marketing plan coordinated action program for reaching the firm's target market and for motivating this customer group to purchase the firm's product/service.

Market niche specific segment of a larger consumer or business market that the firm can profitably exploit.

Metropolitan category system method used by the U.S. Bureau of Census to classify market segments. Market segments are divided into three metropolitan categories: Standard Metropolitan Statistical Areas (SMSAs), Primary Metropolitan Statistical Areas (PMSAs), and Consolidated Metropolitan Statistical Areas (CMSAs).

Net operating income amount of profit that is generated by operations that are normal to the firm. Net operating income is the amount of profit remaining after cost of sales and normal operation expenses are deducted from sales revenue.

North American Industry Classification System (NAICS) is a six-digit uniform number-coding and verbal-description system created by the federal government to classify business firms according to the specific business activity in which they engage.

Operating plan identifies the intended set of activities and procedures that create value for the firm's customers.

Operations the activities that converts resource inputs into valuable outputs for the firm's customers.

Organization structured group of human, physical, informational, and financial resources combined to accomplish specific goals.

Organization plan blueprint of the firm's organization structure. This plan identifies the key positions in the organization, authority/responsibility relationships between them, flow of information and communication between them, and job qualifications needed to fill them.

Percent-of-sales method technique for estimating the value of a given variable by expressing it as a percentage of estimated sales.

Planning the art and science of deciding what future course of action the firm will take to meet established objectives.

Primary task the activity or set of activities that form the reason for the firm's existence.

Primary information source information gathered through the research of original data sources.

Prime rate interest rate a bank charges its most credit-worthy customers on short-term loans.

Producers goods the six major product classes that identify the goods that businesses and organizations buy. These are installations, accessory equipment, raw materials, components, supplies, and professional services.

Pro forma balance sheet projected balance sheet used in financial planning.

Pro forma income statement projected income statement used in financial planning.

Promissory note legal document showing the borrower's debt obligation to the lender.

Promotion strategy and techniques used to communicate information about the product or service between seller and potential buyer.

Receivables-collection pattern the estimated percentages of the credit sales from a given month that are expected to be collected in that month or subsequent months.

Resources those tangible and intangible assets that are used in the business to create value. They include physical assets, such as equipment and buildings; human resources; monetary assets including cash, investments, and credit capability; and intangible assets, such as goodwill or technical know-how.

Return on investment (ROI) a financial ratio that indicates the percentage of income generated per dollar invested in assets.

Risk uncertainty surrounding the occurrence of some future event.

Sales forecast estimate based on assumptions about the future sales during specific time periods.

S corporation corporation that has elected under subchapter S of the Internal Revenue Code to be treated for tax purposes as a sole proprietorship or partnership. This status avoids double taxation and provides other benefits as well.

Savings and loan association financial institution that raises its funds by offering savings deposits and makes residential and commercial mortgage loans.

Scenario (what if) analysis method for treating the uncertainty inherent in planning by preparing multiple sets of plans using different sets of assumptions.

Seasonal business patterns are changes in business activity within a calendar year.

Seed money financing needed to develop and refine the business concept.

Secondary information source information gathered from published sources.

Secret partner a co-owner of a partnership who is active in management and has unlimited liability, but is unknown to the public as a partner.

Silent partner a co-owner of a partnership who has unlimited liability but does not have an active voice in management.

Small business investment company (SBIC) a venture capital firm licensed by the U.S. Small Business Administration.

Sole proprietorship a business firm established, owned, and usually operated by one person.

Spontaneous sources of financing temporary sources of financing, typically accounts payable and accrued liabilities, that rise and fall automatically with changes in the level of business activity.

Standard Industrial Classification (SIC) system is a government system for classifying industries by a four-digit code. It was supplanted by the six-digit NAICS system that was released in 1997. However, certain government departments and agencies still use the SIC codes.

Startup capital financing needed to initiate business operations.

Stockholders owners of a corporation. The proportionate ownership interest of a stockholder is represented by the number of shares of common stock held.

Table of contents document that identifies the content of the presentation package and the components of the business plan by name and page location.

Target market group of potential customers identified by the entrepreneur as having characteristics to which the firm's product/service should appeal and toward which the marketing effort is directed.

Time-series analysis mathematical tools used to identify the basic trend, cyclical movements, and seasonal patterns in time-series data.

Title page cover sheet for the business plan.

Unlimited liability with the sole proprietorship and general partnership forms of ownership, the assets of the business as well as the personal assets of the owner(s) are subject to the claims of the firm's creditors.

U.S. Small Business Administration independent agency of the U.S. Government created by Congress to provide assistance to small businesses.

Venture capitalist typically a high-risk financier who provides equity financing to ventures that promise supernormal growth in sales and profits and a high rate of return on invested capital.

Working capital those temporary current assets, primarily accounts receivable and inventory, that are expected to turn over or release funds within a short time.

Working-capital financing short-term debt financing used to carry the temporary buildup in working capital.

Business Resources

Writing a Convincing Business Plan is an important book for someone who is starting a business or operating a small- to medium-size company. But don't ignore other resources that may help you succeed and grow your business. Whether you're developing a business, writing a business plan, or trying to solve a specific business issue, these agencies and organizations may provide advice or referrals:

American Management Association
135 W. 50th St.
New York, NY 10020
(212) 586-8100
www.amanet.org

American Marketing Association
311 S. Wacker Drive, Suite 5800
Chicago, IL 60606-5819
(312) 542-9000
www.marketingpower.com

International Council for Small Business
St. Louis University
3674 Lindell Blvd.
St. Louis, MO 63108
(314) 658-3896
www.icsb.org

International Trademark Association
655 Third Ave., 10th Floor
New York, NY 10017
(212) 768-9887
www.inta.org

National Federation of Independent Business
Suite 700
600 Maryland Ave., SW
Washington, DC 20024
(800) 634-2669
www.nfib.com

Office of the U.S. Trade Representative
Executive Office of the President
600 17th St., NW
Washington, DC 20506
(202) 395-7360
www.ustr.gov

Procurement Automated Source System is a computerized list of small businesses. If you'd like to be listed, write to:
U.S. Small Business Administration
409 3rd St., SW
Washington, DC 20416

Small Business Administration, Information Office
Office of Public Communications
1411 L St., NW
Washington, DC 20416
(202) 653-7561
www.sba.gov

SBA Small Business Development Centers. Call (800) 827-5722 for the nearest location.

U.S. Patent and Trademarks Office
Commissioner of Patent and Trademark
P.O. Box 1450
Alexandria, VA 22313-1450
(571) 272-1000
www.uspto.gov

U.S. Customs
1300 Pennsylvania Ave., N.W.
Washington, DC 20229
(202) 863-6000
www.cbp.gov

U.S. Government Purchasing and Sales Directory
Superintendent of Documents
U.S. Government Printing Office
Washington, DC 20402-9371

Internet Resources

The Internet is another great source if you're planning a business expansion or a start-up. There's a wealth of information for entrepreneurs. Consider these web resources:

BankWeb
www.bankweb.com
On-line service with directory of banks and interest rates.

Center for Business Planning
www.businessplans.org
This site offers planning resources and examples of business plans. In addition, it provides analysis of business strategy and business planning products.

Commerce Clearing House Business Owner's Toolkit
www.toolkit.com
Features small and home office guides to everyday business concerns.

Minority Business Development Agency
www.mbda.gov
This site offers capital investment aid to minority businesses.

National Association of Women Business Owners
www.nawbo.org
This organization promotes and aids women in business.

Safe-Bidco Small Business Loans
www.safe-bidco.com
State Assistance Fund for Enterprise, Business, and Industrial Development Corporation

Small Business Administration Online
www.sbaonline.sba.gov/
This site provides information on Small Business Administration programs and publications on starting, financing, and expanding a business.

Small Business Exchange
www.americanexpress.com/smallbusiness
The exchange is a comprehensive resource that provides planning information and small-business plans.

Small Business Search Engine
www.allsmallbiz.com
This site can perform searches of business web sites relevant to needs of small businesses.

Small Business Square
www.isquare.com
This site offers content for the entrepreneur and a resource center to search a database of franchise opportunities.

U.S. Business Advisor
www.business.gov
This site offers access to guides and government forms needed to comply with regulations or apply for government-based loans.

Tax Guides

The following publications from the Internal Revenue Service are filled with timely information for anyone writing a business plan. Two must-reads for small-business owners:
Publication 334, Guide for Small Business
Publication 583, Starting a Business and Keeping Records

Other Useful IRS Publications:

Publication 463, Travel, Entertainment, and Gift Expenses
Publication 509, Tax Calendars
Publication 534, Net Operating Losses
Publication 560, Retirement Plans for the Self-Employed
Publication 587, Business Use of Your Home
Publication 917, Business Use of a Car

Library Resources

Don't forget to stop by your local library for useful directories and business sourcebooks. Here are a few examples:

American Manufacturers Directory—Lists manufacturers with 25 or more employees.

City and County Data Book (U.S. Department of Commerce)— Updated every three years with information on population, education, employment, income, housing, and retail sales.

Directory of Directories—Describes more than 9,000 buyer's guides and directories.

Dun and Bradstreet Directories—Lists companies alphabetically, geographically, and by product classification.

Encyclopedia of Business Information Sources (Gale Research)— Lists handbooks, directories, and more for more than 1,200 industries and business subjects.

Pratt's Guide to Venture Capital Sources—New York, Securities Data Publishing, 1999.

Small Business Sourcebook—Contains listing of consultants, education institutions, and government agencies offering advice to businesses.

Sourcebook for Franchise Opportunities—This annual directory of U.S. franchises contains data for investment requirements, royalty and advertising fees, services provided by the franchiser, and locations where franchises are licensed to operate.

Index

NOTES

NOTES

NOTES